A Century of Squatting Strength

Table of contents

Pg 2 Forward

Pg 8 Chapter 1   Into the past

Pg 22 Chapter 2   The squat, greatest single exercise

Pg 29 Chapter 3   Peary Rader, the man and his methods

Pg 44 Chapter 4   The Shrug

Pg 64 Chapter 5   Back to Peary Rader's excerpts

Pg 84 Chapter 6   Mark Berry

Pg 91 Chapter 7   Bob Peoples

The mighty **Paul Anderson**

Pg 123 Chapter 8   Bob and Paul

Pg 131 Chapter 9   Paul Anderson's methods

Pg 160 Chapter 10   J.C. Hise

Pg 170 Chapter 11   Revamped 20 rep squat program

Pg 177 Chapter 12   Hepburn and Harry

Pg 191 Chapter 13   Starting strength squat Q & A sessions

Pg 214 Chapter 14   Bill Starr's big 3

Pg 220 Chapter 15   The Westside influence

Pg 237 Chapter 16   Jumpstretch COO Interview

Pg 247 Chapter 17   The original Westside

Pg 256 Chapter 18   George Frenn

Pg 260 Chapter 19   A bodybuilder's perspective

Pg 290 Chapter 20   Dr. Fred Hatfield

Pg 312 Chapter 21   Some other voices of experience

Pg 325 Chapter 22   Wrapping it up

Pg 332 Chapter 23   One last subject

Forward

This book will contain no new, earth shattering idea that has never before emerged from human brain cells until now.

It will not describe some exotic new supplement discovered by Tibetan monks 1000 years ago and somehow kept secret until I decided to publish this information as my gift to mankind.

I am not touting some incredible new piece of equipment that can only be purchased through me, which will take you from zero to hero over night.

What the heck do I need this book for, then??? You may be asking right now.

Who the heck is Dave Yarnell, and why should I give a rat's tail about anything he has to say, let alone a book on weight training?

I'll tell you who I am and why you should give a rat's tail about what I have to say here.

I am probably a lot like many of you; a student of body culture and strength, trying to wade through all the hype and BS in the weight training game that is available on internet forums galore, magazines, blogs, books, e-books, etc, ad infinitum.

I have been training with weights and virtually every other means of gaining strength I could get my hands on without going broke, since I was knee high to a grasshopper.

Your author in the days when he still had a full head of hair

Circa about 1973-ish.

I have tried to keep an open mind, not rule out anything that seemed remotely promising or worthwhile, and have read thousands of pages of training related info from just about every imaginable source. My goal is to simplify and clarify things for myself and all who would seek to make the best natural progress that they are humanly capable of, without being sold a load of crap designed only to fatten someone's wallet.

I love the feeling of making progress; getting stronger or adding a wee bit of circumference to my extremities or my torso, and have been on a quest to have and to keep that feeling as often and for as long as possible. The fact that you are currently reading this suggests you share the desire to get bigger, stronger, and faster and probably all of the above if you care to actually admit it.

While some of us are afraid to admit such a desire because maybe it smacks of narcissism or selfishness on some level, I would counter that line of thought with the idea that will for self improvement is not in and of itself a bad thing, though seeking **only physical improvement** certainly can be.

There is far more to life than just being big or strong. If you were to neglect family, work, spiritual growth in all out pursuit of physical development, you would indeed be acting selfishly yet you would only be hurting yourself in the long run anyway. While devoting some time to self improvement is a valuable and worthwhile thing, it must be balanced by giving time to God, our families and our community, which are the areas in which we will find true contentment.

Sometimes, devout folks neglect even their own physical upkeep and maintenance in pursuit of serving others, which may indeed be noble and altruistic, but is it wise? If your health and strength fails you because of physical and/or dietary neglect, will you be able to continue serving God or other folks for very long?

There are those who would say that spiritual enlightenment is actually obtained by some forms of physical exercise, but I strongly disagree with that idea. I do believe that a strong and healthy body can facilitate being able to serve God, family & others, and therefore be a positive benefit to spirituality, but I do not think physical and spiritual health are one and the same. It is entirely possible to be strong as an ox and fit as a fiddle while being spiritually bankrupt, in my opinion.

OK, this is not a book about spirituality, religion or faith; I just want to state up front that **I do not espouse the pursuit of physical fitness to the exclusion of all else** or suggest that it is even the most important thing in the world, just that it is a worthwhile endeavor when kept in balance and pursued with some moderation.

With all that being said, **let's talk about the pursuit of strength.**

I have competed in many powerlifting competitions over the years, both steroid enhanced and drug free. I am not on some sort of witch hunt against those who would make the choice to use performance enhancing drugs; I simply make the case that good gains have been and still can be made without them. I have made the choice to train without steroids for my own reasons, though I will be the first to admit I made some of the best gains of my life while taking them.

Here I am in 1988, with the CFI Powerlifting team of Philadelphia

USPF Pa State meet (bottom left)

You may have made a similar choice, and are wondering if you really can get the gains you desire without resorting to shortcuts that may in the long term be harmful.

If that is the case, then we are indeed brothers in arms, and I consider myself as one beggar pointing out to his fellow beggars where he has found a few succulent and nourishing crumbs.

Now where exactly is that, you ask?

To a large extent, It is found in the old school training programs from the turn of the century into about the middle of the century. I won't say that nothing worthwhile has been discovered or written about since that time, but I will say it (the old school methods and ideas) was very **foundational to much of what is still being used with success to this day.**

Why go backward instead of forward?

What happened to weight training and bodybuilding around the middle of the last century that virtually changed everything? If you said "steroids", you get the cupie doll! Steroids were the Pandora's Box of the weight training world, and everything has dramatically changed since it was opened, back around the '50s.

Imagine the result of telling muscle heads of every genre that now there are magic pills that will make you grow like never before, and then make them widely available to those groups of fitness fanatics.

Early on, nobody really knew what the long term effects other than the desired ones, might be, that would show up eventually. The positive effects were so dramatic that any negative effects would be overlooked by their new users as mere inconveniences, and nothing to really be concerned about.

OK, nobody grew a second head or turned green after ingesting those first Dianabol tablets, and personal records were being shattered in gyms all over the world. Did we really expect there to be a free lunch? Wishful thinking tends to get the best of us, far too often. It is just that kind of thinking and mindset that has sold millions of copies of get fit quick schemes and gimmicky pieces of exercise apparatus to the gullible for years.

I'm not pointing fingers, here; after all, I bought into the concept and tried the magic potion myself. OK, so I didn't only try it, I tried it, liked it, and continued using it for quite some time, until I began to see the error of my ways.

I had always been an admirer of great strength and strongly desired it as quality to be obtained. I also considered myself a "hard gainer", which is to say I am like 99 percent of the rest of the world, possessing no tremendous, inherent genetic gifts that would propel me to greatness with little effort involved on my part. As such, when I witnessed contemporaries in the gym making incredible progress, virtually overnight, I wanted in, in a big way. **It really didn't take too long to experience the first disappointment with the drugs.**

This came relatively quickly with the first "off cycle", and the crash that came with it. "What goes up must come down" and such it was with my size and most of my strength gains earned from the first "on cycle".

It was very depressing and dis- heartening, to say the least. But my using friends and fellow lifters convinced me that it had to do with the type of drug I used and the type of training I used.

So, I switched both and was indeed able to keep a bit more of the strength gains from the following couple of cycles. I tried to shrug off the headaches and mood swings that seemed to be part and parcel with the enhancement package. I tried to convince myself that the insane things some of my peers did had nothing to do with the drugs, and that tearing muscles and having a completely black and blue arm, leg or half a torso was just "part of the game".

I have to admit, what really started to eat away at me was the different ways my friends trained relative to whether they were "on" or "off" the juice.

500 pound squats became 135 pound squats, and not just for a week or two. To tell the truth, this kind of made me sick, and I started to question the whole drug culture I was involved in.

Some of the older guys were developing some pretty serious health issues after years of heavy drug use, and I started to seriously question the value of it all. **Was it really worth the potential risks and side effects so that I could earn a few trophies, maybe work my way up to being a state champ some day?** (In those days being a state champ was actually a pretty big deal).

I began to see more and more that drugs were definitely a shortcut to quick gains, but I had to seriously question whether it was wise for those seeking longevity and good health, not just short term super strength. I for one want to continue to train and be relatively strong and healthy right up until my last days. My heart and my brain told me that continued drug use was not a part of that equation; at least not for me, so I made the decision to get off for good, close to twenty years ago now. I have no regrets at all, though I must admit every once in a while I wonder what I could be lifting after a short cycle of the juice. I leave it at that... just a passing thought.

Since giving up the "cheat method", **I have sought healthier and legal alternatives to supplementation from natural sources, and have found some truly beneficial things over the years,** and would have to say that the state of the art in supplementation has steadily improved since the days I first began taking them. **This is perhaps one area where we can actually improve upon the old school ways, and we will explore this area later on in the book.**

It also became clear to me that trying to learn training methods from enhanced lifters and bodybuilders could be miss- leading and even counterproductive, and that at the very least, these methods should be taken in with a grain of salt.

It is actually tough to over train when stacking anabolics, and that is why men can put so many hours of grueling training in and not only survive it, but actually thrive on it.

Sure, there a few freaks of nature who can manage it without a chemistry set, but they are few and far between. For the rest of us, trying to emulate heavily enhanced methods without the enhancement is a dead end street where thousands of would- be strength heroes have ended up.

Yes, you can help your body's ability to recover by wise nutritional supplementation, stretching and recovery techniques such as massage, chiropractic, foam roller use, heat, ice, etc.

Still, all these methods put together will not add up to what you would probably get out of the drugs, but you might get closer than you currently think possible.

But I digress. We **started talking about why we wanted to learn from the old school trainers.**

Well, if you realize that **there was a pretty good crop of very strong people that got their strength before anabolic drugs were ever invented**, you might also be very curious as to how they obtained such strength in those days. If you were on the same wavelength as me (you poor sap), then you might have then started researching and reading everything you could possibly get access to that had to do with strength training in those bygone days. Of course, you may not have been crazy enough or fortunate enough to have the free time to spend on such a project as this. Maybe you would just rather pay the modest price I ask for this book, and learn from me in a quick and easy read what may have otherwise taken you much more time and trouble. I'll tell you right up front that there is no top secret information gleaned by yours truly from the dying lips of some former strength star wishing to come clean in this book.

You could find pretty much everything in this book on your own if you looked hard enough. **Let me make it a little easier for you**. Isn't that worth the price to you?

Chapter One

Into the past

There was a lot of showmanship in the strongman performances of the circus and similar venues in the old days, to be sure. **There were some parlor tricks and even some outright fakery**. Early on, there were many claims of feats being done that went unproven, and even the things that were actually witnessed by multitudes were often done with "smoke and mirrors", much like a magic show. While some primitive form of weight lifting had been around for hundreds, probably more like thousands of years, the barbells, dumbbells and related equipment that we now have only became popular after the 1920-30 range in this country, thanks largely to one Mr. **Alan Calvert.** Calvert caught the "bug" of physical culture when he saw the venerable **Eugen Sandow** at the 1893 World's Fair, performing acts of strength as well as showing off his incredible physique. His reaction at that time was, I am sure, much like my own reaction to seeing **Arnold Schwarzenegger** on the cover of his **"Education of a bodybuilder"** book I read as a young man. **"How do I get a body like that**? " is the reaction I refer to.

At that time, the Europeans were way ahead of us in terms of weight lifting skills and knowledge, and Calvert read everything he could get from the **European experts** of that era, in his quest for training know-how.

In the following photo you will see one of those Europeans, with a bit of accompanying text

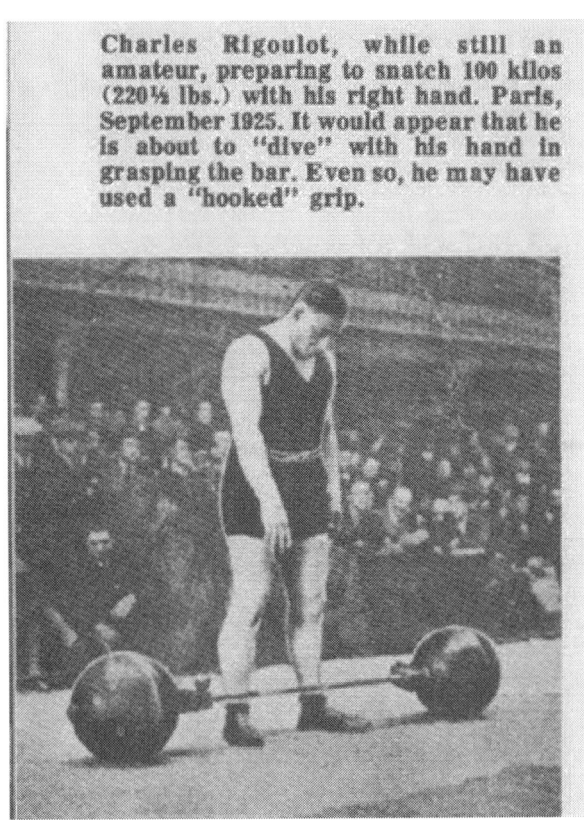

Charles Rigoulot, while still an amateur, preparing to snatch 100 kilos (220¼ lbs.) with his right hand. Paris, September 1925. It would appear that he is about to "dive" with his hand in grasping the bar. Even so, he may have used a "hooked" grip.

It became clear to Alan that barbells, dumbbells and kettlebells were largely responsible for the creation of most, if not all, of the current batch of strongmen, including his revered Sandow. But this knowledge was only of so much value to Calvert at the time, because these items were in very short supply in the good old U.S of A in those days. Most of the traveling strongmen had their own custom made barbell sets that they took along for their traveling side shows, and you could not walk into any gymnasium and grab a dumbbell off the rack.

It so happened that Calvert's family had owned a foundry, and he had grown up with at least some familiarity in working with the raw materials that might be used in the manufacture of barbells and dumbbells.

With some engineering help from others, access to a foundry and his sheer determination to guide him, he started up the fledgling **Milo barbell** company in **Philadelphia in 1902.**

I believe it was as much Alan's drive to get stronger and more fit himself as his entrepreneurial spirit that lead him to start this grand enterprise.

Calvert was also aware of the charlatans involved in the strongman game at the time, and he wished to expose the fakers and record for posterity the **genuine lifts** that were being made and that he hoped would be made by American lifters in the future. **He sought to standardize and regulate the lifting**, much as it had been done over seas for quite some time already.

Calvert wrote this book, "The Truth about Weight Lifting".

It was somewhat of an expose' of weight lifters and strongmen's tricks and fakeries in his day.

He also sought to have Americans catch up to and ultimately surpass their European counterparts in the weight lifting game. It could well be said that Calvert, and his Milo Barbell were the real start of the weight lifting sports and bodybuilding game in the United States. **The first widely available weight training courses in this country were those that one got for free along with their purchase of a Milo Barbell set**. The information was basically that which Calvert had picked up from his reading and talking with the experts from Europe.

It consisted of a limited number of basic exercises done with little more than the supplied barbell and dumbbells. There were no real squat racks or benches for bench pressing even available at the time, so the bulk of the exercises were "ground-based".

Milo's **"First Course in Bodybuilding"** described curls, rows, cleans, various forms of presses, kettlebell swings (something that has seen a big resurgence of late), deadlifts, the heels together squat, walking with tiptoes and a barbell in squat position, barbell pullovers, good mornings, shrugs, Jefferson squats, weighted sit-ups, wrestlers bridge/press, reverse curls and some free style abdominal and stretching movements done at the start of the workout. There was nothing too fancy or frilly there, just the basics. All these exercises could be done without machines or equipment other than supplied by Milo with their basic setup. **These exercises are still the backbone movements of many a solid weight training program, be it for power, bulk, or strength/endurance work.**

The lack of benches and racks had advantages and disadvantages. Basically, every lift had to start from the floor or ground, if you were like most and had no type of rack or bench to rest the weights on. While this may seem like a huge inconvenience, **it added difficulty which in lifting is not a bad thing.**

Lots of differing methods of getting the bar from the floor to overhead or even up to the waist or shoulder height were developed, and some of these are still used commonly today. Some of you may be familiar with or at least have heard of a move called the **Turkish get up**, which can be done with a barbell, dumbbell or kettlebell. In this exercise, one starts lying on the back, on the floor and holding the weight in one hand. Holding the weight overhead at the start, one simultaneously lifts the upper torso from the floor (ala a sit-up, but turning to the side), bringing one hand to the side and bringing the corresponding leg underneath the body.

As you are holding the weight overhead in the initial position, you bend that leg on the same side, as it will become the supporting leg as you bring the opposite one underneath for the drive upward. So you basically lift the body upwards and to one side, bracing yourself momentarily on that elbow. Then you start to lift up the other side of your body using the bent leg, and at the same time start drawing the opposite leg backward and under the body, until you are resting that side on that knee.

From that point you drive upward starting with the leg that was bent at the start, until you can get the other leg positioned to assist the thrust upward and ultimately stand up straight.

Obviously, this is not a model of efficiency in terms of getting the weight from point a to point b. It is however, one very efficient exercise in terms of getting just about every muscle in the body involved in one exercise.

See following picture of Milo's first course book cover:

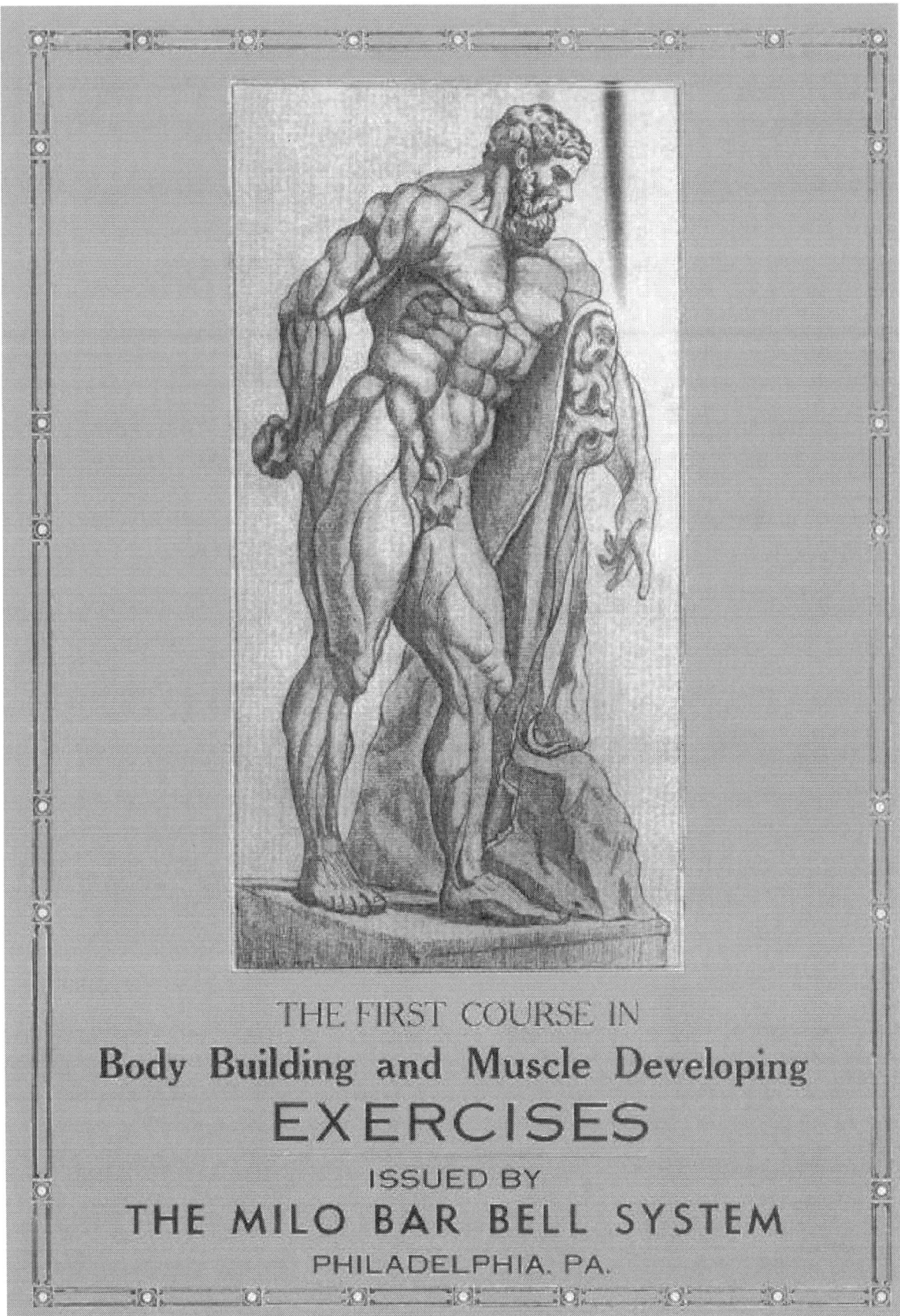

THE FIRST COURSE IN
Body Building and Muscle Developing
EXERCISES
ISSUED BY
THE MILO BAR BELL SYSTEM
PHILADELPHIA, PA.

The point I make is that the lack of racks, benches and similar accessories in those early days made barbell students work that much harder and probably got them that much stronger for it. In order to do a curl or an overhead press, one first had to lift the weight off the floor and into position, which got more muscles involved. If you wanted to squat a barbell, you had to find a way to get it in position on the shoulders. The most common, original way to do this was first do a clean from the floor to the shoulder position, and then do at least a partial overhead press to bring the bar over and behind the head and resting on the upper traps. Of course, this limited your squatting weight to whatever you could manage to get in position in that manner.

Later on, one of the earliest strong proponents of the squat exercise developed a method in which the loaded barbell was tilted to one side as one got down into the squat position and bought the barbell into position from the vertical to the shoulder position. A bit awkward, yes, but **Henry "Milo" Steinborn** managed to do this with quite a bit of weight loaded on the bar. We will discuss Milo in more detail later. The legs found involvement in many exercises other than the squat, so it was not an absolute requirement to learn either of the above methods of getting a bar in squatting position to get some leg strengthening done. Any time one bent the legs in order to pick up a loaded bell, and then straightened them or almost straightened them in the process of lifting the weight to the desired end position, the legs were being used to lift some of the weight. Various techniques used various levels of leg bending and leg strength, and some developed the legs more than others, accordingly. Also exercises like lunges and step-ups could be done for leg development, which did not require the awkward bar shouldering techniques. Iron boots with weight plates attached were another means of attacking the leg muscles in those early days. Harness lifts also used the legs a lot, and were one of the common things done in a strongman show early on. Massive weights were done with these types of lifts, and **Sandow** was one of the guys who performed these. Deadlifts were done, and these will build some leg power, especially the backs of the legs (hamstrings). Other forms of the squat were done, such as **the Jefferson squat**, which involved straddling a loaded bar and doing a partial squat movement that way.

Henry Steinborn, former world's weight-lifting champion and record holder, considered to be the strongest man in wrestling.

The man who started the squat craze in America, Henry "Milo" Steinborn

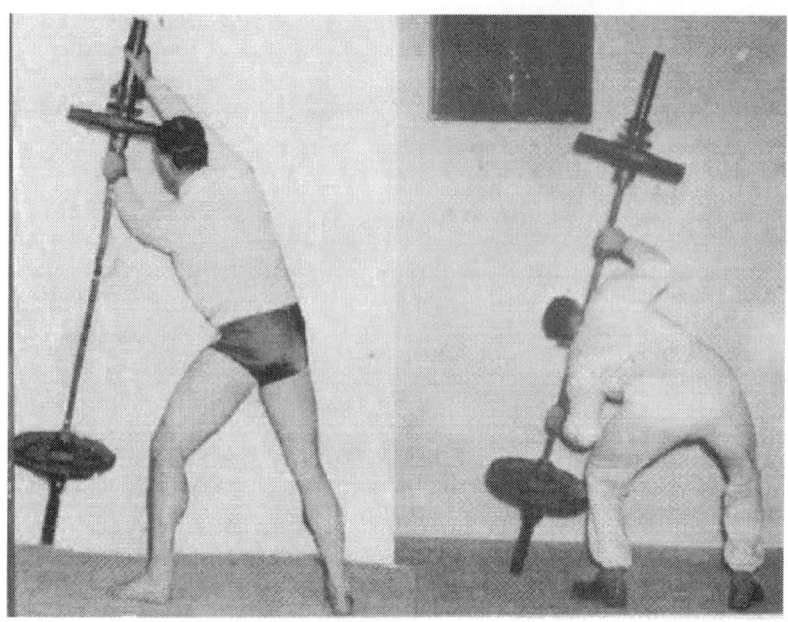

Peary Rader in photos

Setting up for the jerk behind neck or squat, with the "Steinborn lift"

Ed Zercher, another old time strongman, is credited with inventing **the Zercher squat**, which is similar to what most of us know as a front squat, but the bar is held at about waist level as opposed to shoulder level. The original lift consisted of 2 parts; deadlifting the bar into position and cradling on the forearms (not very comfortable!), and then straightening up with it until you were erect or very close to erect. One could then continue squatting to the mid position, or do the entire 2 part motion again. These days, the movement is usually only done from the mid position, having the bar supported in a power rack for the start position. The new way is tough enough, from my experience.

Louie Simmons is a big fan of these for improving both the squat and deadlift. One of the toughest parts of doing these is having the bar cradled on the forearms. This is painful with a considerable load. This can be alleviated by using some sort of yoke to assist in holding the bar, which takes much of the load off of the forearms.

Here is an early illustration of the Zercher squat

Here is an interesting device enabling a higher bar position for the Hack Squat

Yet another early squat form was the **"Hack" squat,** sometimes credited to early wrestler and strongman **George Hackenschmidt**. According to the **"Old time Strongman Training"** website, this is a false notion. The term comes from the German word for ankle, which is where the lift comes very close to touching at the start. **The original version simply used a barbell that was placed behind the ankles and lifted as in a deadlift, as opposed to the machine based variation commonly done these days**. These are a bit tough to get one's balance with, at least at first, in my experience. Again, no squat rack was needed for these.

Even when the more conventional style squat was done, with the bar across the back of the shoulders, it was done with the feet close together and the heels raised, which did not require much weight to really hit the old "quads". This was commonly called a **"Hindu style squat"** as the Eastern wrestling schools squatted just using bodyweight for high repetitions this way in the old days.

Here is a photo of the author depicting a "Hindu Squat"

Note the heels together position which is tricky.

Here we see Bob Hoffman doing the lift with some heavy old style barbells.

One of the greatest early wrestlers was a gentleman named the Great Gama, said to have been undefeated in perhaps 5000 matches. He was also known for his tremendous feat of doing 9000 straight Hindu squats!

See photo below

The Great Gama

Henry aka "Milo" Steinborn came up with the "**Steinborn lift**" in order to handle larger weights in the traditional behind the back squat move.

In my first book that was dedicated to the old school greats. "**Forgotten Secrets of the Old time Strongmen**", I had a section about **Peary Rader**, and his influences (**largely Steinborn, Mark Berry and J.C. Hise**) Not to be redundant, but I think that small section bears repeating here, as it speaks greatly towards the subject matter I am focusing on here, so here goes. Forgive me if you have already read the first book, but stuff this good sometimes needs to be reiterated:

Chapter Two

The Squat: Greatest Single Exercise

By **Peary Rader**

Heavy squat by Hugh Cassidy

The squat is absolutely and without exception the greatest single exercise known to man, for conditioning the entire body, improving the health and energy, strengthening the function of the internal organs, giving the most rapid gains in bodyweight, adding to all-around athletic ability. That's quite a large order, but it's true.

There was a time in the history of American bodybuilding when the squat was given very little consideration. It was thought that the arms and shoulders were most important to either a bodybuilder or a lifter.

However, in time, that way of thinking was changed, largely by certain teachers who had found the squat to be very valuable, and also by bodybuilders and lifters who used it. **Lifters found that the only way they could become superior to other lifters was to develop great power in the legs and hips.**

In the days of **Alan Calvert's and George Jowett's** teaching, the squat was thought to be just another exercise of average importance, like the curl or rowing.

Author's note:

In the early days the squat was usually called the deep knee bend, just like the barbell free, callisthenic version you may have been instructed in during gym class as a youngster

In the following photo, see a drawing of George Jowett with Anvil

Jowett

Because it was hard to do, and little importance was attached to it, many lifters and bodybuilders never included it in their programs. By this omission they greatly limited their progress and ultimate possibilities, although they weren't aware of it.

Old-time wrestler and strongman **Henry (Milo) Steinborn** came over here from Germany and **brought the squat with him.**

He had practiced it a great deal with crude, homemade barbells while in a prison camp in World War I and had reached a very high standard in poundage used and found **his other lifts had greatly increased so that he was able to snatch and clean and jerk record poundage**.

He was a man with a very rugged physique and for many years was a top wrestler. Another young fellow, who, although a lifter, had always been quite slender, caught a spark of enthusiasm from Steinborn and began practicing the squat. This man's name was **Mark Berry**. **He succeeded in gaining about 50 pounds of bodyweight in a short time through use of the squat.**

He later became editor of the old *Strength magazine* and through it encouraged others to adopt the squat for greater progress in lifting and bodybuilding.

When Steinborn did not have access to a squat rack, he did not compromise. He improvised with this:

The Steinborn Lift

- Load the Barbell - use the collars
- Put the bar on its end
- Get under the Barbell
- Let the Barbell fall on your shoulders
- Squat the needed reps
- Reverse the movement when done

See: http://stronglifts.com/ways-to-squat-when-you-dont-have-a-squat-rack/

Author's note:

Another "odd lift" that is attributed to Steinborn is the "jerk behind neck",

This begins with getting the bar in a squat position via the Steinborn lift, and follows with ascending and jumping off the ground while raising the bar to arm's length overhead.

I personally have never seen this done in person at any gym.

Peary Rader in photos

Jerk behind neck

Some unbelievable gains were made at that time by men who had totally failed to gain before. These men were written up in Berry's magazine, and the fad for the squat exercise started.

One man in particular made astounding progress—**doing nothing but the squat and presses behind the neck. J.C. Hise.**

Hise gained 29 pounds in one month, probably a record up to that time.

It was about here that the sets system began to be used effectively by a lot of men, for Hise used about three sets of the squat. Of course, they weren't called sets at that time, so in recent years others have claimed to have invented them.

Actually, sets were probably never discovered by anyone in particular, as is the case with most of what some call modern methods. Sets have been used more or less since barbells were invented, though their real value wasn't recognized until more intensive bodybuilding was practiced in recent years.

Up until the time of Hise's experiments with the squat, I spent about 12 years in fruitless effort trying to develop a physique or gain weight. **I weighed 128 pounds at a height of 5'10" during those years, and training methods at that time didn't alter my physique even slightly.** *

*Author's note

Talk about your "hard gainer", huh?

On publication of the gains of Hise, I decided that this might be what I needed, so I wrote him, and in his characteristically enthusiastic letter I felt I had at last found the secret of gains, so I immediately started working out with ****squats, chins and behind-the-neck presses. ****

*Author's note

Later on you will see this routine laid out fully

I worked out twice per week and used one set of 20 reps in the squat part of the time and two sets of 10 to 15 reps part of the time.

I gained 10 pounds of good muscle the first month. Not much, perhaps, by today's standards, but a lot for a fellow who hadn't been able to gain a pound for years and in fact was even too weak and run down to hold down a job for any length of time.

In two years I gained 70 pounds of bodyweight.

In addition to this I had become heavy weight lifting champion of the Midwestern AAU district, including South Dakota, Nebraska and western Iowa.

I'm not alone in praise of this exercise, for virtually every weightlifter to ever reach his maximum lifting ability has used it as his **key power-producing exercise**. Most of your top bodybuilders have at one time or other specialized on **some version of the squat** and they owe much of their physical development to it.

What is more important to most of you who read this, thousands of fellows just like you who found it almost impossible to make desired gains discovered, as I did, that **the squat was the secret to fast and certain progress.**

Many years ago **Bob Hoffman** was opposed to the squat as an exercise for lifters and classed it as just another exercise. Yet during the intervening years he has gradually been converted to its benefits and now admits that it is **the king of exercises.**

For many years **Iron Man** was almost alone in promotion and publicizing of the squat as the best exercise, and yet it finally forced its way to the recognition it deserves. There are those who feel that we overdid our pushing of this exercise, but such methods often have to be used in order to get the public to accept even the best of new ideas.

We don't recommend that bodybuilders and lifters do nothing but squats, or that they train to excess on it, as some of our critics would have you believe, but we do feel that too many bodybuilders neglect to do even a minimum amount of work on this exercise.

It is especially necessary and valuable in the early stages of a bodybuilder's training. An advanced man can often cut down on his squatting work after he has gotten the desired bulk and use other leg exercises for obtaining the definition and shape he desires, but in the early training programs every man should work very hard on the squat.

Editor's note: **This article was published in the July 1955 Iron Man Magazine.**

The above short article is a perfect introduction to this book, though written many years ago by **Mr. Peary Rader.** The remainder of the book will go on to embellish on the topic of **the squat, its importance as a foundational strength builder, and the many related exercises that go hand in hand with it.** Since Peary was so influential in making the squat so popular, as well as being a strong advocate of hard work on the basics, I thought it fitting to spend some time on this lifting game icon.

Chapter Three
Peary Rader, the man & his methods

Here is a brief article about Mr. Rader by **Bill Hinbern:**

"They Called Him...

    The Iron Man

        Dear Friend,

One of the truly great pioneers of modern weight lifting was born in 1909.

Peary Rader, strong man, writer, publisher, and founder of the famous Iron Man Magazine gave an open forum to those that wanted to share their methods for success. It All Started From Humble Beginnings.

From humble beginnings in rural America, young Peary Rader had a burning desire to go from a skinny lad to a strong man.

He tried every type of physical training course that his meager allowance would provide. Nothing seemed to add weight, or strength for that matter, to his scrawny frame. He decided to experiment on his own with a variety of methods. After several years of trial and error, young Rader managed to develop his own method for gaining weight and developing strength.

His Results Were So Obvious To Family and Friends that it earned Him the Nickname, **"Iron Man"**.

In August of 1936, in the midst of The Great Depression, he began publishing his own magazine to spread the word. The first issue was called, "Super Physique", but later was changed to, you guessed it, "The Iron Man".

It was a primitive affair; digest size, with only a few pages and a 'huge' first time print run of about 25 copies. He printed it with an old mimeograph machine found in the trash. Rader's new magazine was published bi-monthly and available by subscription only. It grew dramatically as well as the methods of printing.

Peary Rader's reputation was personified through Iron Man over the years. It was a clean magazine that could be left on the kitchen table. Rader was an elder in his church. No need to worry about any offensive language or photos in Iron Man. He wouldn't have it!

He didn't preach religion but occasionally would go off on a rant about some of the "modern supplements" used by the big names of the day.

Peary welcomed other points of view in his magazine offering an open forum to anyone who had something worthwhile to contribute.

He gave a start to many successful writers such as **Anthony Ditillo, Bruce Page, Michael J. Salvati, Bradley J. Steiner**, etc.

I remember when I would get my copy of Iron Man in the mail. I would drop whatever I was doing and open the brown envelope. Immediately, I would go to my favorite author and begin reading.

Great stuff in those days. Valuable information from a variety of sources.

    Best wishes,

    Bill Hinbern

I thought I should throw this in for a bit of interesting background info on Rader.

Here is an excerpt from a "specialization" training program, with this particular section on the legs. You may well imagine what Peary is going to say, but here goes:

LEG SPECIALIZATION

Almost every fine, powerful pair of legs in existence today is the result of the squat.

You should do many sets of from 10 to 15 or 20 reps. The number of sets you can work up to will depend on your energy and ability. It may be as high as seven sets, or you may be able to obtain sufficient results with only two sets. Always perform your squats with a flat back. Use as heavy a weight as you can for the required number of reps.

Follow the methods of deep breathing as advised under the paragraph on breathing. You won't have to concentrate on it to the extent you do when trying to gain weight or build a large chest. You will find that you need considerable rest between sets as this is a very strenuous program.

If you want to develop the lower part of your leg more than the upper part then you should squat with the heels on a block of wood or you can squat on the toes with your back against the sliding post. Keep feet close to the post. Sit erect and go straight up and down.

For general thigh development, however, with equal development for the front and back of the thigh, **nothing can equal the regular flat footed squat with the back flat, or even arched a little.**

Three workouts per week are ample and two is often best. Leg specialization is hard work and requires lots of energy, **necessitating lots of rest and sleep, with a full diet.**

AUTHOR's note

You will not often find modern training regimens or programs suggesting 20 reps in the squat, but you will see this was pretty commonly done back in the "old days".

You will also note that this rep range is fairly uniquely suggested for the squat, with a couple of other exercises such as those for calves or forearms. The Hise Shrug is also one that calls for high reps, again because it is considered as "breathing" and conditioning exercise.

Why so many reps?

You will see that the squat was considered not just a leg exercise, but an exercise to boost the metabolism, create expanded lung power and was a general conditioning exercise for the overall system. We will explore some other exercises that employ many body parts and are certainly worthy additions to a strength building arsenal, but none will serve as a substitute for the squat.

Squatting with heavy weights, five sets of five reps with 450, is an important part of John Davis' training for power. Here he shows his style with 500 pounds at an exhibition staged by John Terlazzo in New York. (Ralph Mazzaro photo)

In another section from the same program, Rader describes an abbreviated program **for those with limited time to train**, as shown here:

AN ABBREVIATED PROGRAM OF BODYBUILDING

Many times a pupil may find himself without sufficient time for a complete and heavy workout period for one night or for a lengthy period of time. Others will find that they never have time for a long program of exercise. For these we present the following program as being one of the very best for the purpose. Not only is it the very best for the purpose. Not only is it a good program for keeping in condition but it is also **a good program for all-round muscle development**. We have used many abbreviated programs but find this one is the very best that we have found so far. It is also a good foundation program from which to build up a more varied program. If you have time for it you could add a press from behind neck and a curl. If you have a tendency toward adding weight around the waist you might want to add some abdominal exercise. Or you can add any other exercises where it seems you need work. But, as we have said before, this is an abbreviated program developed and arranged for those who find they haven't time for a larger program of exercises. Also it is ideal for those who are low in energy and cannot gain well on a heavier program. It is also a very ideal weight gaining program, in fact, one of the very best, using, as it does, the largest muscle masses in the body. For all these things we can recommend it very highly.

There are only three exercises – the **supine press** on bench (of course, if you do not have a bench or anyone to hand off the weight, you can perform the exercise on the floor), the **two arm rowing exercise** (if you do several sets of this exercise we recommend you do part of the sets with bar pulled to abdomen and the others bar pulled to chest. This will work all the muscles across the back) **and the squat.**

John Davis, York Barbell Club's heavyweight champ, says heavy bench presses are a valuable auxiliary exercise to build power for overhead pressing. Here Marvin Eder shows how it's done with 350. (Ralph Mazzaro photo)

The Bench Press, aka Supine Press shown above

We recommend that you do the supine press 12 repetitions and the rowing exercise 12 repetitions and the **squat 20 repetitions**.

You should also develop a similar breathing system with the rowing and supine press. That is, take two deep breaths while weight is on the floor between repetitions of the row, and two deep breaths while weight is at straight arms length in the supine press*. Hold the breath while doing the supine press just as you do in the squat.

*Author's note

This breathing suggestion is not commonly seen being used today, but much later in the book, you will see that Pavel makes a somewhat similar suggestion for building pure strength

You should work up to 4 to 6 sets in each exercise. If you do this, you should perform some of your sets of squats with different repetitions, as for instance; the first set with 20 reps, the second set with a heavier weight for 10 reps, the third set with a little less weight for 15 reps and the fourth set with more weight and 10 reps.

In any case you should always follow each set with a set of **pullovers**. Follow other training advice as given earlier in the course.

Followed properly, and with many sets, the above program can become **one of the fastest weight gaining programs in existence as it uses nearly all the large muscle masses of the body.**

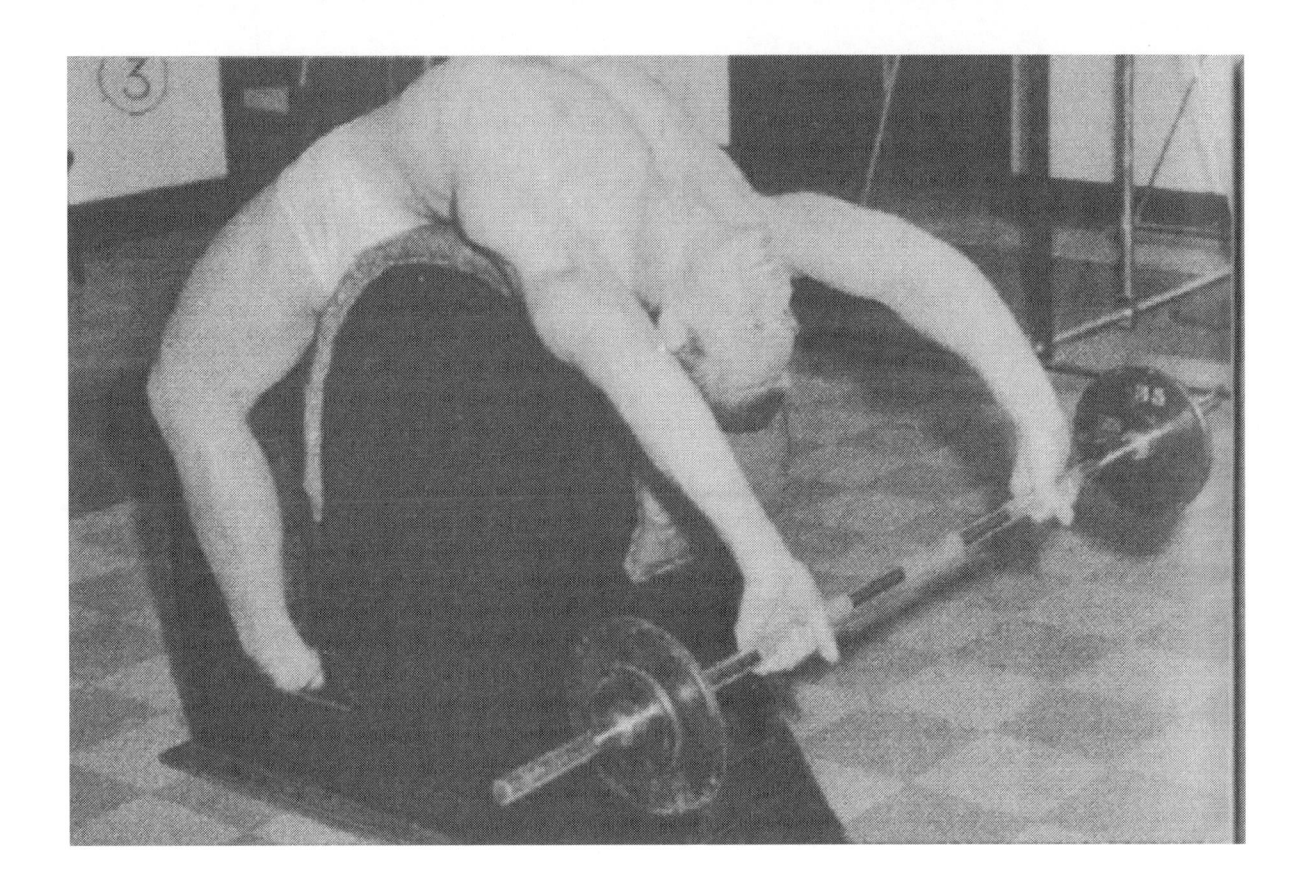

Here is a special bench especially made for the pullover called the moon bench or yogi bench.

I'll bet your gym does not have one of these!

More unique advice from Peary

REBOUND PRINCIPLE OF DEVELOPING MUSCLE AND STRENGTH

This principle is not new but it has never been used extensively and conscientiously by bodybuilders until it was analyzed and presented in "**Iron Man**" magazine.

It is one of the key secrets of developing great strength as well as unusual muscularity. It is performed naturally in the squat by most men, as well as in the supine press. It is the real secret for the success in developing great strength through the dead hang snatch and clean. The dead hang lifts are rebound lifts. We present the idea behind this method in the following so that you can apply it to any or all of your exercises. It would require too much space to describe its application to every exercise, but **once you grasp the principle it is easily applied by anyone.**

In the dead hang clean you grasp the bar and pull it to the shoulders in the regular style for the clean, then lower it with fair speed (to lower too slowly will defeat the purpose of this style of performance), then when the plates are about 3 inches or so from the floor, stop the weight and pull it again into the shoulders for the clean.

The sudden stop and reversal of muscle action against the resistance of the weight places a much greater strain on the muscles than can be obtained in any other way.

The same identical method can also be applied to the two arm snatch; dead lift and one arm snatch and clean.

When applying it to the squat you start the squat in the regulation way but when the thighs reach parallel position with tops of thighs you immediately tense the muscles and come back up. Remember, do not allow yourself to go to the bottom of the squat and stop there. **You catch yourself with muscle tension** and start back up. Do not squat too low or you will not get the effect you would otherwise get on the muscles. At first, you will not use as much weight, perhaps, as in the slow squat, but later on you will be able to use more and you will find yourself making added gains in strength and development. (It is never advisable to squat clear to bottom in the squat with heavy weights due to danger of a strain in the Sacroiliac area, or lower part of hips where spine and hip bones come together*). Of course you hold the breath when performing any rebound exercise.

* *Author's Note*
You will see dissenting opinions about this later on

When using it with the supine press on bench you perform the exercise in the usual manner, except that you lower the weight comparatively fast, and just before the bar touches the chest you stop the weight and start back up. In other words, you rebound it from the tense muscles – it gets what might be termed a muscle bounce from the tensed muscles. Here again we find that this is the reason for the superiority of the supine on the bench to the supine on the floor. On the bench you are almost forced to use some kind of rebound with a heavy weight due to the fact that you can't allow it to rest on elbows on floor between repetitions.

Here again, you may, if you desire, use the rebound method by stopping the weight's downward movement just before the elbows touch the floor.

Of course, this shortens the movement, which in any case is not complete when performed on the floor, and therefore, it is advisable to perform the supine press on the bench whenever possible.

*Author's note

This is not a method that is seen often being done in gyms these days. Please do not confuse this idea with the much more commonly done "bounce method" in which the lifter bounces the bar off his chest on the bottom of a bench press, or bounces off the bottom of squat position. This is a form of cheating, as opposed to actually making the movement more difficult by dead-stopping at a position that generates no associated momentum. There is a monumental difference between these 2 modes.

The Ironman take on the Hise Shrug:

THE HISE BREATHING SHOULDER SHRUG

This is a rather recent discovery made and developed by **J.C. Hise** and has had amazing success in the **development of a high arched chest, good posture, stronger diaphragm (termed the LIFE muscle by Hise) and weight gaining in cases where nothing else seemed to help.**

Doubtless many new improvements will be made in the future, but we present you the best methods to date.

Originally, rather light weights were thought to be better. It was later learned that heavy weights are better. You will, therefore, have to have loading standards for your bar as you may reach 600 or 700 pounds or more in this exercise. You will start out with rather light weights however, and gradually work up, as there is possibility of strain if you start out with heavy weights. **Most fellows will do well to start with about 100 pounds until they have learned the correct movements and positions.**

You take the weight on the shoulders as if you were doing the regular squat. Then, standing with feet in solid position you take a deep breath – always striving to breathe into the upper part of the chest, as high as possible while shrugging the shoulders upward as high as you can. You will **also tense the front of neck muscles as this greatly aids in lifting the chest higher**, causing you to make quite a face.

You will also **make every effort to breathe in as deeply as possibly.** Then breathe out and sag down, then go through the same procedure again and so on until you complete 20 repetitions.

You will probably, at times, find it helpful to work up to 30 repetitions and even 40 repetitions. Most men perform about 3 sets of this exercise. However, this will be governed by the amount of energy you have to expend. Some men find that they like to rock forward on the toes when performing this exercise, however, it is not necessary.

When you reach heavy weights you will find that you are not able to shrug the bar very high.

Mr. Hise says that this varies in different people and is **not too important as long as you are shrugging it as high as you can.** Sometimes it may rise 2 inches, but with others possibly only about a half inch or so.

It is not necessary to use any other exercises with this shrug but we recommend that you use at least the two arm pullover. Most fellows using it will add other exercises for all-round development. You will probably need to use a pad under the bar at first until the shoulders get toughened up to stand the weight on the trapezius muscle.

To most people this will not seem like an exercise and they are likely to dismiss it without a fair trial.

This is a mistake, as its virtues have been proven. **You will soon see your chest becoming higher and larger and it will take on a better taper.** You will have better posture and your waist will probably become smaller.

This exercise has also been used as a reducing exercise with success, though this use has not been widespread enough to prove its value or make any definite schedules for its use for this purpose other than a note that heavy weights must be worked into this.

The shoulder shrug has been very effective in developing the chest, giving great sustaining power and general well being.

You may get dizzy at first from taking so much oxygen into the lungs but this will not injure you in any way.

Author's note

This exercise seems to have gotten lost in the shuffle these days. It is hard to imagine that this is because it was/is ineffective, considering the high praise given by the likes of Hise and Rader. Perhaps it is something we modern day iron heads should experiment with in our current programs before we write it off. Just because something falls out of popularity for some time does not really mean that happened for sound reasons.

Look at the current success that the kettlebell exercises are seeing. There were decades when these things were relegated to grandpa's basement or attic, and were never seen in most gyms. I just offer some food for thought, here.

Start position for Hise Shrug in Smith machine

Top position for Hise Shrug in Smith unit

While I am showing the exercise in the smith unit, it would be better done with a standard Olympic barbell in a power rack.

While we are on the subject of the shrug, I thought it a good time to bring up and discuss Mr. **Paul Kelso**, inventor of the **Kelso Shrug.**

Chapter Four

The Shrug

Featuring

Shrug Variations
by Paul Kelso

January 1986 – Part One

Over a year ago, I promised **Peary Rader** an article about **the Kelso Shrug** explaining what this principle is and how it may be applied. As I state in my course, the Kelso Shrug is **not a single magic exercise**, but positive and negative **applications of the shrug principle to a variety of movements**. I experimented for years to apply these moves to Olympic and powerlifting needs, testing them in conjunction with different lifts and on every type of machine available. A large number of bodybuilding benefits came to light during this tinkering and I will present some of them in this article.

Naming an exercise or training principle after oneself may seem rather conceited or presumptuous.

I am hardly a **Zottman** or **Hackenschmidt** and there is very little entirely new in weight sports. I merely attempt to identify the various movements without causing confusion or being unnecessarily cute.

If there is a **Kelso Shrug**, it is the first I discovered and still find to be very effective. One day, quite by accident, I picked up a bar with a combined rowing and shrugging movement. I felt an unfamiliar response across my upper back so I spent the rest of the afternoon doing bent-over shrugs; underhand, overhand, close grip, wide grip, rolling motions, noticing the different muscle responses. **I worked these movements into my program and realized more sharp, visual gains in my lats and traps in six months than I had in years of training.**

Most are familiar with the usual standing shrug; it is a fine movement, but try something else.

Here's how to do a Kelso Shrug . . .

The Lat Shrug: Assume a position for bent-over rowing. Select a weight that can be used for 8 to 10 reps. Using a close, underhand or curl grip, shrug the weight up toward the chest, aiming the direction of contraction toward the lower trapezius and further to the rear, NOT up toward the ears! Do not bend the elbows. Use only the natural mobility of the shoulder blades while "thinking" the lats into action (this may take a little practice). Lower the weight to a full stretch. The lats should feel like they are tearing loose about the 9th rep.

That's the original Kelso Shrug.

Bent Over Shrug: same position but using an overhand, knuckles up grip 8 to 10 inches apart depending on the lifter.

This variation produces much more emphasis on the middle trapezius and less on the lats. Concentrate dead center between the scapula and crunch them together, not forward or backward along the spine. This overhand style will do more to develop the middle trap specifically than any other exercise I know.

The Rolling Motion: Also performed in the Bent over rowing position. Shrug the bar toward the ears and then roll the contraction, with scapular movement, over and back toward the rear and then return to starting stretch position. Or, contract toward the rear and roll forward toward the ears and then back to start.

As this movement works almost the entire upper back area from the back of the neck to the lower lat inserts, it is excellent as a general movement for the first year man or intermediate who does not wish to further specialize.

Many published back routines include four or five of more different rowing or pulling exercises practiced 4 to 6 sets each.

It is my observation that such a routine becomes less effective about two-thirds through because of fatigue to the biceps, brachialis, rear deltoid and other assisting muscles.

Next time in the gym, do several sets of heavy bent rows. Take the last set to the point of failure so that no more reps can be performed without cheating or heaving the weight. Then, while still holding the bar at arms' length and in the same position, start shrugging. At least three or four shrugs should be possible. **This indicates that the muscles assisting the movement have failed before the muscles targeted by the exercise!** Therefore, I recommend that the shrug movements be placed after arm pulling exercises in a program. If the lifter is working with pre-exhaustion techniques, he should do the shrugs first in his routine. I have also 'super-setted' using lat shrugs and bent over rows on an every other set basis and even every other REP with the overhand grip. I do not advocate using these shrugs in place of standard movements unless specializing. A combination works best as full involvement of all the major and assisting muscles is necessary for full development.

The shrug principle may be applied in many ways on a large variety of machines varying the direction of the shrug on a line of contraction from the hands to any chosen point along the spine between the neck and the lower Latissimus.

Author's note:

This statement seems to be at the heart of the Kelso Shrug book and is probably its core idea. As Paul state early on in this article, there is more to the Kelso Shrug than simply one exercise. It is more a way of adding a shrug movement and or applying the principles of the shrug to a variety of other exercises, In addition to getting the most out of the more traditional shrug movement.

For instance, the Lat Shrug (curl grip) practiced at a normal angle for rowing can work both the middle trap and the lat depending on direction of contraction. Leaning forward so that the upper torso or spinal plane is closer to parallel with the floor will work the lats more sharply. The "lat angle" may be enhanced further by leaning forward while using a seated low pulley or leaning back using an overhead pull down machine. A variety of hand spacing and grips produces different effects on muscle groups. The possibilities have not yet been exhausted because of the wide variety of equipment available. I encourage lifters to boldly experiment with what they have at hand.

Wide Grip Shrugs: These movements may be done several ways and are performed with a very wide snatch grip on an Olympic or power bar. In the bent over position, the contraction is to the middle of the back. Standing, there are two basic alternatives: to the rear, as in finishing a deadlift, or up toward the ears. **All the wide grip movements aid in widening the shoulder girdle**, especially with young people.

The bent over position works the middle trap and contributes to the 'spread' while the standing shrug to the rear, shoulders back deadlift style, could be considered a basic exercise in a general program as it works the entire trapezius. Shrugging up with a wide grip is specific to the upper trap and strongly involves the attachments high on the back of the neck area. **Prepare for some exquisite soreness after the first couple of workouts with this one!**

In all of these shrugs it is important not to use a weight so heavy that the full range of motion is impaired!

However, after several months the lifter probably will be able to shrug more than he can properly row or pull in the corresponding position. Some experience lower back stress in the bent over position – bending the knees and "sitting" back will help. (Getting to work on the lower back wouldn't hurt either!) Placing the forehead on a rack or high bench also relieves the strain but the best method is to do the Bent Over or Lat Shrugs while lying face down on an adjustable incline bench set for the angle of attack. This takes the legs and lower back out of the movement and allows the upper back to do the work. **Lat and bent over shrugs work best practiced at very low angles with the upper body close to parallel with the floor.** Wide grip shrugs may also be worked on an incline bench. A setting of 45 degrees up to nearly perpendicular provides lots of angles for attack. Training partners can help getting the bar into position and there are any number of racks, benches and uprights in a gym that could be used.

Use some imagination!

Wide grip shrugs also may be practiced on the cable crossover machine set on low pulley. **This supplies negative resistance.** Unfortunately, these machines differ widely in cable length and amount of weight available.

The Lat Flair: Inexperienced bodybuilders often have trouble developing the extreme flair or outspread needed for a lat pose.

Muscle control is involved and the complaint is that the scapula won't cooperate. Try this: stand in the cable crossover machine with it set on high pulley. Arms should be extended straight out to the side or slightly up and forward.

(The height of the lifter may be a factor; some do this movement seated.). Use enough weight so that the relaxed arms are stretched and the lats and scapula are under strong stress. The feel should be one of semi-dislocation. Then, without bending the arms, shrug the scapula toward each other while concentrating on the lower trap area as a focus. Return to full stretch, keeping the weight under control. **Reps in the 10 to 12 range result in increased scapular mobility**, muscle delineation and striations of the entire area involved.

By the way, **this movement is similar in negative to an old spring set exercise**. Remember holding the springs behind the back and pressing the hands straight out, rep after rep? Find that old set, put some springs on it, grab the handles and stretch it across the upper back. Press it out and then extend and contract it with scapular and shoulder girdle motion. That's right, a lat spread with resistance. A few sets of this and the crossover machine movement in a program will improve anybody's 'spread'!

Author's note:

It is fascinating that Kelso advocates the use of the spring expander set here, yet another old school tool that seems to have been abandoned in recent years.

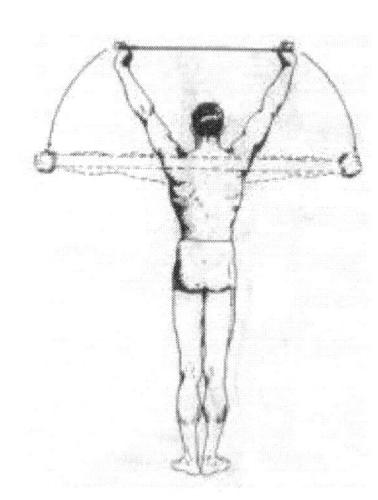

For a full manual on cable training exercises, check out the free downloads section of Christianiron.com, here:

http://christianiron.com/Freedownloads.aspx

There is a free Cable Training guide by Brad Reid available there, as well as many other useful free resources!

My original course stated that **multi-angular shrugs strengthen the entire shoulder girdle and build a foundation for heavy training.** This involves the front of the girdle and calls for PUSHING movements. How can there be a shrug for the chest? There are several and the **dipping shrug** should interest bodybuilders.

Shrug Dips: Warm up with several sets of parallel bar dips. Resume the position but this time raise and lower the body on straight arms using only the action of the shoulder girdle. **This is the direct negative of the common standing shrug**. Lower the body by allowing the shoulders to rise toward the ears. Raise the body by forcing the shoulders down. Varying the angle of the body activates or stresses different muscles. Leaning forward Gironda-style will make the lats, serratus and pectorals scream and will promote mid-chest pectoral cleavage. A dip belt makes this one a winner.

This exercise is best done last in a chest routine following parallel bar dips or decline work. This can be a very tough movement and may take lots of practice. Many will find the standard width dipping bars too close for comfortable performance; **using dip bars that open in a 'Y' shape will allow for experiments in hand spacing.**

Related movements can be performed in the pushup position, or upright with the hands on boxes with the feet elevated to the front, and so on.

Programs: My guess is that most of the lifters reading this article are not doing 15 to 25 sets per body part like the great champions. Advanced men will be able to work these shrugs into their routines using their own experience. But for the more average person training 2 to 4 days per week using far fewer sets per body part, let me make a few suggestions:

Lats: 1.) Bent over rows, seated pulls or overhead pulldowns. 2.) Lat shrug – close, curl grip.

Traps: 1.) Standing wide grip – shrugged up or toward rear. 2.) Bent over shrugs – overhand grip.

Chest, Torso: 1.) Parallel bar dips – wide grip, elbows out. 2.) Shrug dips – lean forward.

Lat Flair: 1.) Wide grip pulldowns or chins. 2.) Crossover machine shrugs. 3.) Spring set shrug – if desired.

These suggested combinations should be worked in with current programs as needed. **Adding them all is just too much**. The lifter should choose either the "Lats" group or the "Lat Flair" section. Experienced men with a separate back day might cut their programs back one third and add several of these shrugs.

Two to four sets apiece, 8 t0 12 reps, should be plenty of work for first year and intermediate men. A really ambitious lat and trap program for split training might include bent over rowing, standing wide grip, bent over and lat shrugs. A more specialized lat program would include rows and pulls, crossover machine shrugs and lat shrugs. Again, these shrugs should be performed after an arm pulling or rowing exercise they closely resemble unless pre-exhaustion is being used, then do them first.

Results from using these shrugs include increased thickness, separation and a thickening of attachments along the spine. A generally enhanced sculpturing of muscularity can be expected.

The lat shrug not only works the lats and middle traps but aids the shrug dip in carving out the line of the lat along the fib cage as seen from the front. One fellow performs lat shrugs while lying face down on a decline bench. He reports better results this way than in the bent over position. The bench is raised on blocks so that the bar doesn't hit the floor at full stretch.

Others use heavy dumbbells when bent over or using benches. However, the underhand grip effect CANNOT be achieved properly with dumbbells because of the difficulty in maintaining the palms front rotation. Finally, the overhand grip bent over shrug is just flat FINE for filling up the mid-scapular hollow with muscle.

Doubting Thomas's always appear when anything new comes along. Let me challenge the scoffers to a test of the possibilities of the shrug variation principle. Jump up to the chinning bar and grab on wide. Get a full hang stretch. Now shrug the body up using only scapular mobility and other torso muscle contractions. Do not bend the elbows. Try several reps. several sets. Use a weight belt. Any questions? This move should follow chins or pull-downs in a program.

One other thing about these shrugs and a dozen others I haven't mentioned:

They Increase Strength!

My next article will discuss variations of the shrug principle **for Olympic lifting, the deadlift, and the bench press. (P.K)**

November 1988 – Part Two

I stated in my January 1986 article that:

Shrug movements develop strength and have direct application to Olympic lifting and powerlifting. The "Kelso" or "lat shrug" and other movements were originally designed to act as foundation training for the shoulder girdle to better support heavy exercises and lifts.

These variations of the shrug principle, the adduction, retraction or "rotation" of the scapula, take advantage of the full range of motion possible by the shoulder girdle.

Most weight men have practiced standing shrugs with a barbell or dumbbells; primarily, these work the upper trapezius.

How about other directions, such as to the rear, down toward the lat insertions, forward using the pecs, out to the side or even a negative movement resembling a dip? Before listing movements specific to aiding the five current competition lifts, I want to explain how the exercises can help. **By analyzing a lift and breaking it down into parts, shrugs can be applied to a particular stage of the lift. Sticking points can then be isolated and attacked.**

Lifters familiar with my work will have read this before, but bear with me.

Many exercise routines do not fully work the muscle or muscle group intended because of the failure of assisting muscles. This is common in back routines.

After many sets of bent over rowing taken to failure, the trainee will still be able to crank out four or five reps of bent over shrugs. The biceps, brachialis and rear deltoids fail before the target muscles: the lats, traps, teres. rhomboids, etc. **This situation can also occur with the bench press.**

The Bench Press

Thirty years ago, the common questions among weight men were "How much do you curl?" and "What can you military press?" The bench press didn't have the popularity it has now. The lift has taken over as the standard for measuring another's strength. I would vote for the clean and jerk as a true indication of strength and athletic ability, but I doubt if I'll get much support these days, so let's discuss the bench press first.

Magazine articles about "the bench" have concentrated for years on lockout problems, hand and arm position, "finding the groove" and so forth. Less has been written about the initial drive off the chest than any other stage of the lift.

Watching top lifters can be revealing. What is the first thing that happens when the referee calls "press?" Most would say arm drive or explosion in order to gain enough height to allow the elbows to rotate into position to begin the follow-through to lockout. Well, look again. **Not only is there arm drive, but a spreading of the lats and a shoulder thrust upward. Not all lifters do this; some don't know to, but many of the best use this technique.**

Record breaking **Rick Weil** has written about it, describing the use of the back and shoulder girdle as a timed and sequential part of the lift requiring considerable practice. **This thrust can be developed by using the movement I call the bench shrug.**

The Bench Shrug: Take the bench press position on the bench. Hand spacing should be the same as regularly used or perhaps a finger width or two closer.

Lower the bar with straight arms by dropping the shoulders down toward the bench and crunching the shoulder blades (scapula) together; force the bar upward by spreading the scapula out to the side (like a lat spread) while raising the shoulders off the bench.

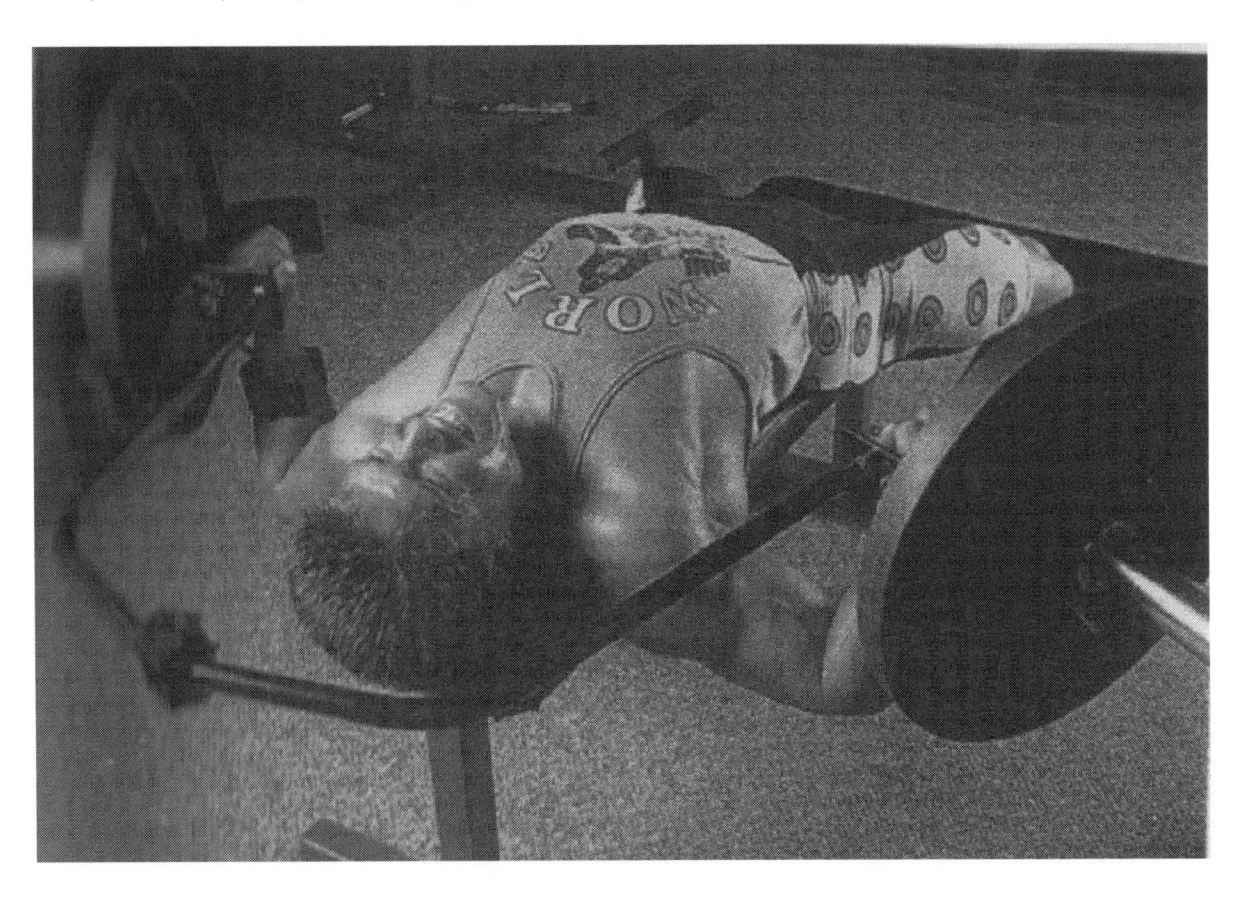

Use pectoral contraction to roll the shoulders up and in toward the sternum. Keep the arms straight at all times during the movement. **The bar will travel only three or four inches either way.**

Not only will the initial drive be enhanced by raising the bar, but control in lowering the bar will increase.

Always use spotters when doing the bench shrug. It is performed with straight arms and can easily land in the lifter's lap if the bar travels off line. If spotters aren't available, power racks will suffice. Just set the pins below the low point of bar travel, and **start out with a weight that can be benched six to eight reps.** Keep adding poundage over time.

It is common for a lifter to eventually handle several reps in the bench shrug with the same weight as his best single bench. For example, I have done four reps with 15 percent over my best single several times.

I suggest adding two sets of the bench shrug at the end of a bench workout.

Several of my college lifters experienced a gain of 20 pounds in the bench press after one month.

This had two causes: **added shoulder girdle strength and control coupled with learning to use the upward "shrug" and roll during the initial drive.**

It is possible to do this movement on the incline bench, but it is trickier to control and more limited in range. Olympic lifters may want to try it on an incline as a support move for the clean and jerk. I no longer recommend an unusually wide grip unless working with moderate weights because very heavy loads with an extra wide grip can cause injury to the shoulders. But closer grips are worth experimenting with for pectoral work, as is the shrug dip.

The Shrug Dip: These dips are the direct negative of the regular standing shrug. These should be done immediately following parallel bar dips.

The lifter assumes the position for dips but raises and lowers the body on straight arms by allowing the shoulders to rise toward the ears and then lifting the body by forcing the shoulders down using pectoral, serratus and Latissimus contractions. **Use of a heavily loaded weight belt is a must if shrug dips are intended as an assistance exercise for the bench press.**

Lance Dreher, Mr. Universe, told me recently that he had learned the shrug dip in the late '70s from former A.A.U. Mr. America **Bob Gajda**. He called the move "monkey dips" and also advocated lean-forward shrugging. Why lean-forward shrugs at a variety of angles, and how do lean-forward shrugs affect the lifts? Let's analyze the movements and see.

(See Lance Dreher photo on following page)

Snatch, Clean and Jerk, and Deadlift

I am not going to discuss the performance and techniques of these lifts as I assume readers are familiar with them. These lifts are different but have similar stages. The first for our purposes is the initial drive off the floor to the point where the bar is roughly just below the knees. This varies depending on the size and proportions of the lifter. The second phase includes thrusting the hips forward while driving the upper body toward the vertical. Third, as the body extends vertically, the shoulders are shrugged upward and pulled to the rear followed by arm pulling. In the deadlift, the shrug part of the lift is directed primarily to pulling the shoulders back instead of up (there is no arm pull in the deadlift, of course).

At this point I'd like to ask a few questions: Why do 95 percent of all lifters practice only the regular standing shrug when the upper body in the first stage above is angled at 35 to 40 degrees in relationship to the floor and 55 to 65 degrees in the second stage?

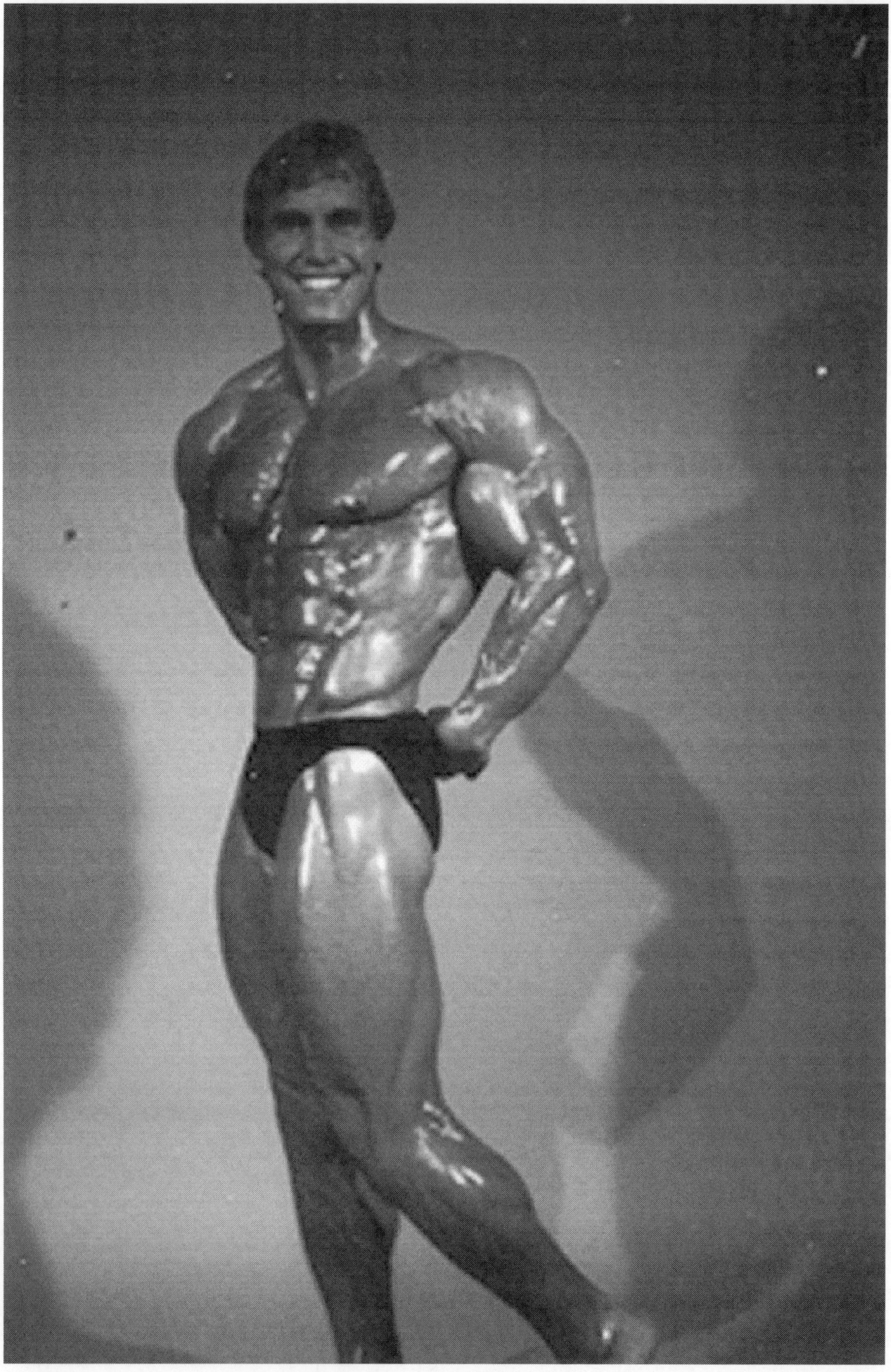

Why do Olympic lifters use only a clean-width grip in shrug training when the wide grip used in snatching causes a different direction of pull force during contraction of the muscles involved?

Why are deadlifters not using their competition (over and under) grip when shrugging in the gym?

I am not leading a crusade against the standing shrug. It is a specific movement within the clean and jerk and the standing shrug is absolutely required for gym training so that maximum bar height may be obtained. However, **it works the upper trap primarily, and it is not necessarily the best assistance movement for the lower stages.**

In the lower stages of the three lifts, the traps and lats are engaged in maintaining and gaining bar height as well as stabilizing the bar and keeping it close to the body. The upper traps have only a partial role in pulling the shoulders to the rear.

Here's what I recommend in answer to the three questions above:

First, lie face down on a heavy duty adjustable incline bench set at about 35 to 45 degrees. A free standing bench is best. This angle should match the angle of the spine in relation to the floor during the initial drive of the pull. Have training partners hand you the bar. Get a full stretch every rep and shrug the bar up toward the chest. Grip selection depends on which lift or muscle group is being targeted.

Then, move the bench up to 55 to 65 degrees for a set or two. This setting aids the second stage of the lifts, as the lifter begins driving toward the vertical. Mentally focus the contraction on a spot between the shoulder blades. Crunch the scapula together. **Don't contract up toward the ears.** Never use a weight so heavy that it prevents full stretch or contraction. The lower the angle of the bench, the more the lats are involved, especially if an underhand grip is used.

Second, because of the angle of the arms during the snatch, the direction of contraction during the shrug at the top of the lift is not just up but at an angle from the hands to the base of the neck. The scapula move toward each other as well as up. Olympic lifters should practice snatch grip shrugs at several angles as well as with the clean width grip. Using a wide grip is the way it's done during the snatch itself, so why not during the assistance exercise?

Third, from what I read of top deadlifter's published routines, most do 25 to 30 lifts per workout. At least two-thirds of those reps do not seriously challenge the lifter's ability to get his shoulders back. A few sets of lat pulls and shrugs are tacked on at the end.

The standing shrugs are usually pulled up first and then "rolled" back. **Why not practice shrugs on the bench using the two angles mentioned above and work all the muscles for the upper back involved in drawing the shoulders to the rear?**

Lean-forward shrugs will increase all lifters' ability to "set" their shoulders at the beginning of all lifts and keep the upper back straight and head up throughout. The lean-forward shrugs should be practiced regularly with the competition grip for two reasons. It's the one used during competition, and secondly, there is a very subtle difference in muscle action between one side of the back as compared to the other when using the over and under grip. **Not only will these back shrugs help get the shoulders back, but they will aid in keeping the bar close to the body as well. This is extremely important.**

I suggest using a bench or some other support so that greater weights may be used and more specific muscle groups targeted. Many lifters are capable of handling huge weights for sets and reps with shrug movements, often more than they can deadlift for a single; this being the case, straps are a good idea.

Author's note:

And now for our segueway back into our key subject, the squat;

The Squat

I said earlier that I'd talk about shrug variations for the five competitive lifts. So, **what kind of shrug variation can help the squat?** I know of no shrug that can build hip and thigh strength, but give me time. I do know one that will build confidence and upper body power which will allow the lifter to manhandle a lot of weight. This **movement will get new trainees past the stage of the bar hurting the shoulders, knit the shoulder girdle together and expand the bone structure.**

I'm talking about the Hise Breathing Shrug. The story of **Joe Hise** has been told many times, so I won't get into it, **but he is known as the first powerlifter.**

The Hise Shrug and high rep breathing squats were the keystones of many bulk and power courses during the '50s. I didn't develop this movement, but it was the first shrug I ever attempted back in 1955.

Back out of the rack with a weight that can be handled for eight reps in the squat. **Don't use a powerlifting stance**.

Keep the bar in a high position and shrug upward toward the ears with trap and scapular action. Try for eight reps. After several months, weights can be handled in excess of the lifter's best squat single. **This will increase squatting ability as the lifter not only gains shoulder girdle strength and stability, but also confidence as he practices backing out and setting up with overloads.** The back shrugs I described will help keep the back straight and the head up during the lift. Combining them with the Hise movement helps prevent losing the bar forward over the head during the squat.

Powerlifters should add two sets of Hise shrugs, bench shrugs and face-down incline bench back shrugs at the end of their squat, bench and deadlift workouts respectively. Olympic lifters will want to try snatch and clean grip shrugs at the positions discussed: initial, midpoint and vertical.

I say try them all, but get serious about those that meet immediate needs, such as sticking points, getting the shoulders back or the drive explosion in benching.

The section above consists of excerpts from old Ironman issues about Kelso's training ideas. For further and far more detailed instructions on Paul's methods and ideas, you may want to purchase his book:

Check out Amazon and ads in Powerlifting USA magazine

The Hise Breathing Shrug as seen from behind

Chapter Five
Back to Peary Rader's excerpts:

SPECIALIZING ON ONE EXERCISE FOR MAXIMUM GAINS

It is sometimes desirable to **specialize on one lift or exercise to the exclusion of all others**. The reason for this is that **you can direct all your energies and effort in one direction.**

This will enable you to make much faster progress and reach greater heights of strength and development than if you spread your efforts out over several movements. **It is not advisable to make this a permanent habit**, as it might result in an uneven development of the body, but it is helpful at times to do this. An example of this is **William Boone**, who has reached a **420 jerk and a 700 deadlift** expecting to do more, as well as a 315 bent press and a 360 jerk press all by this method of **specializing in one of these lifts at a time.** The same thing can apply to the development of increased size as well. For instance, if your legs are rather small then you could specialize on leg work – perhaps the squat alone for a certain period, If your back is weak you could specialize on the deadlift alone for a length of time. In doing this you would work with heavy weights and many sets. **The exact number would have to be determined by the pupil himself.** Find out what you can stand and progress best on. Also you will start out with one or two sets and then work up to more. You will also vary the number of repetitions and amount of weight in the different sets.

You will find that by specializing in this manner you can work up to a tremendous amount of work for the part in question and force the most stubborn muscles to respond.

Of course, if you are working the small muscles, like arm muscles, you would be able to use more exercises. For instance, for the biceps you would use two different types of curls, or for the triceps you could use the supine press and the bent arm pullover or the standing triceps curl.

Or you might be able to work both muscles if they were to be specialized on, and use perhaps 4 exercises. However, you should not get too many exercises, as the secret of this method is to limit the exercises and work them to the limit of your ability to stand it.

You will have to be watchful and not overwork, as you can go stale on this program just as you can on any other from overwork.

Pupils often ask what the sign of overwork is and we tell that that when they feel tired all the time and perhaps become nervous and irritable beyond normal they should check to see if they might not be overworking and perhaps under-resting.

Author's note:

Modern trainers such as Pavel have adopted a version of this idea known as "greasing the groove", which is more often associated with bodyweight movements such as pull-ups and pushups.

Earle Liederman also mentioned the concept, which I referenced in my book "The Secrets To Age Defying Strength", wherein he instructed a pupil looking for pec development to concentrate on the area by doing 150 reps a day of dips, both from the floor and from bars or chairs, and spring expander work. According to Earle, this method worked very well for this pupil.

THE USE OF "SHORT MOVEMENTS" FOR POWER & DEVELOPMENT

It is possible by the following methods to develop very great strength and **help you pass that sticking point in your lifts.**

It will also, in many instances, help you to get added development when other methods seem to fail.

An **example of what we mean by short movements is the half or quarter squat**. In this exercise **you can work up to tremendous poundage**.

This will often bring your regular squat up a lot and in many cases will start you gaining in leg development when you may have been at a standstill. It will also give you great power in such lifts as the jerk etc.

It will give you muscle and ligament strength obtainable in no other way.

Every bodybuilder and lifter should spend a specialized period on half and quarter squats for the power and development he can obtain from them.

The deadlift can be worked in much the same manner. **William Boone**, who specialized on this lift, started out by digging a hole in the ground 8 inches deep. He stood in the hole and did his deadlifts.*

Author's note He did not have a power rack as it was not invented yet... where there's a will, there's a way!

This **enabled him to use about 200 pounds more than he normally could do on the ground.**

He worked up to very high poundage while standing in this hole. Then when he had reached a satisfactory poundage he started filling the hole up and **when he had the hole filled he was doing a great many more pounds in his deadlift than had ever been possible for him before.**

The same system can be used in the supine press on floor. **You can place blocks under each end of the bar and press from this**,

* Author's Note* Here is yet another innovation used before the power rack came around!*

You may or may not know that strongman competitions often have an event based on deadlifting from blocks as in above mentioned section

If you wish you can press up a heavier weight than you could normally supine press by **the belly toss method***, and then do your repetitions by allowing the weight to come down only about half the way before pressing it back up. When you reach satisfactory poundage in this you can make the movements a little greater until you are supine pressing far more than you ever have before. **Your triceps and pectorals as well as the front of the deltoids will have taken on new size and shape.**

* *Author's Note*

The May 2010 issue of Powerlifting USA contained an article by Ron Fernando on Belly Tossing, and Ron compared it to the common modern practice of benching off of boards placed on the chest.

In regard to the deadlift above – **if you do not train out of doors where you can dig a hole, you can place blocks of wood under the plates as we advise in the paragraph on the supine press.**

When you first start some of these short movements you may find that you can't do much more than in the complete movement, but this is because you are no stronger than the poundage you have been using can make you. In other words, you have been cheating your muscles of the full power possible to them because you have limited the poundage to what you could do complete movements with. *

Author's Note what a concept... doing full ROM movements can be a way of cheating yourself

Note that many of the old time strongmen's feats of strength involved "short movements", involving super heavy weights, but just getting them slightly off the ground in some cases.

Such is the case with the photo shown below. Usually, harnesses were incorporated in these types of lifts.

Using a body harness in order to even budge this puppy would be one heck of a "short movement"

This dumbbell was reported to weigh 1650 pounds UNLOADED.

The man in the photo is Warren Lincoln Travis

We do not give all the exercises that can be used this way but only enough to demonstrate the principle of the thing so that you can apply it to any other exercises you happen to be interested in.

We do not advise a man to go on a permanent program of this sort but it is very wise to go on such programs at certain times for specialization periods. **You will be amazed at the all-round body strength these movements will give you.**

A similar method can be used for **developing the jerk.** You should take very heavy weights off the standards in hands at shoulders and do quarter squats in this position, coming up fast and trying to heave the weight as high off the shoulders as you can, which won't be much but it is the effort that does the job. **Then in the overhead portion of the lift you should suspend the bar from chains from the ceiling and load it up, then get under the bar, which has been suspended at the height of the top the head, and take the position of the jerk in split position and lift the bar on straight arms until you stand erect in the finishing position of the jerk.** While holding it thus, lower the weight just a trifle and press it back to arms length again. Do this about three times for each time you get up from the jerk position. If you have no overhead chains you can use high standards but in this case you may have to drop the weight each time, then unload it on the ground, then load it back up on the rack for the next repetition. The practice of this exercise will soon develop great power in the jerk, especially when used in conjunction with the quarter squats with the weight at the shoulders as described above.

You can use the same method for the bent press by supporting weights at various heights. **By a little thought you can devise ways of applying this principle to every exercise and lift to its benefit.** This is a system that was much used by the old timers but has been neglected in recent years by modern lifters and bodybuilders. **It is very valuable and not to be minimized in its importance.**

Here are Peary's thoughts on some other plateau busting methods for the advanced trainee; **building up to the rest-pause system that you may have thought was something new:**

OTHER SPECIAL TRAINING SYSTEMS

In the following programs and systems you will find many **methods for forcing added muscular growth and strength**. Most of these systems and methods are for advanced men though a few of them will assist beginners who have the problem of not gaining as fast as they should. The first, the Split Repetition method is one such.

The following pages are aimed at finishing a complete but condensed education in scientific bodybuilding.

SPLIT REPETITION

If you are of the type that has but little energy, you will find that at first you will gain best on a program in which the repetitions are split up into several sets. In this type of program you get the same strenuous work with less expenditure of energy. In following this split repetition program, it is not always necessary to split up the upper body exercises. However, where this is found desirable you should **split them into two sets of 6 repetitions each**. Use the standard program as outlined before, but instead of doing 10 to 12 repetitions in the press, do only 6. **Rest a minute and do 6 more,** working up to 8 repetitions. Do the same with the other exercises. **Split the squat repetitions into two groups of ten.** Do ten reps, then rest a while and do ten more.

Later on as you become stronger and feel the need of more work you may do another set of 10 repetitions making three sets in all. We advise you to use the same weight, if you can, for all sets. You may find, in the squat that you can make but 9 reps in the second set and only 8 in the third. Some fellows make ten for all sets. Or **it may be that you will wish to reduce the poundage for each succeeding set of squats to enable you to do the full set of 10 reps each time. This is all right.** Remember, **it is the hard reps in each set that benefit you the most. Try to make as many of them as possible.** It is well to do a set of pullovers between each set of squats, as well as to massage the legs lightly as this helps the flow of blood in carrying away fatigue poisons.

SPLIT, PAUSE PROGRAM

This method of squatting is for those with low energy or those who find that they cannot stand a bar on their shoulders for any length of time.

This program is an advanced version of the preceding program. You perform your upper body exercises in the usual manner, but when you come to the squat, instead of performing the full 20 repetitions and keeping the weight on the shoulders for the entire time, you perform about five reps in the usual manner with deep breathing.

As soon as you complete the 5th squat, you quickly replace the weight on the stands and do about 10 deep breaths, or possibly as many as 15, then quickly take the weight and perform another set of 5 squats, doing about 3 deep breaths between each squat. Then replace the bar on the stands for another pause of 10 to 15 breaths, then another set of 5 reps, pause, another set of 5 reps – in **all, 20 reps with 4 pauses.** If you are doing this because of pain in the shoulders from holding the bar you can wrap a pad around the bar which will help some. if the bar doesn't bother your you do not need the pad as it will be in the way for quick changes of the bar from shoulders to stands and back to the shoulders. You will, of course, require some good stands so that it will be convenient for these changes. You may want to make the pauses after but three squat but we do not recommend this where not absolutely necessary. You may soon work up to where you make three pauses in 20 repetitions and later but two. When performing with this method you must stand close to the stands when squatting so that you can quickly place the bar on them.

THE REST PAUSE SYSTEM

There is another version of this method called the **Rest Pause System**. It is performed in exactly the same way as recommended for the squat in the Split Pause Program as explained above.

However, instead of doing it with the squat only, you follow the same plan with every exercise on your program. In the curl, for instance, you will have a pair of boxes, a chair, or rack support at the proper height for resting the weight on between repetitions. You will do one repetition and rest the bar on the support for a count of 3 to 5 then grasp the weight and make another repetition, then pause for another rest for a count of about 5. Continue in this way for the full number of reps of 10 or 12. Follow this same method through your entire program – one rep, then a rest pause and so on. We suggest that you do two reps of the squat and a rest pause, rather than the five recommended in the first section of this method.

Some very remarkable gains have been made by men who followed this system when other methods failed.

☺

Here is a very interesting **isometric style,** weight free exercise for the chest, which incidentally shows up years later in a **Harry Paschall** routine, being demonstrated by his cleverly drawn strongman.

RADER HIGH CHEST PULL

You will find this one of the most unusual exercises for **giving great gains in rib box expansion.** It has given very good gains to advanced men who have trained for years with no chest improvement from any other method.

It can be practiced anywhere without special apparatus and several times per day.

It will give you chest increase in the upper chest where you want it most. It gives a high arch to the chest. No other exercise will affect the chest as does this exercise.

It is a little more difficult to learn than some other chest exercises and the better you learn it the more effective it becomes.

You stand and grasp a bar, a shelf, door, or any other solid, strong object which can be grasped at slightly above the height of the top of the head.

Now that you have a grasp on this object, with the hands spaced about 3 inches apart or less, you keep the arms straight and pull down and IN and at the same time take a deep breath. If you perform this movement properly you will feel a very strong pull in the area of the breast bone, and even a sharp little pain there at times. Don't be alarmed. This is an indication that you are performing the exercise correctly.

Some men find they can pull harder if they bend the elbows just slightly. Don't allow them to bend too much, though. The harder you pull the more benefit your chest will get, IF you are pulling correctly. **You MUST NOT contract the abdominals. If they are tensed they will flatten the chest and prevent any effective pull from the pectoral muscles which do the work in this exercise.**

After a little practice you will learn to give a little yank or jerk while pulling and this will increase the pull that you feel on the chest.

Demo of Rader High Chest Pull move

You can also obtain additional pull by tensing the front of the neck muscles and then pulling the head back. This should be learned last, for if you try to learn everything at once, you will, in all probability, defeat yourself in that you will not learn anything right. This neck tensing lifts the chest high and should be done at the same time you pull down an in with the arms. It is especially important that you should pull in very hard with the arms. Of course, you don't allow the arms to move from their position as that would spoil the effect.

You can do 15 to 20 of these pulls after each set of squats and your chest will feel stretched as it never has before. You **can perform a few reps of this exercise during the day and can do it every day without going stale. Your chest may get a little sore and tender at first, so don't overdo it until you get used to it.**

No other exercise can give you the maximum chest size this exercise can. Don't neglect it. **You won't need to perform the regular pullover when using this exercise, for it accomplishes the same thing much better**.

Next, the Ironman introduces the concepts of **cheating and forced reps:**

CHEATING METHOD OF EXERCISE

There are two methods of performing an exercise – very strict, and cheating or loose style. Taking the curl as an example; a very strict style would be where you stand strictly erect and slowly curl the weight to the shoulders with **no movement of the elbows, shoulders or body**. **It can be made very strict by leaning the shoulders against the wall or a post to prevent movement.**

A cheating curl would be performed by taking the weight in the hands and **starting it with a swing and bending back as the weight comes up. In other words, you use a fast start and lots of body movement – anything to get it up.** There are different degrees of cheating as you can plainly see, and it is used in different degrees by bodybuilders.

Generally speaking, most men will use a very strict style and find it best for most bodybuilding programs. There are times, however, when you reach a sticking point in your training where you will find that a specialized program of cheating exercises will help you get started progressing again.

With these cheating movements **you can use much greater poundage** and work the muscles very hard. This cheating style can be applied to nearly every exercise known.

Just remember in applying it to any exercise, that a cheating movement is doing it the easiest way and the one in which the greatest poundage can be used. In the press this would be a fast start and excessive back bend. In the bench press it would be bouncing the weight from chest and back arch. In the rowing you would start it fast and allow considerable body movement. In the squat you would not go so slow and also would aid yourself with one or two hands to get past the hard stages. This is easy to learn.

You need only release the bar with one hand and push against your thigh to help you out. So you can go on and on adapting cheating methods to your exercises.

You should not **use these methods** permanently – **only occasionally** to help speed your progress.

In addition to giving you added development you will find cheating methods will give you great strength in a hurry.

FORCED REPETITIONS

The method of forced reps has been used for many years and has certain values for a specialized program. In this method you use the help of two assistants who stand by to help you when you reach a point where you can't make another repetition. Let's take the bench press, for example. You have perhaps made 6 reps and as you start the 7th you get about half way up and stop. Your training partners will then place a hand under the bar and help you just enough to complete the movement. You will continue in this manner until you have completed 10 or 12 reps. In other words you do all you can without help, then complete the set with help.

This is a very advanced form of power and developmental training and should only be used by advanced men. You should use care that you do not become over trained and go stale. It can be used on any exercise and it doesn't take much imagination to know how to apply it to any exercise you wish to use it on. It can be used for one or many exercises. .
If you train alone, **one handed movements can be adapted to this method.**

*Author's note

I have to interject here and say that the last 2 methods spoken of by Peary are probably the 2 most overused methods in the gym. Enthusiastic young trainees in particular are guilty of this; thinking that using more weight either by cheating and/ or doing forced reps is the key to progress. Both methods have their place, but should be used as the exception, not the rule!!

A few more **minimalist** programs from the master:

MORE ABBREVIATED PROGRAMS

There are several reasons why some men find it advantageous to practice on an abbreviated squat program. One is that they don't have energy enough for the other exercises, and **as the squat is the key exercise** they eliminate some of the others. **There have been many cases where the pupil practiced nothing but the squat and made amazing gains in bodyweight.** It might be thought that this specialization would result in large legs and nothing else, but such was not the case, as the pupils made gains in the size of the chest, arms, neck, back, etc. These parts likewise increased in strength.

It is because of these characteristics that the squat is termed the "Growing Exercise."

It is often found that such as abbreviated program is the only way to force some stubborn cases to grow. Once they are on their way to gaining, other exercises are added.

Also it is sometimes the desire of some people to gain weight only. They have little interest in general proportions etc. They just want improved health and normal weight.

To these this abbreviated program is ideal. Also, if at some later date they wish to bring their other proportions up they need only adopt exercises affecting these parts.

Many fellows have found it wise to use nothing but the squat and perhaps one to three other exercises. They will perhaps use the press behind the neck – and rowing exercise – or perhaps they will adopt some favorite lift of exercise that affects some part of the body that they are particularly interested in developing. However, **they retain their key exercise, the squat, as their main exercise.**

- In these abbreviated programs the pupil is usually advised to so several sets of the squat. Often he will start with 10 reps, then rest and do 15 with a lighter weight, then rest and do 20 with a still lighter weight. Some men follow the practice of doing as many as 5 sets of squats of various numbers of repetitions and weights.

The same breathing methods and other practices in general are followed as given in the first standard program. We list later variations in programs for those who have tried the first or standard program for at least 3 months and wish to make a change.

PRESS – CHIN – SQUAT PROGRAM

*Author's note

This is essentially the program Peary used himself to kick-start his gains, which was mentioned earlier in the book

Here is an abbreviated program that has given very good results. It consists of but three exercises and yet they are so well chosen that **they cover most of the major muscles in the body.**

You should first perform the two arm press either in the **continental style or the military style**, or if you prefer, the press behind neck. Use only one style in your program. Follow this with the two arm chin. Be sure to make your chins complete by straightening the arms out when you come down and then pulling up until the bar touches the chest when coming up. Follow the chin exercise with the squats. We suggest that you do 10 to 12 repetitions in the press and 10 to 15 in the chin and 20 to 25 in the squat.

If you find it develops you better you can use the split repetition method on this abbreviated program, however, it would be wise to first try the above named repetitions as they are most successful in the majority of cases. **Work out two or three times a week** on this program. Also include the pullover in this program following the squat.

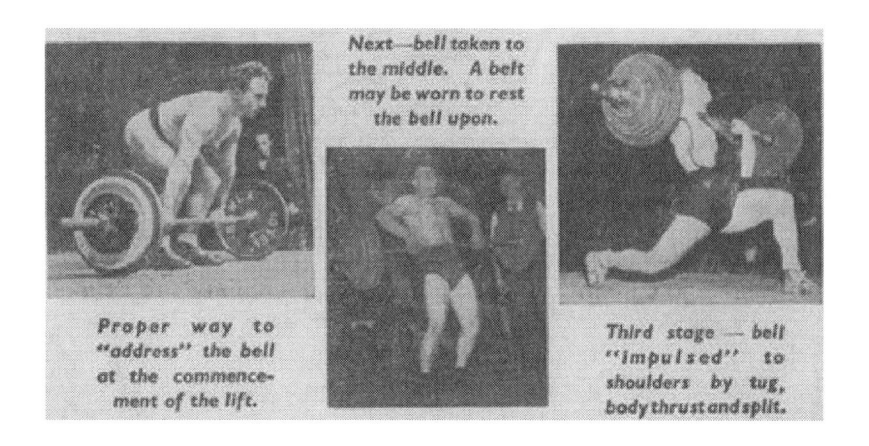

Proper way to "address" the bell at the commencement of the lift.

Next—bell taken to the middle. A belt may be worn to rest the bell upon.

Third stage — bell "impulsed" to shoulders by tug, body thrust and split.

The Continental Clean & press

**THE CLEAN AND PRESS
SQUAT PROGRAM**

Another wonderful program that has proven to be a marvelous all round developer is as follows:

First perform the **clean and press.** This is an exercise that **we rate as a body builder along with the squat. One could perform it alone and obtain marvelous results if he were to work hard enough at it.***

By using it along with the squat and the rowing exercise you have an unbeatable combination. This program would come under the heading of an abbreviated program. It requires considerable explanation.

*Author's note:

I knew a guy in my old neighborhood where I grew up that got very strong by using variations of the press as his primary means. He owned no bench, just a barbell set that he trained with religiously, in addition to doing some manual labor as a stock boy at a local small grocery store. He was the strongest kid in the neighborhood, without a question, and was one of the early influences on my own weight training start.

In the proper performance of the clean and press for a growing exercise you should use the same breathing methods that you use for the squat. You should work up to about 15 reps in the clean and press. Then add more weight. If the pupil will follow carefully, we will give a description of the proper performance.

Bend over the bar and grasp it at a little over shoulder width over grip. While keeping the legs almost straight, stand up, and as you do so pull the weight in to the shoulders. You should take a very deep breath as we have told you to do in the squat, and hold the breath until the weight is at the shoulders, after which you expel the breath and take another quick and VERY LARGE breath. In pulling the weight to the shoulders, make the movement with the arms as much as possible. **Use the legs no more than necessary**. You see, we want to make it as much an arm and shoulder exercise as possible. Now, after taking the deep breath at the shoulders, press the weight overhead.

in starting out you will probably be able to pull the weight up with the arms alone and to press the weight in military style, but as you progress in repetitions you will find that you will have to use the legs a bit more in pulling the weight up and that you will have to bend the back considerably to press overhead. This is proper, as by thus performing it you will be able to do more repetitions with more weight.

As you finish the press you will expel the breath and lower the weight to the floor. Now, while resting the weight on the floor, do your deep breathing, as in the squat. You will probably not take over two or three deep breaths between lifts, then hold the last one and pull the weight to the shoulders and perform another complete lift. Repeat thus until you have completed the full 15 reps. You may perform a set of light pullovers after this exercise.

In the photo,

Ken Patera performing the press portion of the C&P

The next exercise is the **Two Arm Rowing Exercise**. It should be performed as given earlier in the course.

Now perform your squat, also as given earlier, doing 20 to 25 reps. After your final squat perform another set of light pullovers.

You should feel that you have had a very good workout after this.

If you like, you may, on some of the first clean and presses, lower the weight to arms length only and just hold the weight in the hands against the thighs while doing your deep breathing, then pull the weight from here to the shoulders for the next rep.

CLEAN AND JERK PRESS SQUAT PROGRAM

This exercise is the same as the one above except that you use the clean and jerk instead of the clean and press. It is more advanced in that you use more weight and clean with as much leg action as necessary. **Then start the press with a drive of the legs by bending and then straightening them quickly**, then finish by pressing to straight arms length. Do this exercise first then your squats as usual. This program will give you rugged power as well as unusual development and is **a favorite program of Doug Hepburn.**

SPECIALIZED SQUAT PROGRAM

We have mentioned this program before. It is very effective where the pupil desires nothing but added bodyweight. Some pupils have found it a very fast method of gaining and they later adopt more varied programs.

It is also an excellent program for when a pupil's time is very limited. It has great chest developing qualities. In this program you use nothing but **the squat and the pullover or Rader Chest Pull. ****

You perform the squat first and just as given previously, and then follow it with a set of pullovers. If you feel you have the energy, you may do still another set of squats using either 20 or 15 or 10 repetitions and then another set of pullovers.

Some pupils thrive on several such sets. Other training principles involving diet, rest, sleep, etc, are the same as given for all other programs.

*Author's note:

In Arnold's book "the Education of a Bodybuilder", he suggested super sets of squats and pullovers as a base for a new weight trainee's program

I could go on and on with courses and programs written by Peary, but I really just wanted to give you a good taste of his ideas and some of his methods. You can see Peary Rader's and his magazine Iron Man's influences on all aspects of weight training right up to the present day. Some of the exercises have gone out of vogue in recent days, but perhaps they are worthy of exploring again and incorporating in our modern programs. It never hurts to try something new (new to you anyway)

Chapter Six
Mark Berry

Besides Peary Rader's name, you saw Mark Berry named above as an influence on the squat becoming popular in those early days. One of Berry's protégé's, and probably the most famous and successful one, was one John Grimek, who was one of those rare individuals that was both a great weight lifter and a great bodybuilder. He became a model in Berry's training manuals, and it was claimed that the squat was one of the key exercises that propelled Grimek to greatness ultimately. Berry went on to be an Olympic lifting coach and played a key role in the Milo Barbell Company's Strength magazine in the days after Calvert left. He designed the courses that went hand in hand with Milo barbell sets in 1930.

Here is an excerpt of the Berry course provided by one of the faithful followers of **Dave Draper's Iron online forum**, posted some years ago:

Course #1

Warm up with set ups, Std toe touches, Side bends
WO
1. Two arm curl. 2. The lying press. 3. Bent forward row. 4. Press behind neck. 5. Pull over. 6. Full squat. 7. Shrug. 8. Straddle squat. 9 Leg raises. 10. One arm Press. 11. KB swing. 12. Windup= forearms.13. Wrestlers bridge. 14. Reverse curl. 15. Two arm press.

Course #2

1. Alternating DB press. 2. Front raise with bar. 3. Squat press (as you go down in a squat you also press the bar overhead. 4. Step ups with weight. 5. Leg press. 6. Side bend. 7. Reguler Deadlift. 8. Alt. DB curl. 9. One arm side lateral. 10. Calf raises. 11. Stiff leg Deadlift. 12. One arm curl. 13. Abs ex. of your choice.
All the above is done 1 set of 6 to 12 reps

Course # 3

1. Two hands clean and press. 2. Two hands snatch. 3. Two hand clean and jerk. 4. One snatch. 5. One hand clean. 6 One jerk. 7. One hand Press. 8. Bent press. 9. Side press. 10. One swing catch with the other hand in front then continue to the other hand. 11. Two hand clean and push press. This one used to be called the continental.

John Grimek, perhaps Mark Berry's most famous pupil

Here is another famous Grimek Pose

   In the third course you must do the first three 5sets of 5 reps. After that if you have anything left in you do one or two of any of the DB lifting sets and reps are up to you.
He also wrote about proper bathing and clean clothes. He wrote about proper eating. No junk.
Mark Berry was the coach of the 1932 & 1936 Olympic lifting team.

Bill Hinbern on Berry:

Author and Olympic Coach, Mark H. Berry

Dear Friend,

Most of the training routines used by old time strong men up until the late 1920's used compound movements. Previous to that time the squat, or deep knee bend as it was called back then, was considered just another accessory exercise and was used very little. **It wasn't until a strength pioneer by the name of Mark Berry came along and placed an emphasis on the squat as a real body builder.**

After becoming a National Champion weight lifter himself **in 1925, Berry advocated drinking milk and heavy squats for building tremendous bulk and power.**

Through his insistent writings, Berry proved that the squat was the master exercise thus changing the science of bodybuilding and weightlifting and creating the stream of world champion lifters that became famous in the United States in the 1930's and 40's.

He saw the tremendous potential of a young man he met in the late 1920's and began to train him almost exclusively on his own special training methods.

His name...John C. Grimek.

Later, Grimek became a National Weight Lifting Champion and was a member of the famous Olympic Weight Lifting Team that competed in Berlin in 1936. However, **Grimek's real fame was that of bodybuilding. He became the only two time AAU Mr. America in 1940 and 1941. In addition, he won Mr. Universe in 1948 and Mr. USA in 1949. After that, he retired undefeated in any bodybuilding contest he ever entered!**

In the 1920's and 30's he(Berry) edited a variety of magazines published by the old Milo Bar Bell Co. including **Strength, The Strongman and Physical Training Notes.**

After his success with training John C. Grimek, **he became the head instructor at Milo Barbell Co**. His responsibilities there included setting up the training schedules for everyone who purchased Milo Bar Bells, courses and instruction. **From there he was selected to be head coach for the United States Olympic Weight Lifting Team in 1932 and 1936.**

In 1936 he started his own business called **The Berry Bar Bell Co**. After that, he went to work for **Bur Barbell Co. from the late 1930's to the 1950's as head physical training instructor.**

Best Wishes, Bill Hinbern

Note: **Bill Hinbern** is a big aficionado of all things "old school" and has a website where he sells old courses. Here is his website:

http://www.superstrengthbooks.com/

Another big supporter of the squat, who also had a section dedicated to him in my first old time strongman book, was the mighty **Paul Anderson**, who was possibly the best squatter that ever walked the earth, and was touted by many in his era to be the strongest man who ever lived.

Paul started his early weight training in earnest in order to gain size and strength for his College football team, where he impressed team members, and in particular his first training partner, Bob Snead tremendously with his natural strength, especially in the leg department.

In the photo, big Paul with Richard Nixon

Another great lifter from the era and a guy that was also from Tennessee (where Paul eventually moved), **Bob Peoples** "discovered" Anderson and made him another Iron Man magazine disciple and helped him fine tune his training. **Bob was a deadlift specialist**, but was no stranger to the squat, and in fact it was claimed that he could squat over 500 at under 200 pounds bodyweight(well under, at that), and at a time when squat suits, wraps and the like were virtually nonexistent.

This takes us into our next chapter, on the great Bob Peoples

Chapter Seven
Bob Peoples

Before we delve into the relationship between Bob Peoples and Paul Anderson, let's talk about Bob a bit.

Bob Peoples was a farm boy who **made some of his own lifting equipment, as he had no access to a gym in his early days**. He made his own crude version of a barbell, a setup with barrels full of water and a yoke (the strongman yoke we know these days, in a more pristine form), and actually made the first (or at least one of the first; Berry had a diagram of something like this in his early magazine articles also) prototypical power rack, along with homemade lifting platforms. Paul Anderson was one of the lucky ones to train in what was affectionately termed "**the dungeon**", in Peoples basement. Peoples went on to set world records in the deadlift and **his numbers are still impressive to this day.**

Peoples was very innovative in his training, though he did have some inspiration from the **Farmer Burns** course, Mark Berry, **Health and Strength** and **Iron Man** magazines, **David P Willoughby'**s writings from the magazine **Physical Culture**, and **Alan Calvert's book Super Strength.** Bob was born in 1910, and **started keeping records on his training in his early twenties**, and was deadlifting 500 pounds in 1935, at the age of 25. In those days, this was no mean feat, especially for a man of his size.

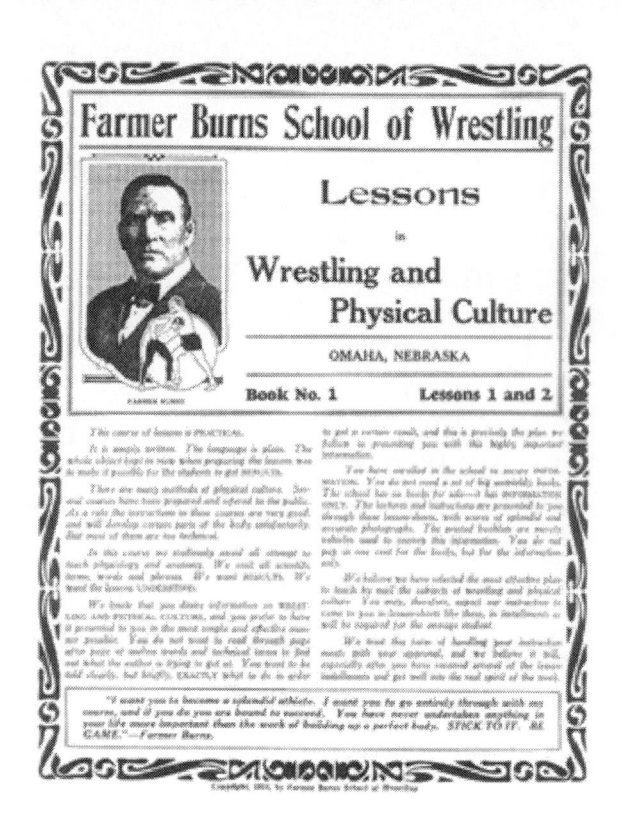

Farmer Burns early mail order training course

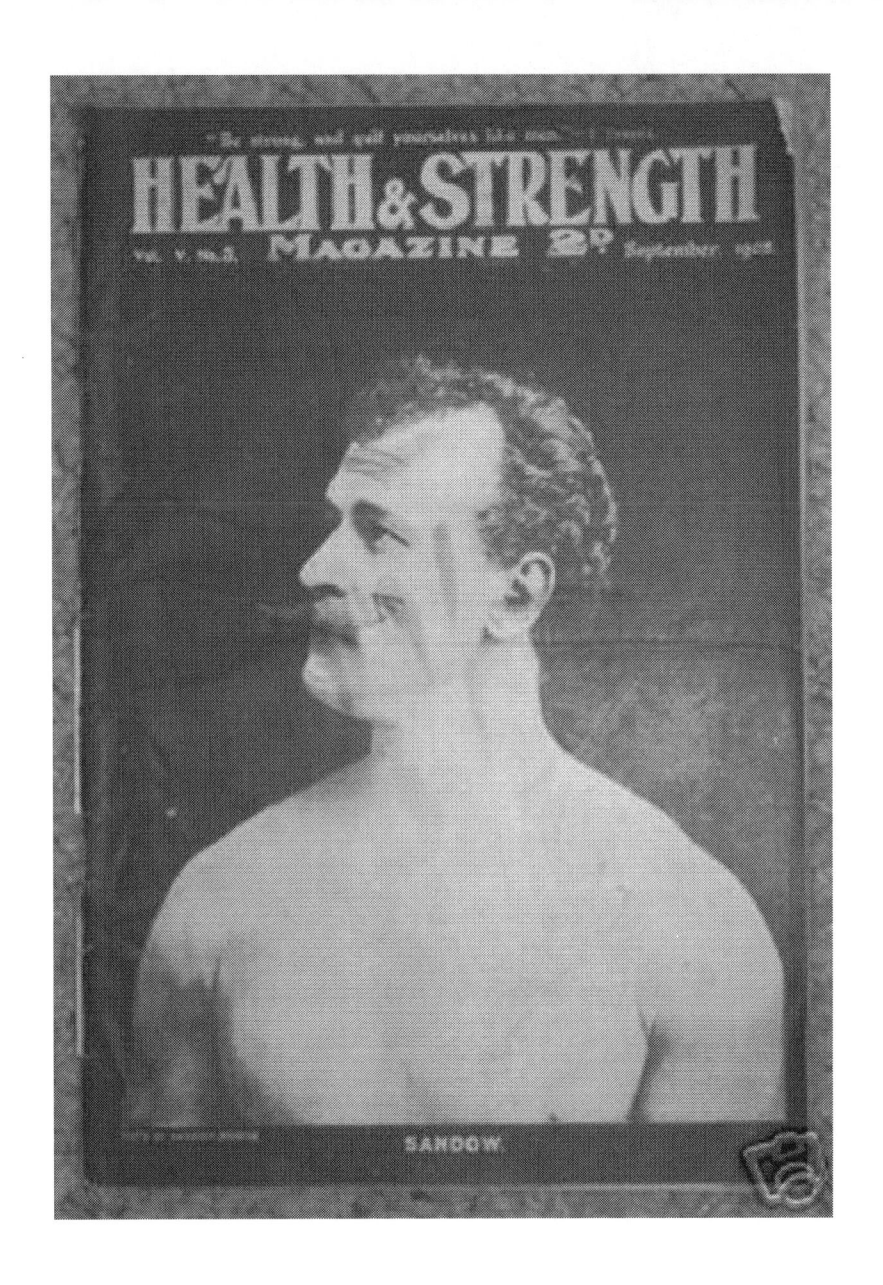

Here is one of the first magazines that came from Milo Barbell and Alan Calvert, perhaps one that Bob would see a second hand copy of years later

Eugene Sandow is the cover man

One of the interesting items Bob trained with to build his lower body sounded a lot like what has evolved into the well known "**trap bar**" of our generation.

He trained with his version using a platform, and going down very deep to start the lift. This was refined and came to be known as the "**magic circle**" Actually, Peary Rader is credited with inventing this device.

Here is a picture of a later version of the magic circle

Another favorite was the **dead-hang clean**, which he claimed contributed greatly to his deadlifting prowess. His **crude power rack** was a great aid to performing this lift, as he could set a loaded barbell on the support pins right at the starting level of this lift.

This movement is a **great builder of explosive strength and is commonly performed by football players in our day**, though many are not big on the conventional deadlift from the floor. It probably helped Bob improve his Olympic lifting, an area in which Bob eventually excelled.

He won the **Tennessee state Lightheavyweight Olympic championship** meet in 1940, and followed this with a **600 pound deadlift and a near miss with 625**. After training interruptions related to WW2, **Bob finally was able to set a World record deadlift of 651 &1/4 pounds at 175 pounds bodyweight in 1946, after defending his Olympic title.** Later on, in 1947 he appeared to reach the then mythical barrier of 700 during the **Bob Hise** Show, a YMCA meet held in Chattanooga, which unfortunately weighed out at 699 upon further scrutiny. This was still good enough for a new 181 pound class record.

Peoples managed to out lift a much larger opponent in this meet that made a record himself, of 680 at 275, one **Bill Boone*** of Shreveport, Louisiana.

Author's Note

We will see this name later on again in the book, and you probably noticed his name mentioned by Peary Rader earlier

What makes this whole episode even harder to believe was that the local reporter apparently missed getting a picture of Bob's 699 lift, so Bob obliged him by actually **repeating the lift so that the lucky fellow could snap a photo!** In 1949, on March 5th, Bob pulled 725 & ½ in Johnson City, Tennessee, one of the greatest deadlift performances in history. He came very close to locking out 750 later at the Junior Nationals meet, but did not quite finish the lift. Consider again that this was done before groove briefs, erector shirts, deadlift suits and steroids were on the map!

It is interesting to note that Mr. Peoples was not one that did weight training and competition to the exclusion of all else in life. **Bob was a family man that was very active in his community. He served his local Boy's Club and the Salvation Army, as well as being involved in a number of civic affairs in his community.**

While Peoples lifted in the 40s in his competitive days, he has been a big influence on many great strength athletes right up until today, including **Louie Simmons** of Westside Barbell. Louie had this to say on Bob's unique approach to using the abs in the deadlift:

"Bob Peoples taught the best method of using the abs in the deadlift to me. He said It was best to breath into the stomach only, not the chest. This will stabilize and support the lower back, and it does not elongate the spine.

The shorter the spine, the better the deadlifter. If you have long legs, a short torso, and long arms, you have the perfect build for deadlifting."

Here is a very young Louie Simmons shot

Bob Hise wrote this tribute to Bob back in **1964**, which will give a more personal and in-depth glimpse of some of what was mentioned briefly above, and much additional info:

BOB PEOPLES –

WORLD'S GREATEST DEADLIFTER

By

Bob Hise (1964)

There has been quite a bit of controversy as to whether or not power lifting competitions should be held and who should govern these lifts. I served on the first committee for power lifting appointed by Mr. David A. Matlin, National AAU Weightlifting Chairman. The purpose of this group was to make a study of the situation and report to the National Committee which met just prior to the 1963 Senior National Weightlifting Championships held at Harrisburg, Pennsylvania, which we did.

One thing that I discovered for sure was that as long as man lives upon this earth, strength will be admired. To develop strength one must practice the power lifts and probably the *King of these lifts is the dead lift.

Author's Note

Ah, the ongoing controversy over which lift is the true King; the squat or the deadlift. It would be easy to side with the latter in my case, as I can do a lot more weight in that one and am somewhat a specialist in it.

Ask a man who knows nothing about a barbell to perform a lift to measure his strength. He will not attempt to press, curl or squat with the weight; he will assemble the plates on the bar and proceed to lift the bar clear of the floor and stand erect. This type of lifting is the most natural way of performing a strength test.

In traveling from my home in California to Harrisburg, my son and I went by way of Johnson City, Tennessee and visited with Bob Peoples and his family for a few days before and after the contest.

Driving from Johnson City along with John Summers and Peoples, to Harrisburg, observing the two days of lifting and returning to Johnson City, allowed us much time for discussing our sport, a sport that we love. It was then that I realized that many of Bob's training innovations, pieces of equipment and methods of performance were still unknown to a vast number of power lifters.

Peary Rader gave clearance to write this article and here I am sitting on the Peoples' porch early in the morning drinking in the beauty of forested, rolling East Tennessee country. As I pen these words that I am sure will be helpful, and watch a fox scamper across the pasture, I'm reminded of what an ideal setting this is to train in; a place of stability and opportunity where rugged mountain folk still like to earn their living by the sweat of their brow and to be free to think for themselves and worship God in their own way. I attended services at the Sinking Creek Baptist Church last night. It is the oldest in Tennessee; a part of the original building which was built in 1783 is still standing and is a part of the old historic shrine.

It was among these settings that Bob Peoples was born and grew up as a boy across the road from where his grandfather was raised. Bob's father, as a young man, was interested in strength. It was with **his father's 50 pound dumbbell that Bob started training at the age of 9.**

A ***Farmer Burns course* of training was purchased when Bob was 15** and he followed this very diligently for three years, at which time **Physical Culture Magazine** published an article on barbell training. This article was written by **David Willoughby** and was very well illustrated. The story helped to steer young Peoples forward on his quest for great body power.

Author's note The original Farmer Burns course referred to above is available for viewing at the "Sandowplus" website, as are many other old time courses. This is a most excellent resource!

Another media resource which helped Bob greatly was "**Strength Magazine.**" It was read avidly until the publication ceased in the early thirties. Peoples has been a regular subscriber of most all the magazines and has just about every copy of the periodicals that have been published. **Through the pages of Strength, Bob learned of the Olympic lifts and the power movements also.**

By the time Bob had reached the age of 18 he had become very interested in the dead lift. He did all around training, but his specialty from this time on was his pet, the deadlift. He made a lift of 350 and in a year had worked up to 450 at a bodyweight of 165. **His first competition of any kind was the 1937 Tennessee State Weightlifting Championships.**

The next two years of training brought much improvement. Again he traveled to Chattanooga and lifted in the 1939 State Championships. His total had improved 65 pounds but the highlight of this occasion was a deadlift of 600 pounds.

After this performance of deadlifting, Bob returned home and did some of the most serious training of his life, only to have his gains swept away by a serious illness that resulted in a major operation.

Bob was sent to Fort Oglethorpe, Georgia Induction Center and it was there, after several days of medical examinations that it was discovered that a kidney tube was obstructed. Fortunately this condition was discovered before too much damage had occurred.

As Bob was told by the Army Medics to see his private physician, he did so upon his arrival home. After a consultation it was decided that Bob should make a trip up to the famed Oschner's Clinic in New Orleans.

Bob made the trip and this serious kidney operation was performed there. The incision was about 18 inches long, reaching from the center of the back to just below the front center of the lower rib.

Bob returned home to convalesce; the **worst part of the recuperative process was the ever-present thought that there would be no more heavy lifting**. After all, that was the verdict laid down by Dr. Oschner. About six weeks after surgery Bob did a little light work on the weights. This convinced him that he should do more training.

We hear so much about **isotonic and isometric training** and many have trained by these non-movement and **short movement types of exercises**. This method of training, as we have read, has played an important part in developing some of our modern day lifters.

Bob built a rack somewhat similar to our present day isometric racks. The uprights were made of 4"x4" hardwood and attached to the floor and overhead beams. These uprights had 1 1/8" by 3" holes drilled in them. Bolts 1"x 8" could be inserted in these holes. At first Bob used this device to work on the press and lockout on his jerks, but his foremost love being the deadlift, he turned his direction of work in this area. **Three methods of training were performed on the uprights.**

1.) The bar was loaded with an excess of his best deadlift poundage and **partial movements were executed at various positions**. Most work was done at positions of just below knees, knee height and just above the knees.

2.) Take weight from the uprights and lower to the floor and stand erect.

3.) A complete static (isometric) exercise in various positions.

Bob felt that he needed more basic starting strength and devised a ring with short extensions by which to hold and to add weight. (Was this the first **trap-bar??**)*

Author's Note, We saw this mentioned above; the "magic circle" The author of the article seems to be crediting Bob with its invention, while I have seen the magic circle credited to Mr. Rader as mentioned previously.

By standing on various height objects he was able to **develop tremendous sub-starting power.**

Bob Peoples' Basement gym, known as "The Dungeon"

By this time Bob was using such heavy weights that it became more and more difficult for him to hold the bar while doing repetitions in his various exercises. **He engineered hooks to facilitate gripping of the bar. These were the forerunner of the straps that are commonly used today.**

Bob's innovative leg press device

Peoples had completely overcome his post-operative and convalescing period by breaking his personal deadlift record.

At the 1946 Tennessee State Weightlifting Championships he surprised the world by doing 651 ¼ pounds in the deadlift. Bob returned to his East Tennessee farm and came up with other innovations that helped gain even loftier heights in the deadlift.

The continuous heavy training would sometimes leave his joints stiff and sore.

Bob invented another gimmick, a sponge rubber was soaked with a good liniment and placed on the knees, back, or other sore area and secured in place by wrapping with a bandage. This not only was soothing, but allowed harder workouts with no discomfort, which facilitated further gains.

Our deadlift champion began to study his body leverages and gravity centers. He would take a bar in a starting deadlift position and view himself in a mirror and notice by the raising or lowering of the bar as he changed grips, using different height shoes, inhaling slightly, inhaling heavily, exhaling slightly, exhaling heavily and observing the positions and conditions that suited him best.

He decided that the best position for him was **rounded back, palms forward, hook grip and to lift barefooted and with a completely exhaled thoracic cavity.** *

In the photo that comes up next, you will see Terry Todd demonstrating the Round back starting position that was one of Peoples' trademarks in the deadlift

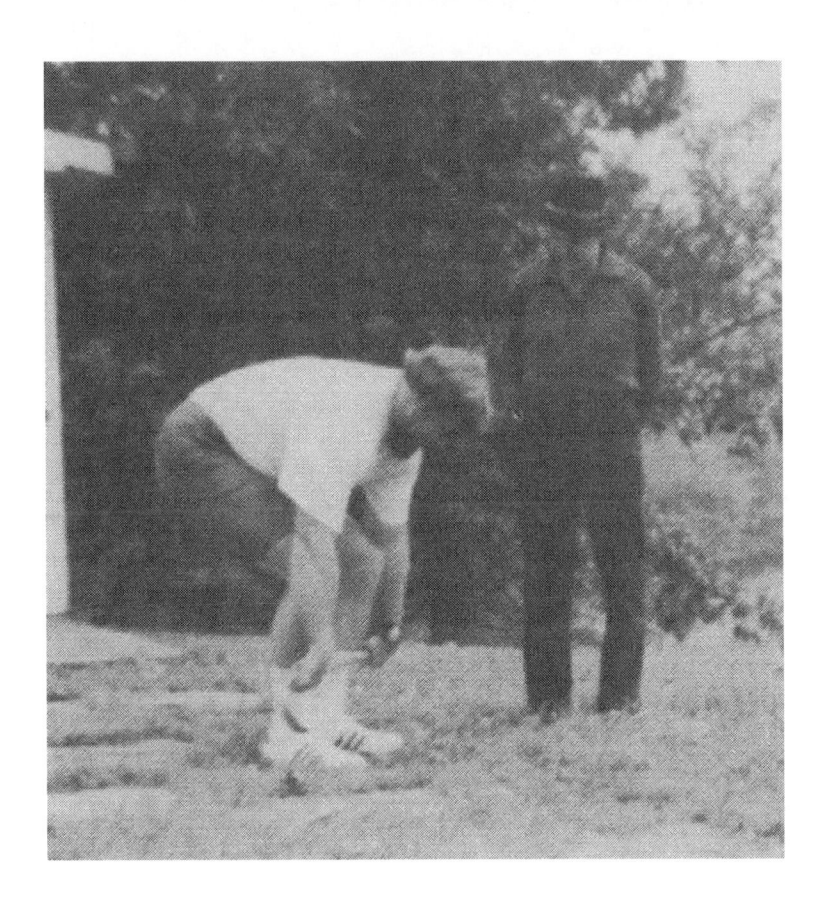

Author's Note: This is a highly unusual style and is not suggested for the vast majority of lifters

With this new knowledge and much training under his belt, Peoples journeyed to Chattanooga to take part in the 1947 "Mr. South" contest and variety show. This event was staged annually by the Central YMCA during the month of October. Top stars were invited to perform in their special events.

As the crowd cheered and Bob heaved and tugged, the stupendous weight of 699 pounds cleared the floor and inched its way upward until it became fixed by Bob at the completion position. Another record to his credit, but this wasn't all;

the newspaper photographer failed to get a picture, Bob went back stage and obliged the press photographer by lifting the same weight a second time. It seemed that Bob had discovered magic formulas – each time he performed the record would go up. As he trained somewhat along the lines of previous training and making a few changes here and there he became progressively stronger.

Though **Bob had always done some squats, he now embarked on a concentrated course of deep knee bends.** His back being very strong, he noticed that coming up out of squats he would do a type of exercise which was between a knee bend and a good morning movement.*

*****Author's Note: you see this a lot among lifters with stronger backs, but again, this is not the desirable way to perform a squat for the masses***

A shoulder apparatus was built to support weight and facilitate the exercise. This and **quarter squats** plus **taking heavy weights from the racks and doing rapid deadlifts by bouncing the weight off the floor increased his strength a great deal more.** An invitation to appear on the Nashville YMCA Variety Show program was accepted. The show was held in December of 1947.

"Pudgy" Stockton was billed as the headline but after Bob deadlifted 710 pounds she was pushed back into the background. March of 1948 found Bob lifting 704 pounds in Detroit. This was the first time that he had performed in public without making an increase in poundage lifted. He did clear the floor with 719 pounds and just failed to stand erect with this weight which would have been a record.

The grand climax of lifting came to John Robert Peoples Jr. during the great Red Shield Boy's Club Variety Show of 1949. What an opportunity – that of being able to perform before an enthusiastic hometown crowd.

A hush fell over the Johnson City Auditorium as Bob approached the bar with a yell from an old Tennessee Mountaineer, "That's our man – come on Bob, I know ye can lift that dang weight!"

It seemed like an eternity before the barbell left the floor. Up, up it went and with a final heave mighty Bob Peoples stood erect to one of the most thunderous applauses that I ever heard.

The lifter weighed 181 pounds and the weight scaled 725 ¾ pounds.

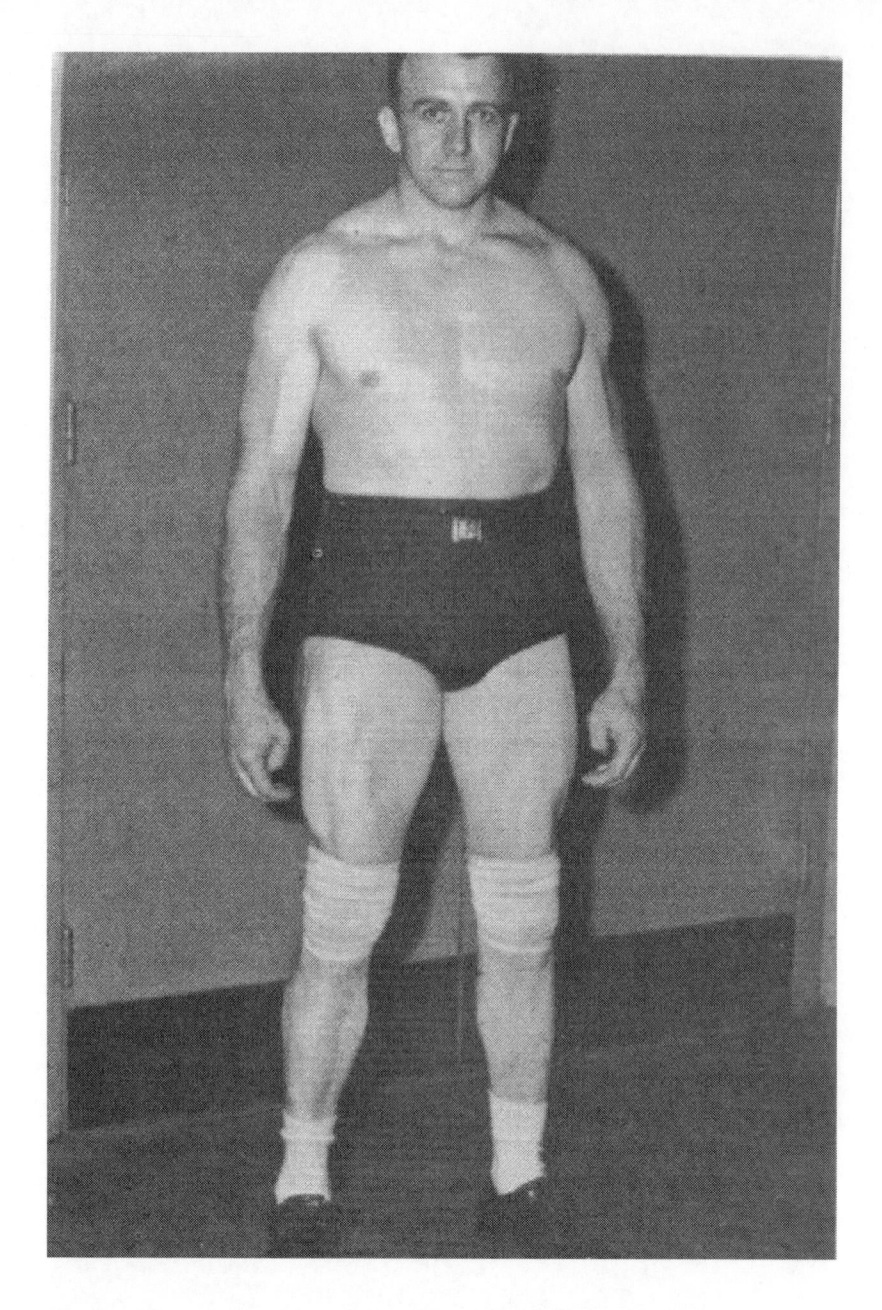

Bob Peoples in his deadlifting gear

In another article written by Mr. Hise, these glowing words were written:

The Bob Peoples I Knew

By Bob Hise II

Some lifters have bulging biceps, some have massive chests. Bob Peoples had robust rhomboids, a spinal column encased with spinal erectors the size of forearms; a back highly developed from the head bone to the tail bone, atlas to coccyx, with **ligaments and tendons that could be equated to steel cables.**

In the 1940s, he deadlifted 728 lbs. weighing 178, minus drugs, wraps and body suits. This was done using a cross hand (knuckles out) grip. He wore no shoes (only socks) and was the forerunner of ballet-type deadlift shoes.

In 1937 the Tennessee State Olympic Weightlifting Championships were held at the Frye Institute (a Mecca for the Iron fraternity) in Chattanooga. Bob Peoples, an unknown lifter from the eastern part of the state was entered. If memory serves me right he did a 190 press, 215 snatch and a clean & jerk of 265. He used a powerful pull and shallow split in snatching and cleaning which denoted tremendous back strength. When the competition was over he asked to put on a **deadlift exhibition**. With no warm-up he opened with 500 which he did for 4 reps. Bob went on to do 600 and 650 with much to spare at a bodyweight of 175.

The most unusual part of his lifting was the way he gripped the bar, a straight no-cross grip and a steady, no pause lift from the floor to a strong stand up finish. We became friends from then and continued until the end when I served as a pall bearer at his funeral.

Many were the times that we visited in each other's homes and discussed lifting. His many innovative training philosophies, routines and inventions guided him as he became the world's greatest deadlifter.

His early training was done with crude objects. Two barrels with a heavy pipe attached, large timbers were placed in the ground and were used for supports of this huge apparatus. The barrels were filled with rocks, each having the weight painted on them. This was one of Bob's first training devices.

Sinking Creek ran in front of the Peoples' home, and a suspension footbridge skirted the creek. Bob would load up his barrels, take them off the racks and walk across the swaying bridge, turn around, walk back across and place the weight on the supports. **I've seen him use 500 lbs. for this feat. He called it building 'super-strength'.**

-

The above sounds a bit like a farmers walk or strongman yoke walk with a big instability factor thrown in for added difficulty* (Author's note)

For deadlifting he would place the barrels on the ground and use different height platforms to stand on – which gave him different lifting positions with bar touching insteps, to medium, and a high finish position.

The only conventional pieces of equipment he owned at that time were a 150 lb. standard plate-loaded barbell and two solid dumbbells (one 60 lbs. and one 75 lbs.). **He would do one-arm swings, presses, and snatches with dumbbells**. Of course, Bob later acquired conventional equipment – a Jackson Olympic 400 lb. set. He had the local foundry cast four 100 lb. weights to use in his various exercises.

Peoples was much in demand for deadlifting performances and I accompanied him to Atlanta, Nashville, Detroit and other areas. Many times we would have to take extra weights because the sponsors would not have adequate barbell plates. One of these times was an event at the Nashville YMCA, an Olympic lifting contest, plus an exhibition by **Pudgy Stockton** and Bob's deadlifting. I had recently been discharged from World War II days in the Army Air Force and had an Army Jeep. Highway 41 was being worked on and we had to detour over the mountains via Richard City (home of famed western film star Tom Mix). Logging and mining trucks had left the road in horrible condition and driving at a reasonable speed carried you all over the road. With weights in back and makeshift bed on top where my wife Billy was sleeping and Bob in front with me shivering, we made the lurching journey as fast as possible so Bob could get back to work. I asked Bob to drive ad get warmed up – his reply, in his usual dry wit, "No, I might get the Jeep in jump gear and we'd really have a disaster."

Bob, along with Pudgy, stole the show. **He lifted 728 weighing 178**. No wraps, wearing only socks on his feet. To quote Bob, "It gave me better leverage." He used his underhand grip here because it is the natural way to lift. Ask any beginner to lift a barbell and they'll start in this manner. He used both styles of gripping but always thought this was the best way to lift heavy weights.

The following photo shows "Pudgy" Stockton

She doesn't look too pudgy to me!

Bob was always cold and when I walked him to the passenger boarding train platform his knees were actually bouncing together from the extreme shivering. He had to catch the Southern Railway train "The Tennessean" and get back to Johnson City for work that afternoon.

This reminds me of when Bob and his wife Juanita visited us in Los Angeles (which as you know is not a cold area). Bob asked me if I'd turn on the forced air furnace so I adjusted the temperature to a good warm setting and opened the vent wide in their bedroom. For the first time ever the thermostat malfunctioned and the burners cut off – blowing cold air into their room. Bob never believed this wasn't intentional.

Some of Bob's training methods were unique. He built a **bouncing platform** of two oak 2x12" boards, 8' long, nailed barbell width apart on 4x4" timbers underneath at each end. By using the lift on his tractor (extending a lowering/raising mechanism *which he could operate by placing his head against the actuator*) 800 lbs. would be lifted to an upright extended position, and he would lower this, with a bounce, and attempt to get the bar to his knees. This would build great starting strength (50 kg. Mav-Rik bumpers can be used for this type of training). **Bob also did a lot of eccentric movements by using his tractor lift to raise an excessive weight and then lowering it himself.**

I witnessed him doing cleans with two 110 lb. dumbbells for ten reps, one from the floor and 9 dead hangs. **He used no straps which showed his great gripping and tremendous back strength.** His theory: **you start most every lift with the hands so they must be strong.** I think many power and Olympic lifters neglect grip strength training.

I've never known a man who did so much: worked in a rayon mill (changing shifts every week), a member of the Johnson County Road Commission, farmed, *and still trained*, and I mean HARD TRAINING – many times at 2 a.m. after he finished his evening shift of work and had a bite to eat.

Bob bought another farm with a huge house sitting on a hill. **Here he built his basement dungeon gym.** Not only did he train here, but **he trained Paul Anderson as well**. Peoples was really an organized man.

He was a mild man, but did have a flare up temper at times. His wife Juanita told me of times he would get so angry *with himself* because he wasn't progressing that he would actually carry his weights from the dungeon and throw them down the hill – swearing never to lift again.

A few days later he would lug all the weights up and back to **the dungeon** and train harder than ever. (A *real* layoff.)

Yes, **Bob Peoples was ahead of his time**. His photo is enshrined in the Tri-City: Johnson City-Kingsport-Bristol Airport, denoting his position in the Tennessee Athletic Hall of Fame. He was a graduate of the University of Tennessee and won honors as a livestock judge.

Yes, Mr. Peoples was a great lifter, a fine gentleman, and a true friend whom I miss very much.

Here is an article penned by the man himself:

Systems and Methods I Have Used

By Bob Peoples

I first became acquainted with weights when very young and **started tinkering around with a 50-pound dumbbell and other odds and ends. I followed no system as I knew of none**. The first lifter I saw was in Johnson City, Tennessee, he was a sidewalk strongman who lifted a set of boxcar wheels by means of a harness. I was neither big nor strong but continued to try my hand and do some exercises. Then came the time I became acquainted with some magazines and acquired some knowledge of training.

The **first system I followed was the*** *double progressive system**, taking a given weight (for example, 100 pounds) and performing five repetitions and working up to ten. Then more weight was added and you began with five repetitions once again. This can be applied to all exercises and the number of repetitions varied from three to five, add weight and repeat. This, in my opinion, is the most foolproof method known. It is easy for the beginner to follow and a system whereby he can gauge his progress more easily.

Author's note this is the system used in the Milo first course in bodybuilding that came with their barbell sets early on

More often I used the system in this manner: three repetitions to five, five repetitions to ten, and seven repetitions to fifteen. I did not use the seven to fifteen very much as I considered fifteen repetitions too much for strength building purposes. I never lost sight of this method and used it in perhaps eighty percent of my training.

As to the time of training, I found in my case late afternoon to be the time of my highest energy peak. However, I trained any time I could find time or when circumstances permitted.

The number of times per week varied. More often I trained on an average of four to five times a week but have trained on Monday, Wednesday and Friday, or every other day.

I have also made good progress one or two days per week, but I did not follow a one or two day per week pattern very often. **Very early in my training I built a power rack and included in my routine the heavy supports in yoked position.** I also did **half and quarter squats and lockouts.** I also have used the rack with slots for leg pressing and press outs over head and lockouts over head. When I got down to serious training, a routine of the following was used:

1.) Warm up with light or medium weight to warm muscles and joints.
   2,) Dead Lift
   3.) Deep Knee Bend (squat)
   4.) Press
   5.) Snatch
   6.) Clean and Jerk

2.) All for 3 to 5 repetitions.

I kept strict records and when five repetitions were reached, I added weight and started again, making as much progress as possible on each of the individual lifts. Along with this, I used some heavy lockouts or half and quarter squats. I always did sit-ups with weight and some leg raises along with the above routine. At times, I would mix other exercises in with my regular routine. **Some of these were chin-ups, neck work, curls, toe raises and others.**

I usually used one set of low repetitions for strength building. I used the most weight possible and went for as many repetitions as I possibly could, going the limit **every day.**

About every two weeks or less, according to the way I felt, I would try a personal record on the dead lift, deep knee bends and the three Olympic lifts.

I used the alternate press with dumbbells to a great advantage. I made good progress here but the two dumbbells simultaneous press, I never mastered. I never used single arm presses to any great extent.

I did not use the strictest form in training but would strive to get the weight up in some form. But for training for a contest, one must work on good form so that his lift will pass the judges.

Many have used the set system and have built huge muscle and strength by taking a certain weight and going five repetitions, then resting, and going another five, and so on, until three sets or more were made.

In my case, I found this to be more tiring and as I always used maximum weight and repetition, I felt I could not make as much progress for strength building with the set system.

I used the heavy and light system some but saw no advantage in lightening the load and doing more repetitions. It seemed a waste of energy.

I used the system of taking a certain weight and performing the same number of repetitions each training day. I made progress here but found it more difficult to gauge my progress. For example, if I could use 450 pounds for the dead lift each day for about two weeks, I was good for 600 pounds in a single dead lift. However, I abandoned this method for the double progressive system as I felt I made much greater progress with it. **For example, I take the dead lift from the rack at top side and lower to where you can pull out, then gradually lower the rack setting about one inch at a time as you improve, continuing over time until you can perform one full dead lift with the weight**. Then add weight and got through the process again. This is the double progressive in a different form. Some progress can be made but I prefer other methods.

Another system uses high repetitions with heavy weights or using maximum repetitions with maximum weight. I have experimented with this system using a heavy weight and going as high as 40 to 50 repetitions and then do the maximum weight dead lift. But, **using this system any length of time used up my energy and I found myself losing strength. I abandoned this in favor of lower repetitions.**

I used the method of taking a given weight and doing maximum repetitions and then lowering the weight by 50 pounds and doing more repetitions. The weight was lowered a second time by 50 pounds and more repetitions and more repetitions done.*

*Author's note: These have been called "Strip sets" and are a bodybuilder favorite

I found this exhausting so I did not pursue it.

I have used the method of doing upper body work one day and lower body work the next day. This worked well for me.

I have used and experimented with leverage and cam machines. The leverage machine had a terrific kick back. I used this for special work.

Another system, using maximum resistance in each exercise all the way through, where the weight and the leverage must change. For example, in the press, you can use 360 pounds in the start of the press and 300 pounds in the finish, using helpers through the sticking point. In addition, lowering the weight is done in the same manner. The dead lift and deep knee bend can be performed in the same manner using helpers through the sticking point. The bench press can be performed in the same manner.

I found fighting maximum resistance all the way very fatiguing or exhausting and preferred another method of breaking the exercise into three parts (start, regular and finish movements). For example, in the press, you can start and do five repetitions with 300 pounds. Using this in a separate movement, five starts do not use much energy. Then do the finish movement, starting slightly above the sticking point. If you can use 300 pounds for five repetitions, this can be performed with much less energy. Then do the regular press. For example, in using maximum resistance, 200 pounds is the maximum weight at the point of longest leverage (sticking point). By using 200 pounds in a regular movement, more repetitions can be accomplished. As the sticking point is the crucial point, one gets two or more movements or repetitions through this crucial point than with the maximum all the way movement. This, in my opinion, is a superior method. The maximum resistance all the way method will give results, but, in my opinion, it is inferior to other methods.

The dead lift can be broken into three movements – regular and high movements and doing half and quarter squats for starting the dead lift.

The deep knee bend can be broken into two movements – regular and half bends.

A more modern Deadlifting hero, **Vince Anello** did an interview for a lifting website/forum (At Large Nutrition) a while back, and I think this excerpt shows some influences from Peoples:

Vince Anello is a living powerlifting legend. He was the first man in history to pull over 800 lbs at a body weight of less than 200 lbs!

Vince competed over the course of 3 decades and during what might be considered a *golden age* in the sport when mastodons like Casey, Reinhoudt, Kuc, Williams, Cole and many others ruled the platform. A tremendous all-around lifter, Vince's legacy as one of the all-time great deadlifters is etched in the annals of powerlifting history.

Chris: Vince, first, I want to thank you for agreeing to this interview. From the first time I read about you in Fred Hatfield's *The Complete Guide to Power Training* I have always been in awe of your deadlifting prowess. My goal with this interview is to pay homage to your tremendous accomplishments in the sport of powerlifting and to deadlifting in particular. I want to introduce you to a whole new generation of powerlifters and to remind those who know of you just how great you were.

To that end I would like to start this interview with you providing a brief highlight of your powerlifting career to include some of your amazing accomplishments.

Vince: Thank you Chris. My competitive powerlifting career spanned 3 decades. Below is a list of some of the highlights (in reverse order):

1998 Inducted into the Strength Hall of Fame (York, Pa.)**

- 1988 Drug Free N.A.S.A. National Champion, Open Division
- 1987 National and World Champion, Masters Division
- 1980 Senior National Champion and World Champion
- 1979 Third Place World Championship (Dayton, Ohio)
- 1978 Hawaii Invitational Champion, Senior National Champion and World Champion (Turku, Finland)
- 1977 Senior National Champion and World Champion (Perth, Australia)
- 1976 Senior National Champion, 2nd Place World Championship, Pan American Champion
- 1975 National YMCA Champion, Pan American Champion Became First man under 200 to pull over 800lb
- 1974 National YMCA Champion
- 1973 National YMCA Champion
- 1972 World Champion, Light Heavyweight Division (York, PA)
- 1971 National YMCA Champion
- 1970 Broke World Deadlift Record - National Champion
- 1970 National Collegiate Champion

Above: Vince looking THICK!

Note: This picture also hangs in the **York Barbell Hall of Fame, and is the first in a series of pictures I took there in 2009.****

My best unofficial pull was 880 lbs at 200 lbs body weight. In competition, my best pulls were:

- 821. 2 lbs in the 198 class
- 811. 3 lbs in the 220 class
- 750. 5 lbs in the 181 class

Chris: You had a *very* unique deadlifting style. Tell us a bit about that and how you developed your technique.

Vince: You know, I was never one to over-analyze my training technique. My particular style was something that came naturally and felt best and strongest for me. I always felt the KISS (Keep it Simple Stupid) principle was best. On the opposite end of the spectrum, I had a training partner who was very methodical is his approach. He studied and analyzed every nuance of his form. This guy truly had the potential to be one of the strongest men in the world, but I felt he cheated himself out of that chance with paralysis by analysis.

Above: Vince pulling BIG!!!

Chris: Vince, everything about powerlifting training was different when you were at your peak. The gear (bench shirts, suits etc.) were either non-existent or dramatically different than the gear of today. The training equipment was different as well; chains and bands were not part of the repertoire back then. With that said, yourself and the best of your generation were able to build absolutely awe-inspiring strength and set some records which still stand today.

Tell us a bit about your training. What methods did you find worked best? Do you have any "secrets" that can help the strength trainees of today?

Vince: Chris, I have always kept my training fairly simple. There are many different training methodologies these days and there have been champions from each camp. In the end, heavy progressive resistance training coupled with recovery is what makes you bigger and stronger. The "secret", if there is one, is the bulldog mindset! You set a goal and you don't let go of it until you have achieved it. The best of the best in any endeavor all share that common trait, **dogged determination**!

Chris: Vince, your point is well taken. I definitely think there is a place for the conjugate method and various other training modalities and apparatus, but the end-game is heavy and hard. A current strength **freak** that comes to mind who exemplifies this is Jeremy Hoornstra. To my knowledge, his training routine is much like that of a bodybuilder, yet the guy is probably the strongest bencher ever having done well over 600 lbs raw at only 242 lbs.

Vince, this talk about hard and heavy training has me curious, was your training influenced

at all by the great Bob Peoples?

Vince Anello of Cleveland, Ohio, winning the 198-lb. class at the Intercollegiate Championships with a deadlift of 715 lbs. Vince holds the record at 724. (Borden photo)

Above: A young Vince showing his tremendous potential!

Vince: Well, I did not pattern my training after that of Bob's per se, **but I had and have a tremendous amount of respect for the man. When I first was coming to prominence he was a living strength legend. In fact, I had read about him in junior high and to this day have a book he wrote. Actually, I have an interesting Bob Peoples story.** I was the first man to pull over 800 lbs at under 200 lbs of body weight. The first time I did it in competition was at the 1975 Senior Nationals. After the pull, this older gentleman approached me to congratulate me. Surprise, surprise, it was Bob Peoples! I wanted so badly to get a picture taken with him, but as things go I got sidetracked speaking with other lifters and by the time I tried to find him for the picture he was gone.

Chris: I have that same book Vince! It is titled *Developing Physical Strength*, no? Bob was an absolutely amazing strength athlete. For our uninformed readers, Bob was a powerlifter before the term existed. In fact, he pulled 725 lbs at roughly 185 lbs body weight using a hook grip and no other supportive apparatus in **1949!!!**

Vince, I think you and Bob were cut from the same cloth when it comes to being master deadlifters. To me, you are the living deadlift legend that Bob was to you.

Vince: Thank you Chris. I don't think of myself in those terms, but if you or anyone else feels that way I am truly flattered.

Chris: Please provide us the specific deadlifting routine you followed prior to your all-time best pull.

Vince: I worked my way up to heavy singles. I would warm-up with sets of 10, 8, and 6 reps. I would then start my singles with 80% of my estimated or tested 1 rep maximum (1RM). Next, I would do a single with 90% and then a final one with 95%.

The readers may find it interesting that I almost never pulled from the floor. I did what I call "negative accentuated" pulls. I would take the bar from the rack and emphasize the eccentric portion of the movement by slowly lowering it to the ground. I would allow the bar to come to a dead stop. I would then perform an explosive positive.

Partials from varying heights were also regularly included in my training. I was able to move some pretty crazy weight with the partials. I once got 1050 lbs from mid-knee level.

Author's note

(I think the section highlighted above points towards training tips garnered from Bob's book, don't you?)

Chris: There is a saying that great men stand on the shoulders of giants. If we want to be great, we must build on the foundation laid by the giants of the past. Thus, I am always excited to pick the brain of someone who has done something I aspire to do (in your case pull over 800 lbs at less than 220 lbs). I firmly believe in learning from the experience (sometimes the mistakes) of others. What, if anything, would you do differently relative to your strength training if you could do it all over again?

Vince: I wouldn't really change the way I trained per se. As I mentioned above, I once pulled 880 lbs at 200 lbs body weight in training. About my only regret is that I did not cycle my training to hit that peak in a meet!

Note the mention in the interview above about Vince's induction into the York Barbell Hall of Fame. There is a thread on my website forum with Vince's picture at the top of a group of many pictures, a sort of virtual tour of the York Barbell HOF. Check it out here:

http://christianiron.com/forum.aspx

I know I have spent quite a bit of space on the deadlift here, but hey, I am a deadlift specialist, so cut me a break! Besides, **both the squat & deadlift are key exercises that are considered indispensible. It is ill-advised to neglect either one.**

Chapter Eight

Bob and Paul

Now let us begin to explore **Bob Peoples' relationship with Paul Anderson**, by starting with an intro article from Paul himself:

Here is a photo showing Paul doing what he did best

My Beginnings

by Paul Anderson

When I was in college, all of the football players lived together in one large athletic dorm called McGee Hall, on the old Furman University campus. As strange as it may seem there were no coaches or any other adults living in the dormitory with the athletes, so we had a free run of the old dilapidated building and often there would be folks afoot into the wee hours.

Mischief abounded. You might, for instance, wake up in the morning to find your door had been nailed shut as you slept, or find a horse had been led into your room, or you'd come into your room tired and fall into bed before you noticed there was a ten-pound catfish under the covers. Even so, or perhaps because of, many close friendships developed in old McGee Hall.

I had several real close friends on the freshman football team and one in particular, an outstanding linebacker from West Virginia, was very close to me. His name was Bob Snead.

Bob explained to me that weightlifting was his hobby, and that he did this exercising in the off-season to prepare him for football. This seemed quite strange to me because **through the years I had been warned that weightlifting would make you muscle-bound and ruin your athletic ability**. Bob explained to me that this wasn't true and that **he had done it for years and attributed a lot of his football success to lifting weights.**

His argument made sense to me, so I helped him set up his weights in a corner of the athletic building. He not only had assorted barbell plates but racks and benches. The next day Bob asked me if I would like to work out with him. **Remembering with pleasure the times during my high school years when I had lifted various objects to test my strength**, I was happy to take part in a workout, although I still had fears of becoming muscle-bound. I feared that there might be some truth in the stories I had been told by my coaches and other interested individuals. I joined Bob in the gym and proceeded to follow him through a workout. **The first lift that he was going to do was the deep knee bend, or squat.**

This was Bob's favorite exercise, so I helped him set up his weights in a corner of the athletic building. He not only had assorted barbell plates but racks and benches.

This was Bob's favorite exercise and he was quite good at it. He put a poundage on the bar (about 300 pounds) and did a couple of squats, then placed the bar back on the rack. He asked me with a smile if I would like to try, and to **his amazement I did ten reps very easily.**

It was very evident that I could handle much more. **Bob was very encouraging, saying that I had more leg and back strength than anyone he had ever seen.**

I was fired up by his words and by the workout itself and made plans to join him lifting from that moment forward. Not only was I thrilled over the fact that I had natural strength, but it **seemed that the weights satisfied a deep need in my nature**. I got enormous satisfaction out of working out with the barbells. Until that point in my life nothing had given me such peace of mind and satisfaction.

Bob and I hadn't been working out for more than three or four days when the head football coach surprised us one day with a visit. He came there not to observe, but really to condemn.

Naturally with all the clanging of the barbells our workouts were no secret. The coach explained that weightlifting was not for good for us and would keep us from running fast or making any quick movements.

He said we were to stop or he would have to take our scholarships away. In his defense I should add that the position he was taking was not unique, but was a position most all athletic coaches took just those few years ago. He was sincere in his concern and really had our best interests at heart, wrongheaded though he was.

Naturally I was discouraged by our coach's words and really felt that he knew more about athletics than my friend Bob. But Bob proceeded to convince me once again that the coach was wrong and explained that lifting simply got more done in less time. To be honest, Bob convinced me of something that I wanted to believe in, so his task was none too hard.

I gained strength so rapidly that it seemed unbelievable to me. From one workout to the next my strength would noticeably increase. We were quite handicapped in training now and had been forced to gather up some old wrestling mats, and even some old mattresses to cushion and quiet our weights so as not to alert the coaching staff downstairs.

During that time my schoolwork was really suffering, mainly because of lack of interest. I wasn't really happy at Furman and I couldn't seem to put my academic work into the right perspective. The feeling was not dissatisfaction with my particular college, but rather a desire to be doing something else. I felt this in a very real sense almost every day.

I felt that my calling was elsewhere. Even **my desire to play college football and eventually professional football was overcome by this overpowering desire to follow my interest in lifting**.

However, when I would think of a career in weightlifting, I realized that to become really successful I would have to give up college and football because of my coach's attitude. The problem was that when this thought took charge of my mind I would feel rather foolish.

How could I ever explain to anyone, especially my parents that I wanted to quit school to lift weights? That I wanted to give up a full athletic scholarship and become a strongman? For about eight weeks a daily battle raged between my common sense and my heart's desire. In my room at night my better judgment and common sense would overrule my desire, but every other day when Bob and I would take our workouts the desire would return and the battle would begin once more. No matter what my better judgment or common sense had to say, it still seemed *right* for me to become a competing weightlifter. I knew this could never be at Furman for I needed much equipment and more space to perform the overhead competitive lifts. Also, Bob and I were barely getting away without workouts and we felt that out weights might be confiscated at any moment, along with out scholarships.

I remember so well the day that I made the final decision to leave school and devote my life to competition lifting. Not one minute had elapsed after I had made this decision before I felt extremely guilt-ridden. I would be letting so many people down – my high school coach, who had great confidence in me; my parents, who had sacrificed to allow me to pursue a higher education; and of course the coaching staff and my teammates. I realized that if I went to talk with my coaches about this decision they would either talk me out of it or cancel my scholarship on the grounds that I was mentally deranged.

So, late one night I packed all of my bags and left school before daylight the next morning. Perhaps this was not the manliest way to handle the situation, but I felt at the time that it was the best thing for me to do.

I hitchhiked from Greenville, South Carolina, to Toccoa, Georgia, and as I look back, I remember hoping that I wouldn't get a quick ride home. I'm sure this feeling resulted from the fact that I was still feeling guilty about leaving school and I really hated to face my parents with the news that I was giving up my scholarship. My hopes went for naught, however, because one of the first cars that came by gave me a ride all the way to Toccoa.

I remember so well walking in the house and being greeted with real alarm by my mother, who feared that only sickness could have brought me home. When I told my parents that I had decided to give up college temporarily, they naturally wanted to know what I had in mind. The real shocker came when I told them that I wanted to be a weightlifter.

Naturally they knew of no one who made a good living lifting weights, since there was no one in America who did, and they reacted just as most all parents would have.

They felt that I was giving up a tremendous opportunity, choosing instead to pursue something which had no future whatsoever even if I did become successful in it.

Finally, however, they allowed me to follow through on my plans, with my solemn promise that I would enter college again next fall. Their understanding and assistance during this stage of my life meant more to me then and means more to me now than I am able to put into words.

My first problem up in **Elizabethtown, Tennessee** (where my father was then employed) was solved when I decided to use the garage for a gym. It was not being used for car storage but contained everything that one could imagine. After relocating lawnmowers, various washing machines and other appliances I found that I had enough room to place the equipment that I felt I needed. The *real* problem came up now: where would I get the weights? I investigated all the places where standard weights would possibly be available, and not only did they not have the heavy equipment that I would need but the price for such equipment was too staggering for me to even consider.

Naturally I could not approach my parents on the venture, as I was determined to do it on my own. They kept me fed, clothed and housed and this in itself seemed more than generous to me then. It still does, in fact.

I began to visit all the junk and salvage yards in the area and the prospects for my gymnasium started looking a little better. I found that weights could be made out of old auto parts and other pieces of discarded machinery. I found that flywheels from automobile engines usually weighed around 35 pounds and could be used for lifts that did not take extreme precision and accuracy. Automobile drive shafts and truck axles made good bars. To supplement the weights that I could pick up from these salvage yards I poured many out of concrete. I would secure a bucket, barrel, box or anything that would serve as a mold, and then by putting a pipe through it and pouring it full of concrete I would have a large weight that I could slip on one of the drive shafts or axles.

This surprisingly enough served my purpose, and **after several weeks of raking and scraping through the scrap yards I had a well-equipped, though somewhat crude, gym.**

Author's note

Notice all the trouble Paul went through just to facilitate his training, let alone the long & crazy workouts that would then ensue. Refer back to Vince Anello's quote earlier about "dogged determination" This was one quality that big Paul did not lack for in the least!

I also admire his frugal equipment making mentality, which is something I aspire to myself, as those who know me might tell you (my wife, in particular)

In fact, check out my website page dedicated to frugal fitness here:

http://christianiron.com/FrugalFitness.aspx

I started training as soon as I got everything set that I actually needed to work out with. **On launching this training program I put all my heart into the exercises. I trained every day from nine o'clock until four.** I worked my upper body one day and my lower body the next. After a few weeks I not only felt more strength coming into my body, but I found that I was getting a great deal larger.

I weighed about 250 pounds when I began my home training and immediately my bodyweight shot up to about 265 pounds. I felt a few inadequacies in my training program, for at this time I was only doing the basic lifts that I had learned from Bob Snead in college.

So I started thinking up new ways to lift, new ways to develop my strength by lifting at different angles. I did this by rigging up a series of pulleys, thus enabling me to do exercises that I could not do with a free barbell or dumbbell movement. This began to pay off because I found that in the power lifts I quickly became able to handle far more weight.

Big Paul having some fun with the camera man at the capitol

To learn something about the weightlifting world, and to keep up with what was going on, **I started to buy the standard muscle magazines found on the newsstand.**

Since most of these dealt mainly with bodybuilding, I could find out very little about strength records. **One thing that I did find out was that in the deep knee bend I was approaching the world record. Much to my surprise it was about 600 pounds at that time, and I had done almost that much in training**.

At that time the squat was not a lift that was performed in competition, as it is today, even though throughout the years records had been kept.

One day during a heavy training session a fellow came up to my garage and introduced himself. His name was **Bob Taylor** and he lived in the adjoining Tennessee town of Johnson City. Bob was a dyed-down-in-the-wool weightlifting enthusiast. He was extremely interested in all phases of the strength world and had done a great deal of lifting himself. He watched while I trained and seemed especially interested in my lifting in the squat. He could not really believe that the weights I had on my makeshift barbell were quite as heavy as I told him. After testing some of them to authenticate the poundage he was quite impressed, since some of them were heavier than I gave them credit for being. He told me about another gentleman, **Bob Peoples,** also from Johnson City, who held the world record in the deadlift with 725 pounds. **Bob Taylor told me that he was sure that Mr. Peoples would like to meet me, and naturally I was enthusiastic about meeting him**. I was generally enthusiastic about making contact with people who were interested in weightlifting and with whom I could exchange ideas.

A few days later Bob Taylor called to ask if I would be interested in going to Bob Peoples' home on the coming Saturday to do some lifting. I told him that I would be delighted, and on the Saturday morning he came to pick me up. We drove about 10 miles to Mr. Peoples' farm. I soon met the owner of both the farm and the world record. He was a very powerful looking man with long arms and rounded shoulders. He looked as if he weighed about 200, extremely wiry and muscular, and seemed to be in his early or mid 40's. Even though he was balding somewhat he gave as overall impression of vibrant, youthful strength. He was also very amiable, and quiet by nature.

He took me down to his gym, which I later began referring to as "the dungeon." It was a hand-excavated basement, **holding a huge conglomeration of barbells and dumbbells**. He had also made some weights similar to those I had built.*

*(See Page 60 picture)

After a guided tour, **Mr. Peoples asked if I would care to do some of the deep knee bends that he had heard so much about.** I replied that I would.

When he asked what I'd like to warm up with I told him that I did very little warming up and asked **to put about 600 on the bar**. He seemed amazed but he politely proceeded to help Bob Taylor load up the big bar.

I then put the bar across my shoulders, stepped back, went into a full deep knee bend and came back up. Being young and sort of frisky, **I did a second repetition and then replaced the barbell back on the rack.** Mr. Peoples was mighty surprised.

Chapter Nine

Paul Anderson's methods

Some Squatting routines from big Paul

Here is an article written by Paul about several of his **squat routines**, we will skip over the first section, as he simply states that one must find his own groove and style which is most appropriate for his body type, leverages, etc. Then, the first 3 routines are basically 3 sets of 10s for number one, and 3 sets of 3's for number 2. Number 3 kicks in quarter squats, obviously with heavier weight. In routine 3, one starts with a warm-up, then goes to a set of 10, add weight and do 5 reps of quarter squats, with the time between the 2 sets as short as possible, in more of a super set mode.

Here are the remaining routines:

Routine Four

In this routine we will keep the **quarter squat** and arrange it in a position that I feel is most advantageous in an advanced program. First do 10 reps in the full squat after a proper warm-up. Then 3 quarter squats with a weight that is adequate for that amount of reps. next, do three full squats with a weight that works you quite well, and then round out the set with **one-legged squats.**

One legged squats can be performed in many ways with many degrees of results. I personally have found the best way to accomplish these is to do them by standing with the leg to be worked on a bench or low table that will allow the athlete to go down into a full knee bend position on the one leg and rise again without the other leg touching the floor. To better explain, the leg not in use is to hang off the end of the bench or table as the exercise is being performed. Do as many of these as possible, working up to about 20 reps.

The following photo shows a one legged squat using only bodyweight, as advocated by Pavel and also called a "pistol"

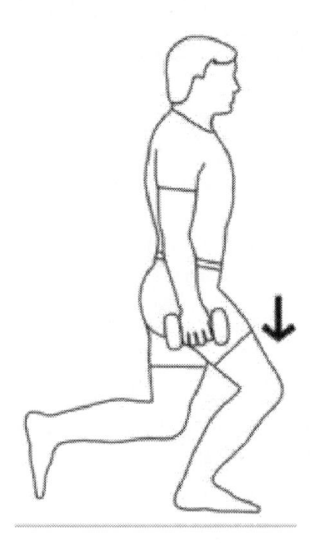

This drawing shows another variation of the lift in which one holds dumbbells in each hand, and the non-working leg goes behind instead of in front like the above version

The photo above is more like the version Paul was talking about

If balance is a problem, there is no harm in placing a hand or finger against the wall or a near object to keep balance, just as long as it is not used to help the lift itself.

Again, three sets of this routine are preferred. A set consists of 10 squats, 3 quarter squats, 3 full squats, and as many one-legged squats as possible, working up to about 20.

Routine Five

At this time I would like for you to consider an exercise that I have found to be quite productive along with my squatting routines, and I have read that some of the European lifters have discovered that **jumping movements** have also been good for them. This is exactly what I am talking about: jumping. When our weightlifting team was traveling for the State Department in 1955, I remember I would get some real strange looks and sometimes many questions when I would go leaping around the warm-up room or stadium grounds in what we would call **jump-squat movements**. In performing this, I would **go all the way down into a full squat position and leap forward and as high as possible**.

By exerting as much leaping power as possible, much strain is put on the muscles, and in turn, the groups being exercised are stimulated and strengthened just as though a slower movement was being done with weights.

As years have gone by **I have found that the best way to perform this type movement is to leap up on a table**. *

Author's note

Let me interject here to note that this method was a favorite of the great George Hackenschmidt, whom I wrote about in my book "The Secrets of Age Defying Strength and how to obtain it" Here is a quote from the book:

The Russian Lion was renowned for jumping over tables and chairs and excelled at the long jump and the high jump as a teenager.

Interestingly, George also ran and rode a bike frequently, and here is another tidbit from the book about George:

While many of the other strength greats of the day mentioned deep breathing practice as a big part of their regimens, George had a bit of a different angle on this idea than most.

He suggested running, especially up hills, as being the best deep breathing exercise one could do, and that it was very simple to do this way, as opposed to some of the other trainers of the time's methods for deep breathing. He suggested that the technique came naturally when running and required little in the way of thought or study.

．．．

Also in the book mentioned above was William Bankier aka Apollo the Scottish Hercules

Here is a quote from the book on his take on jumping: "Making short jumps and skipping on one leg were a couple of his lower body favorites".

You will also see later on in this manual as we progress to modern day methods, references to Paul's jumping squats by Louie Simmons, who still uses these currently.

These are a form of what has more recently become known as "Plyometrics"

Back to Paul's article:

Just like different poundage is handled by different lifters, **a different height table is required for those with various abilities to leap flat-footed with a single leap landing flat-footed on the table.** Make sure that the object that you are leaping up on is fixed so that it cannot slide when it is receiving your total weight. Do these leaping movements in sets of 10's. Leap onto the table, descend to the floor, and leap again until ten have been accomplished. I believe that you will find this a new and strange sensation in your regular work at this point, making for a different stimulation to the muscles and continuing them on their way to personal records in the squat for you. To incorporate the jumps into a set, do 10 going down about halfway into a squatting position for your leaps, 5 in the regular deep knee bend, and 5 in the quarter squat. These three movements will constitute a set. Work up to 3 sets.

If, as time goes by, your leaping power increases, surely it is wise to make your table a little higher to compensate for your new **explosive power.**

Author's note:

In more recent articles by Louie Simmons, he suggests using caution in adding these types of Plyometrics movements with more conventional training and he says one must be very careful not to over train using both, as the Plyometrics work really drains the muscle power.

Routine Six

This sixth routine I will give you **is a real killer**. I have waited until last because you must be in tremendous condition to do this particular routine.

It has to do with the theory of **lowering a heavy weight with as much resistance as possible.** I will first describe how I like to do the exercise, and then talk about the "whys."

A set is as follows: warm up and do one set of 10's with a weight that works you, then with two strong spotters and **the bar loaded to a heavier weight than your natural squat**, or more than you can do in one rep in the natural deep knee bend, have the spotters help you lift the bar from the rack and assist you as you step back into the squatting position.

Variations of this can be worked out on a power rack by removing the pins when the bar is brought up and **then the spotters help to force the weight down**.

Or other safety devices can be used such as parallel bars at the squat position, weights large enough to hit the floor when the athlete can't get back up, etc. **The latter is the reason that I have used the large wheels for my deep knee bends in training for years. Many people have been impressed with these tremendous wheels that weigh about 400 pounds apiece. But the real purpose of them has been to just touch the floor if I have added more weight than I can get up with.** This helps as a safety factor such as the others I have named, and allows me to use a heavy weight, heavier than I can return to upright with, in safety.

Practice with lighter weights before going to something that will actually do the work.

To continue with our instructions on actually performing the lift: as the spotters back up with the lifter, they should help him get in position and then, when ready, the lifter should start down himself naturally in the lift. Many lifters would have ten times strength enough to hold all the poundage the spotters could place on the bar, **if the knees were not voluntary broken**. *

*Author's note

This is what is referred to as a support lift, which many of the old strongmen performed regularly

After the knees are slightly bent and the bar is being brought down, the spotters are in control of how much downward pressure, or weight, they are putting on the bar as they have their hands in a position where they can either lift up or push down. If this weight is adequate to work the higher position in the squat, which is not as necessary as the sticking point in low position, the spotters will have to be quite careful that they **allow the bar to slow down as the sticking point and lower positions are reached**. Of course, working the high side of the squat is not as important since we are doing so many quarter squats. The **main thing we want to consider is the sticking point and low position as the lifter fights the weight, when the spotters are pressing it down. When the bottom is reached, the lifter should try to drive up from the low position 3 times.** Coming up as high into the sticking point as he possibly can, and fighting it, and going down to the bottom and attempting it two more times.

After this, the spotters can pull the weight back up to standing position, and they will probably have to handle most of this weight, because the lifter is going to be pretty well exhausted after his 3 attempts on the bottom. Pushing him down two more times with each bottom position being a foundation for the three upper tries again, these spotters should then help the lifter up for the last time and carefully place the bar back on the racks.

As I have said, power racks are very good for this movement to be performed in, since the lifter doesn't have to take a step backward or forward from the racks before doing his lifts. In performing a set of this particular routine, which consists of 10 repetitions in the deep knee bend, and the 3 downward movements with each containing 3 attempts to rise before the spotters help the lifter up, the athlete to decide exactly how to modify the routine for his particular use. If, at the start, one force down knee bend with the lifter fighting as hard as possible against the spotters and then doing the three upward attempts at the bottom before being lifted up again exhaust him, he should call it a day without doing the other two repetitions.

Anyway, how many repetitions you choose to do in the down position is up to you, but I would recommend working up to 3 even though you cannot do but one set consisting of the 10 deep knee bends and the 3 force down movements. 3 sets should be the limit.

Routine Seven

Although I am not claiming that this routine is new with me, I feel that I have done more experimenting with it than anyone else, and in turn have written more about it than any other instructor. My personal name for it is **Progressive Movement Training**.

This is the only time I am going to ask you to deviate from my rule of thumb of always doing the actual movement, because I feel with all the reps you have been doing in the deep knee bend you are pretty well in the groove and will not get out of the groove in the time that you spend on the Progressive Movement squatting routine.

The real trick to it is repetition variation as well as lengthening the movement. The idea of doing this in the squat is to **start off with a quarter squat lift in a power rack**, or a squat rack with some type of guards running up each side to keep the weight from falling out in case of a loss of balance.

By starting off in a quarter squat, **you should use a weight about 100 pounds more than your best full squat.** I realize this is a very light weight in comparison to what you can quarter squat with, but this is part of the plan. I recommend doing about **20 to 25 repetitions in the quarter squatting movement with the particular weight that fits your ability, performing 2 sets.** The 20 to 25 repetitions will constitute a set. I want you to do this every day.

After doing the two sets you are going to feel, especially in the beginning, that you are not accomplishing very much and you will not get very tired. **Every three days, lower the bar or raise the body, which will come out to the same results, about three inches. When lowering the bar three inches, knock off 3 reps. Continue the 2 sets of 17 to 22 reps, according to what you started with, for three days, ten raise the body or lower the stands again some three inches, knocking off 3 repetitions per set.** Continue doing this until you have worked just as far down as you possibly can into a full squatting position. **Always start the lift in the bottom position. After you have worked down just as far as possible, cutting your repetitions all the way down to 2, rest about two or three days and then try your limit in the squat.** I believe that you will find that you have gained quite a bit of strength during this drawn out Progressive Movement routine. You can do your upper body and back exercises as usual, if you feel you can perform all of them.

Much of your recovery ability and your strength progression is up to you as an individual. I am giving you **routines that I feel are the ultimate in power building, and many of them quite unique. Much thought and experimentation have gone into these**, but one thing I have learned through experimenting with other athletes and on myself is that each and every one is an individual.

You must learn to judge your repetitions, and especially your sets according to your personal ability and responsiveness to the exercises themselves.

Another tip on doing this routine is to use one-inch sheets of plywood for the height graduation. If you will cut these one-inch sheets of plywood just square enough for your stance in the squat allowing safe foot room on each side, you can stack them up as you lengthen the movement. I have given some ideas on squat racks for this including the power rack's use, but you may even go so far as I have in the movement, if finances will allow. I use the heavy quarter squat racks with bumper jacks built in and I can just raise and lower them at will.

If you cannot afford to build such equipment or if at this time you do not wish to, either power racks or squat racks with extra guards built up on each side will work out more than adequately for the exercise.

I have suggested in the squatting routine that you build on the program of using the routines in sequence, but if you happen to be a very advanced lifter and would like to choose them at random, that is also up to you.

(*Article close*)

....

Author's note Now I will have to say the eccentric (negatives) movements he suggests will be impossible to duplicate without very reliable and strong spotters, but some variation of these may be accomplished to a degree using the more modern methods using bands in conjunction with weights.

These were not available when Paul penned the article above, and I suspect he'd have made great use of them if they had been. I'd also suggest extreme caution and light weights starting out with Paul's eccentric methods as they are extremely demanding.*

In the next section, Paul gives his deadlift routines, and it is in this article that homage is paid to his mentor, Bob Peoples

Training for the Deadlift

By Paul Anderson

I have spent much time and thought on the deadlift, and the main reason is that I am the world's poorest deadlifter. I believe at the date of this publication I have actually raised more poundage in the lift than anyone else, but in comparison to some of my other lifts I am rather ashamed of what I have done. Ashamed possibly is not the word to use, because I have a tremendously bad leverage for the lift, as most large-bodied people do. The ideal deadlifter is as person with long limbs and a short body, but no matter how we look at it, we are usually favored or discriminated against in one of the three powerlifts, no matter how we are built.

This usually evens it all out and makes it relatively fair for everyone. The point I am making is that if you are rather poor in a lift, you do more thinking on it, and consequently come up with better ideas and training methods.

I must also give credit for some of my knowledge in the deadlift to Bob Peoples. Bob lifted back in the day when powerlifting was not a recognized sport, and was quite alone.

At 181 pounds or actually less, he raised 725 pounds. **Considering everything I know about Bob Peoples and his training conditions, I must say that he is surely the greatest deadlifter that I have ever known.**

To dwell just a moment on philosophy and my friend Bob Peoples, let me say that **he has always been one of the greatest thinkers in the weightlifting world.** Because of this, I was able to learn various things about the deadlift that would seldom come to most athletes because of my close association with Bob.

From the instructions and philosophy so far, you can see that I am always very sensitive and aware of a lifter's position and procedure in carrying out a lift. I have called the correct manner in each athlete performing the desired movement the "groove," and that is exactly what we are discussing: the particular manner in which each individual finds it easiest to make the lift, always considering, of course, performing in a legal manner.

I have observed lifters who looked like they made all their attempts in one motion. To better explain this, personally I have found that whether I am pressing, bench pressing, squatting, etc., I seem to have to change gears as the bar travels through its particular cycles. On the other hand, I have seen fellows who rammed a press to arm's length or stood straight up with a deadlift in almost a sudden gesture, without any evidence of this changing of gears, which could very well mean the changing of the direction of the bar as it traveled to arm's length, upright position, or as you would stand to finish position in the squat. These thoughts may seem trivial, but every individual must learn himself and know how he is performing the lift. Working out in front of a mirror, or better still, seeing a film or videotape of one's performances can be of great help in finding out just how the bar is traveling, and deciding whether or not this is the proper manner in which you should perform.

These suggestions concerning the groove are important, and this is one of the reasons I have recommended repetitions in some of the lifts as we went through other routines. Doing the higher repetitions not only helps pump a great deal of blood into the muscles, which is part of strengthening them, but also gets you accustomed to allowing the bar to move along the strongest route. Also this is why I say that a lift should be practiced along with assistance exercises to strengthen the particular lift. **Coordinate the strength that you are building, while keeping the lift in the groove.**

Before going into our first routine for the deadlift, let's consider the fact that we are going to be doing some variations of the deadlift, and in doing so, we well be performing repetitions.

Doing repetitions with a bar loaded heavy enough to work the lower back and other muscle groups used in performing the deadlift makes for one big problem. This difficulty is the tenderness of the human hands, resulting in blisters, calluses, torn skin, etc.

The hand is naturally going to get tough as it is called on to do any particular work that puts a strain on the surface, but the soreness that results from each workout, as the lifter holds onto a bar for repetitions usually cannot be overcome by the next workout. This means that the entire muscle groups worked by the deadlift and its variations are going to be at the mercy of the condition of the lifter's hands.

There is an answer to this and it is not original with me, although I have worked out some variations as the years have gone by. **The first answer I saw to this problem was developed by Bob Peoples and as I have said, I will be mentioning him a great deal in this article. He had made two hooks to perform repetition deadlifts with and fastened them on his wrist by wrapping the upper ends with cloth tapes about 2 ½ inches wide.** In this same manner, many have used straps to help secure the bar while performing repetitions, but I really believe that the hooks are the best idea. When straps are used, the hands still take a pretty good beating, while they can be far more relaxed when hooks are applied.

Also before going into the routines let's think about the manner in which the bar is to be gripped. Many reading these instructions will already have their minds made up and through personal experience know exactly how they would like to grip the bar whether it is concerning the width of hand spacing or manner of holding the bar in the hands. The vast majority of deadlifters I seen use the reverse grip, securing the bar by hooking the thumbs. The main thing I would like to point out here is that if you use a reverse grip on your heavy singles when attempting a record lift, please also use that same reverse grip when using hooks of straps to do the repetitions. I think much has been lost in the past by lifters who have chosen to go to a straight overhand grip when using these aids in holding the bar, and found that even if they did not recognize it at the time, they were a little handicapped with their reverse grip on the heavy single. I say handicapped referring only to the fact that they were not using the power that they had developed 100% from repetitions. The simple reason is that the bar was not in the groove, because of a change of grip.

To once again put the burden on the individual, allow me to instruct you to **lift without the aid of hooks or straps enough so that the hands will be tough and strong when doing heavy singles.** This must be left up to you and your own judgment. The **aids in gripping are just to allow the back and other muscle groups to be properly worked to gain your ultimate in deadlifting strength.**

Author's note:

There are a couple of schools of thought on this matter of whether or not to use hooks or straps to aid the deadlift (and other lifts). Brooks Kubick (author of the Dinosaur Training book), for example is not big on using such aids, saying that doing so bypasses the needed hand toughening and grip building that is part and parcel to a strongman's or powerlifter's repertoire. In fact, Brooks goes to the opposite extreme in suggesting training with fat bars and the like to increase the grip building component of the deadlift and other lifts. I have had grip issues with my deadlift and I have found Brooks' ideas more to my liking. I have tried straps and hooks but I am not a big fan of them.

I feel that over using them will certainly be detrimental to the grip that is needed in a maximum single deadlift attempt, but if you feel the need, they may well enable you to "overload" the back muscles when used sparingly. I will also say that doing fat bar deadlifts with moderate weight on my light, speed work days was one of the best grip building methods I have ever used. This is a matter of personal preference and something one should experiment with for best gains.

Routine One

After warming up, the first routine is very simple. Do 8 repetitions in the regular deadlift, lowering the bar all the way to the floor and stopping each time for a new start.

Follow with 8 repetitions in the stiff-legged deadlift, with the bar just touching the floor and no hesitation each time. 8 reps will be the most I will give in deadlifts because breathing is a little difficult while performing the movement.

With the bar hanging at arm's length and all the weight extending from the shoulders, the rib cage is cramped. **A set of 8 reps in the regular deadlift followed by 8 in the stiff-legged.**

Routine Two

It is almost imperative to have three bars loaded for this particular routine, or at least have helpers to make some **fast changes if enough weights and bars are not available.**

The **routine consists of three different lifts and each set should be done in a relatively short period of time.** First, after a warm-up, do 5 repetitions in the regular deadlift.

As soon as recovered do 5 repetitions in the "top side" of the deadlift, by raising a bar some four to five inches off parallel racks, boxes, or any other apparatus that you would like to use in raising the bar to a position so that there is only about four or five inches left when lifting the bar to a finish position. The weight used on this should be something that works the body well for the 5 reps, and **your starting stance should be in the same position that it would have been if the bar had not been brought from the floor to this point.** In other words, I do not want you to get in a real advantage position to handle more weight in this top side lift, other than the position you world ordinarily have been in had you lifted the bar from the floor. The weight you can handle in this "finish out" should be quite a bit more than in your regular deadlift.

Next, continuing to handle more weight than the regular deadlift, do 5 repetitions with a bar originating on the floor, and the body in the original starting position for the deadlift. The bar should be loaded to a point so that it can only be raised about four inches from the floor.

The two assistance exercises here are naturally to give a good "finish out" and "starting pull" for the dead lift. Many lifters will find that they are extremely strong in one or the other of these positions, but very few will find that they can handle a great deal more weight than their regular lift in both.

No matter what the poundage that can be handled for the five repetitions either in the top or bottom position of the deadlift, load the bar to what you can handle with a good exertion of strength. Work up to 3 sets in this routine with the regular, the top side and the starting position movement constituting one set. Five repetitions in each, then repeat the three movements. This is a routine that you may want to come back to occasionally, for it is a very good one.

Other routines in the various lifts may work so well that they become favorites and you will want to repeat them every few weeks or months, but also remember that if a routine does not produce now, it very well could later. So try them again.

Routine Three

For an assistance exercise on this particular routine let's use **the good morning exercise**. I realize that there are several things that will pop up as objections to the good morning lift, but let's do it in a little different manner than usual.

The first time I tried good mornings as a strengthening lift for my lower back, I was very satisfied. I started out with a weight that I considered to be ridiculously light, for I wanted to do some high repetitions and also knew that sometimes discomfort resulted from a heavy bar resting in this position. I did this lift just as strictly as I thought was possible for quite a while and certainly did receive great results from it. The results I am speaking of came basically from my pulling power in the regular deadlift and also the clean and snatch.

Overly delighted with this particular assistance exercise, I continued doing it and even found I was getting much, much stronger in it, but then my progress in the lifts that I was actually performing this assistance exercise in order to increase stopped advancing. My first reaction was to consider what was wrong and give it some serious thought. I was not going stale because I was getting stronger in the good morning, so there must be something else wrong. On real close examination, I found that even though I was continuing to perform the lift with stiff knees, and bending the trunk of the body at least into a parallel position to the floor before rising again, there was indeed something different.

I had, without knowing or planning it, learned to cheat on the movement. I was counterbalancing the lift by extending my hips backward, which accounted for lifting more weight with less of the desired results. Because of this experience, I developed a good way to do the good morning exercise, producing tremendous results.

Make a wide belt that can be pulled up just above the knee on each thigh. This belt can be made of leather or some type of webbing, and should be about five or six inches wide. On each belt there should be a ring sewn in, or attached in some way just about midway of the width.

By attaching a rope, chain, etc. to each of the rings and joining it to a single rope about three feet from the rings, you will have yourself an apparatus that will help you perform good mornings in a strict manner. Attach a rope that the two original ropes or chains are fastened to on to something stable that is just a little higher than the position that the belts are in around the thighs. When taking the bar from the squat racks, have enough length on the ropes so that you may step forward into your stance for the movement and tighten the rope. (Photos – figures 29 and 30)

Lean forward, do the exercise with tension being on the thigh belts. Keep a good footing so that you will not be apt to swing onto the belts and that way fall forward.

Figure 30

The photos above and next show what Paul is talking about

Figure 29

To better explain, keep a great deal of weight on your feet and only use the belts as stabilizers to lean against and not swing all your weight on. This can best be done by using a very light weight for experimenting until you get it down pat.

There have been other such methods developed, such as leaning on a board and different variations on such, but to me this is the best method I have used.

Do about ten of these good mornings for part of the set in this routine. For the second portion of each set I want you to get a weight that is almost your limit in the deadlift, approaching it without hooks or straps, using your regular grip, and do one repetition. Put this weight down, stand erect, take several deep breaths, and once again do a single repetition. Continue doing this for 10 repetitions. Try to do the lift as rapidly as possible, although I do not want you to sacrifice poundage for speed in performance.

Author's note:

This is a variation of the rest-pause idea Mr. Rader spoke of earlier

During the first few times you try these singles, work up just how many breaths it takes between each lift. This way you can gauge your performance. Also try not to leave the original stance, keeping chalk nearby so that you can just pick it up and re-chalk your grip when necessary. These lifts will not only build strength but will really put your heavy deadlift in the groove.

Summing up this routine, do ten modified good mornings, ten of the heavy singles and you will have accomplished a set. This is another one of the real killers, so be conservative on your sets, hoping to work up to three.

Routine Four

I would like to start this routine by saying that **there is no one who cannot deadlift more flat-footed than with heels on their shoes**. I say that I would like to start by making this statement, but there surely is an exception to every rule when it comes to lifting.

This is because of the many body make-ups and sizes of people. So, let us just say that, as a rule, there is no one who can't lift more flatfooted than with heels. I think this can be emphasized by many of the lifters who have caught on to what some are calling "deadlifting downhill."

This expression describes those who would actually build up the front of their shoes, raising the ball of the foot higher that the heel so that when the lift is started the lifter is really pulling back and has a **better leverage on the bar than if he was flatfooted or barefooted.**

Now, operating under the assumption that being flatfooted is an advantage, let's take a great disadvantage.

After a proper warm-up, I would like you to do a set of deadlifts with the first being in the regular form, the next four stiff-legged, and a final repetition going back down into your original regular deadlift stance and completing the lift. This is the only exercise in this routine I would like you to do, performing 4 sets.

Do not misinterpret this as elementary, for **we are going to do it the hard way.**

That is, with the heels elevated. I would like for you to elevate your heels just as high as possible and still be able to put weight on the entire foot. Maybe by wearing a shoe with a regular heel and putting on top of a 2 x 4, there will be enough elevation. If this does not seem enough for you, put even more under the heel so that you are really lifting uphill instead of downhill. This is going to put a unique strain on the entire deadlift movement, and should help overcome the sticking point that you personally have.

Routine Five

You're going to have to use hooks or straps for this one. The "down movement" as discussed in training the squat. Prepare for the heavy down movement by doing the maximum reps in your deadlift, which we have said is eight.

After the proper rest, your spotters are to give their help in bringing the heavier than you can manage weight to the finish position and, as you voluntarily start to lower it, they will push down so that in no way can you stop the bar even though you should try with all your might. Repeat this four times.

A set in this routine will be 8 deadlifts, after warm-up, and 4 repetitions in the down movement. If four repetitions are too much, cut them down, and even though you are working up to a hopeful 3 sets, judge this by your progress and endurance.

There are many lifting routines I can give you in every lift that is done in power lifting competition. A different combination of the routines I have instructed you in can be worked out by you as you advance and experiment on your own.

My tendency has always been to over train, and on occasions it has caught up with me just like it will with you. I point this out because some of the routines I have given you are quite strenuous and some of you possible cannot bear up under the full thrust of them. Even though I have said this many times throughout these instructions, play it cool, and work into them slowly.

Indeed, you will have to work hard to make progress in lifting – as in any other thing in life. You will get out of this work just about what you put in. From many of my comments you should have gathered that weightlifting takes not only hard work to be successful, but also much thinking. I challenge you to THINK!

Some of your best ideas will come when things are not going well.

This is why I have offered you the possibilities of rearranging the lifts that I have recommended in the routines, or even rearranging the routines themselves where I have put them in sequence. First, I would like for you to try them as I have given them to you.

Yes, there are many other exercises that I could give you, but most of them take special equipment and as a rule, they are not any better than the ones I have projected. One is **the inverted stiff-legged deadlift**. This takes a bench, something like an incline board but not quite as steep. The lift is done by the athlete hanging by his feet in an inverted position on this bench and pulling the bar from the starting to the finish position of the stiff-legged deadlift. **The weights are attached by a cable hooked to the bar going up over the top end of the bench through a pulley. The weights themselves are, of course, suspended at the other end of the cable.**

Author's note:

Wow, here is another exercise I have never seen being done... what a concept!

This is only an example of the many things that I have worked out through the years for special problems in lifting.

Paul's Thoughts on eating

At this time I will add a few tidbits from an article by Paul about nutrition.

Keep in mind that Paul was diagnosed with Blights disease as a very young boy and was playing "catch-up" with his fellows until his mid to late teens.

Many of the older routines do not offer a great deal of detail on diet, but Paul obviously feels this area is important and deserves some detail, accordingly.

On Raw eggs:

I ate many raw eggs, which gave me much strength, and I personally feel that eggs are quite good for this, in spite of the cholesterol jag we seem to be on.

On meat & fish:

On many occasions I can remember, instead of taking my extra spending money and buying sweets, I would buy various types of canned fish that my body seemed to constantly crave. Most of my attention in high school turned toward eating meat (beef and lamb) that was cooked quite rare. Heretofore I had always preferred meat that was well done, even to the point of almost being charred. This is actually the way my family had always prepared meat dishes, and my taste naturally developed in this way. **I found that not only did the meat taste better rare, but it seemed to digest faster and give me more strength.**

On Protein consumption:

I knew basically that I needed a **great quantity of protein** to build and repair the muscle tissue I was tearing down with the heavy lifting. It made sense to me that the more protein my body could assimilate the greater progress I could make in my quest for weightlifting championships.

Milk and eggs together:

As I examined the situation, I came to the conclusion that even though I could not eat a great deal of solid foods, I always consumed large quantities of liquids. Much of my diet had been made up of milk, from which I received much good digestible protein.

Throughout my junior high and high school years, I had sometimes consumed three to four quarts of milk per day. Now part of the task before me was to figure out a way to put protein in drinkable form.

My first pursuit of a higher protein diet, in a liquid form, was to go back on the **raw eggs and sweet milk.** By beating them up in a blender, I could drink about a dozen eggs at a time, which would give me much extra protein along with the milk. I found that this once again enhanced my ability to gain weight and to build strong healthy muscle tissue, after it had been torn down earlier in my workouts.

The introduction of Soy

I read somewhere that soybean powder was very good for protein deficiency, and it was being shipped overseas for starving people in various parts of the world. I thought surely if this was good for someone with a gross lack of protein, it would be extra nourishing for a person that needed more protein because of his strenuous exercise. Finally I was able to buy some soybean meal. This product was quite course in comparison with the finely crushed powder we know in protein supplements today. Although it was in this crude form, I was able to grind it a bit finer by beating it in a milk solution for a long period of time with the aid of a blender. I could immediately tell the difference in my diet and thought actually that two protein supplements I had tried thus far, both being good, should be combined in some way, which would give me the better quantities of both. I started varying my diet, making ice cream and milk shakes with the soybean meal, raw eggs, milk, and varying the type of flavor used. Even better results were obtained from this particular procedure.

Adding animal and vegetable proteins together

One day I was reading the label on a plain gelatin product, and saw that they advertised it to be very high in protein. I thought this would be something to try, so I started putting it into orange juice, stirring it up briskly and drinking it. I used this along with the diet of milk, raw eggs, and soybeans. Now there was a greater vitality in my life, and certainly a marked difference in my training.

I varied the gelatin products, many being on the market, and started buying it in a bulk form. Now I started to learn that both animal and vegetable proteins were better when they were used together.

The value of using animal and vegetable protein in a blend proved itself more as time went by.

Sweet tooth:

Occasionally I would drink soft drinks during my training and noticed when I did this I could perform much better, and my digestive cycle would work much faster. This proved to me that I needed a great deal more sugar. It seemed that the more protein I took, the more sugar I needed to help digest the protein, and also give me quick energy. I turned to the greatest sugar supply I could find, which was honey. I soon found that much of the honey that could be bought in grocery stores did not do me as much good as honey direct from the beehive, bought from a farmer. It was my personal belief that much of the honey that was on the market had been heated in a pasteurizing process and had lost some of its quick digesting qualities.

Some days I would consume even a half pint of honey, when I was working out strenuously and carrying on my tremendous traveling schedule.

On Raw proteins:

I guess the first distasteful food I started to use was the extract from raw beef. I have always been very careful about the beef I chose for such a dish, since I was eating it without any type of cooking. The procedure here is to take good ground beef, of the lean variety and put it in one of the better centrifugal force extractors. This will extract most of the liquid, which looks mostly like blood. I usually add a little salt to this liquid, and drink it. Considering all the liquid supplements I have used, this is one of the greatest. This meat extract can be disguised by drinking it in tomato juice, or adding some type of meat sauce to it to change the flavor.

I expanded this through the years, and not only used beef but all types of raw seafood. With a diet of all the protein supplements that I have mentioned, and also using the raw beef extracts and raw seafood, whether liquefied of used in a solid form, I found that I could put in some eighteen hours a day in my traveling and speaking engagements, plus carry on a workout routine.

Not a vampire:

I have experimented with many other typed of extra protein foods. Some I can half-heartedly recommend. Some I condemn completely.

I tried one time to drink **pure beef blood. This food that many of the old-time strongmen used** is quite hard to secure, but I found one meatpacking house that would furnish it for me. Especially in this procedure, one has to have a person that he can trust to secure the blood, and of course to secure it in a sanitary manner, and then be quite discreet in what type animal the blood is taken from. To keep the blood from coagulating I found that a little citric acid mixed with water, previously placed in the container would do the trick.

Concerning this diet of beef blood, I never found it as rewarding, in a strength-building sense, as the beef extracts. I believe that from the extracts not only blood is obtained, but also other fluids and meat tissue that are also valuable.

Vitamins:

Along with all of these foods that I recommend, I have always used a vitamin-mineral supplement, and on most occasions taken large quantities of cold-pressed **wheat germ oil.**

In closing:

Diet cannot do it alone. There are many qualities that make up the champion, or just the person who wants to live a full and vibrant life and get the most use out of what God has given him.

Certainly all will agree, the type of fuel we put into the wonderful machines we call bodies is what determines the efficiency of their operation.

Author's note:

It is interesting that Anderson sought a great variety of protein sources in his diet, whereas many modern bodybuilders seem to get caught up in using one or 2 sources almost exclusively, at least for periods of time. I have come across recent dietary suggestions that seem to agree with what Paul was preaching way back then; that the body thrives on a variety of sources and this may be a better approach. Besides, it's a lot less boring!

More about Bob Peoples

I recently purchased and read Bob People's book "**Developing Physical Strength**", which is not voluminous in nature, but provides a nice look at Bob's training methods, style, and innovation. Bob built a number of devices in order to help him train heavy and safely even when lifting by himself.

Bob did a whole lot of rack work, having built his own rack in his basement gym, and was also very much into negative training or eccentric work. His intensity coupled with the volume of workouts he did was mind blowing.

There were times when he deadlifted 4-5 times per week, which is unheard of these days.

He did freely admit to being a deadlift specialist, and in truth his other lifts were far less remarkable when compared to his insane deadlifting power. I would not try to emulate Bob's training as it would likely cripple me, yet there are many things that can be learned from him.

I suggest you read Bob's book to fully comprehend the man and his methods.

In the preface to the book, **JC Hise** speaks fondly of Bob, as he was one of his contemporaries and friends.

Hise was quite the lifter himself and as he was mentioned above as one of the most successful students of the squat we can think of, I thought we should present this nice article excerpt on him here:

Chapter Ten

J.C. Hise

J.C. Hise, Pioneer of Powerlifting
by Fred Howell

"**Someday a weightlifter will clean & jerk 500 pounds**," said Joe Hise to the gang of lifters around him at a meet. Most of them told Joe he was daydreaming, for at that time, in 1936, that poundage was a good deadlift!

But Joe went on to say it will take a combination of hard work on the legs, back and bodyweight, plus plenty of lifting practice and a mind that will accept the fact that it can be done. In 1970 his "pipe dream" came true when in Columbus, Ohio, **Vasily Alexeev clean & jerked 501½ pounds.**

It was **during the early 30s that Joseph Curtis Hise started to train with barbells**. As a youth he had a couple of bouts with pleurisy and found with exercise he never had the trouble again. With the standard routines of the day, Joe found himself gaining from 160 lbs. to 200 after a little leg work, but then hit a sticking point.

After reading some of Mark Berry's articles in the deep knee bend, Joe decided to give it a try. Using the press behind the neck for 15 reps, and the deep knee bend in which he did 8 reps then rested and did 8 more; he then removed 100 lbs. from the bar and did 20 more reps. Thirty days later Joe found himself weighing 229 lbs. with a chest of 46 ½ and thighs reaching 28 inches.

It wasn't long before Joe and his growing exercise were the talk of the strength world. His fast results were reported in the February issue of "**Strong Man**" and the August 1932 issue of "**Strength**" magazine.

He wrote Mark Berry and said, "Although I exercised for years **I never knew that leg work increased the chest and lungs. I thought it was the chest exercises that spread the chest until I read your article in Strong Man."**

Joe then kept right on squatting, now **using a straight 20 reps in the squat,** and soon found that he weighed 237 lbs. at 26 years of age. He continued his experiments and finally reached a bodyweight of 298 lbs. and had an arm of 19½ inches, chest at 56 and thighs that measured 33 inches at 5'10" tall. During his training **Joe made sure to eat meat twice a day and drink plenty of milk.**

Suddenly the name Joe Hise was famous throughout the barbell world, with lifters coming to see Joe in Homer, Illinois to "check" and see if he was all that was reported in the magazines of that day. As Joe said to Mark Berry, "Some of the fellows who visited me thought it might ghost writing or just plain hot air when they read my gains in strength, measurements and bodyweight!"

At a lifting contest held in Postl's gym, the minute Joe showed up, out came the steel measuring tapes to see if his "claims" were fact or printing mistakes.

John Grimek was one of those visitors to the home of Hise, while John was working in Urbana, Illinois. **The two were to become good friends and train together many times.** During his visit with Joe, John got a good look at **the rugged and primitive training quarters that were used by Hise to toss the iron up and down.** Joe never had a real chance to practice the three lifts as he had only exercise bars and trained outdoors or in a cold garage. John had this to say about his visit with Hise –

"The one thing I remember well, when visiting his home in Homer and watching Hise train, was his unusual system of squats and deadlifts.

For all his ponderous weight, Joe moved with the agility of a lightweight."

As Joe Hise reported his bodyweight ad strength gains, many barbell fans who were without such startling results him wrote Joe and asked him for his help. Joe wrote back to all of them and soon had an army of exercise pupils using his methods.

Peary Rader gained 75 pounds after reading about Joe in Strong Man and trying on the squat. Other men such as **James Douglass, Leo Murdock, Rodger Eels, Earl Stout, Tom Bruno, Doc Kelling and Foster Mays**, to name just a few of his fans, all received letters and results from this friendly strongman's instructions.

One day Joe came to do his workout and found that his brother had used his bar as a tool for a Model T driveshaft housing and bent it. Joe gave the bar a whack and bent the bar straight again and did his squats with 395 lbs. The straight bar bothered his neck every time he did squats, and he got to thinking about the bent bar. He grabbed a pinch bar and "un-straightened" the bar, **putting a camber in the bar** and tried 20 reps with 300 lbs. When he finished he found the **bar did not roll up and down on his neck as before, and the weights had a perfect hang for squatting!**

After that Joe used only a cambered bar for squatting, and suddenly everyone was putting a camber in exercise bars. For many it was a way to exercise in comfort when doing that tough exercise, the squat.

Early cambered bar squat shown in photo

After having used the squat for months Joe decided to give deadlifting a try. He used the regular bent leg style and then tried the stiff legged version. This caused him to have a stiff back following each session. Using his inventive mind, Joe came up with a hopper so he could bounce the weight past the danger point. He discovered that if he bounced the weight from wooden planks that were raised about two inches at each end he relieved the over-stretch and this allowed him to handle 550 for 5 reps in the exercise. Then Joe got annoyed with kettlebells pressing down on his wrists, cut holes in some buckets, and made what he called bucket-bells.

An even earlier bent bar

Hise had many hobbies including reading books on philosophy, the classics and other nonfiction material. Here he found a way to relax and independently increase his knowledge of the world. Joe was also a traveling man and loved to visit his correspondents, many times unannounced and much to their surprise.

One time he rode a freight train to Springfield, New Jersey to visit **Andy Jackson**, then the owner of the **Jackson Barbell Company**. When he got to Andy's house he was covered with soot and his eyes were full of cinders. Andy's dad spent an hour getting the cinders out of Joe's eyes. **Riding a freight train is a rough way to travel, yet after his eyes were cleaned and with no rest after a long, hard trip, Joe went downstairs to Andy's shop and deadlifted 700 lbs.**

After watching him lift that weight Andy said, "It was far from his limit. He lifted it way too easy to be his top poundage."

Joe was a bachelor and enjoyed his freedom, but Andy said to Joe, "You're not getting any younger. Why not settle down and find a good gal to take care of you?" But Joe didn't want any part of the domestic life at all, for he liked to be free to come and go as the mood moved him.

Andy had a better idea and took Hise to the wrestling matches one night, and Joe sat there in silence watching the bodies bounce back and forth. After a while Andy just casually mentioned to Joe that he could make some good money using his bulk and strength as a wrestler. Joe looked at Andy for a long moment and then said, "NOT ME! I'm not going to get hamburgered and busted up plus hat-pinned by some nutty little old lady; not this man!" That was the end of that deal.

One time Joe had to flatten a couple of hobos who thought he was easy pickings while waiting for a freight, but he wasn't going to look for that kind of exercise five nights a week.

During this period in his life, Joe continued to wonder why some men made great gains both in muscle and power, while others seemed to train for years with little results. One other thing that bothered him was the fact that some people seem to be healthy on a very poor diet while others who were very careful about what they ate had physical problems anyway.

As Hise kept asking himself, "Why doesn't everyone respond to exercise?" he evolved his **cartilage mass theory**. Since youth and cartilage go hand in hand, than what he called postural exercises will increase cartilage areas in the body, and help those resistant to exercise gain results.

Joe believed you should not exercise over three times a week on growing exercises, and twice per week on strength-building or lifting routines. The first exercise in a growing routine is the squat. First you **do 10 reps, and then take three deep breaths between each rep until you reach 20 reps**; if you use **heavy weights, one set only**.

This, plus the **wrestler's bridge**, two arm pull-over with a light weight, upright rowing, deadlift and the curl would pack the weight and power onto a stubborn no-gain pupil. **If the course sounds a bit familiar, it should, for a number of "experts" have borrowed a lot from Joe's routines.**

Here I am doing a modified wrestler's bridge

In the original version, your head makes contact, not the shoulders

One day Hise saw a young man, Charles Tiffin, put a light barbell across his shoulders and then do shrugging movements while taking deep breaths.

Joe's inventive mind went to work and reasoned that maybe a heavy barbell would be better and increase chest size and improve posture. This was the start of ***the Hise Shrug.***

Soon letters were pouring in to Hise that, in fact, it did work. It worked so well that a well known barbell company included it in their bulk course, passing it off as their own discovery. **Harry Paschall**, in his book "**Development of Strength,**" included it as one of the strength-building exercises in his routines.

To do the Hise Shrug you take a bar from a rack, several inches below shoulder level. With your back strongly erect and your legs slightly bent, straighten your knees and lift the weight from the supports. Now breathe in strongly and lift the weight by shrugging the trapezius muscles; breathe out as you lower the weight. Use 5 reps for power and 20 for bulk-making. Be sure to breathe high and fill the top part of the chest and not low in the belly.

Remember one thing – **Joe never had fancy equipment, and trained alone under the most primitive of conditions.** Even at home his squat rack was a couple of hedge posts tied up against the garage Because of this outdoor training, his workouts were spasmodic except in the summer months. Yet, even with such conditions he was able to make great progress at a time when Peary Rader said, "We all know that as yet the science of body culture is rather crude and uncertain."

Joe always worked at the hardest types of jobs, in coal mines, uranium mills, cement mills, lumber stacking and as a hobby and in the hope of striking it rich, searching out lost mines and finding his own claims. He had a passion for the old west and its lore. Andy Jackson said that when Joe visited him he would fall asleep at the kitchen table at 2:00 a.m. listening to the western tales Joe could spin.

For Joe, the freedom of prospecting and working at a job until he was tired of it was a way of life for him, and his philosophy. When necessary, he was capable of doing a terrific amount of work. For months on end he would work double shifts and save his money, then retire to train and experiment with his weights. Also, he was supporting a few relatives on the side. **Hise was an able writer with a style all his own. He wrote many articles for Iron Man, Vim, Strong Man, and Vigor.**

It was not until 1956 that I became friends with this mountain man. As Joe became older, still living alone and cooking for himself, time and hard work had taken their toll and had worn this rugged man down. He became ill and, living alone, neglected himself. This illness, along with some personal family problems, plus an old work injury, made it impossible for Joe to exercise or take care of himself. His fellow workers talked him into seeing a doctor who put him in a hospital and insisted on Joe losing weight until he was skin and bones.

It was to be a fatal mistake. Later I was to learn that the director of the hospital Hise was in was arrested, along with his doctor friends, for stealing large amounts of money allotted for the patients' food.

When they got done with him Joe weighed less than 190 lbs. and was a walking wreck.

In August of 1972 Joe knew he was a very sick man, weakened by the stupid "medical attention" he underwent. He then decided to buy a pickup truck and set out to visit his friends across the country for the last time. On a Friday afternoon I received a phone call from my wife, Natalie, informing me that Joe Hise was at our home. I rushed from work and when I shook hands with Joe I was shocked. This once massive man was now a shadow of his former self. Mentally as sharp as ever, Joe was full of plans to regain his health, write, and enjoy life once more.

He said he had just visited John Grimek, and after his stay with me he would head for other friends in Pennsylvania and Ohio.

Joe made many mistakes in life, like we all do, and deeply regretted not trying to become a lifting champion when he was at his strongest physically and had great ambitions for lifting during his twenties. **In his early training days he was able to jerk 300 lbs. behind his neck without much trouble, and may have been the first man in America to accomplish this feat. Joe could also pull 400 lbs. chest-high at any time. This, plus over 700 lbs. in the deadlift and 690 lb. squats shows that he had plenty of power but needed proper training in style and form and access to superior equipment.**

He was sorry he never married as he felt a good woman might have made the difference in caring and meals that could have kept him healthy or helped him regain his health during the dark days of his last two years. But Joe went on to say, "the trick is to find a female who doesn't mind her husband lifting weights."

Although he kept a positive outlook in his future plans, Joe told Natalie when he was talking with her that he wanted to visit his friends now because he felt his time was limited on this earth. When he said goodbye I had a feeling it would be the last time I would see Joseph C. Hise, and it turned out to be true. A month later he died.

Every time someone does a heavy squat, Hise shrug, hopper deadlift, and achieves some muscle or strength progress it will be in part because of this inventive strongman.

As his friend Tom Bruno wrote me, "Joe had a roaming fever which is OK. This is what he wanted to do in life. He was a powerful strongman who lived the way he wanted to in this life, a free man.

Who could want for more?"

This was taken From "Readers' Round-Up", **IronMan magazine**, October/November 1972.

Above is a picture of JC Hise in his prime.

Chapter Eleven

Revamped 20 rep squat program

There have been many modifications to the 20 rep squat program and exercises used to complement the squats, and dietary tweaks over the years. Iron Magazine had this interesting article on the subject:

Written by: Jim Brewster

The 20 rep Squat is without a doubt one of the most demanding exercises you can do. You will definitely know what pain is all about after one set of these! It also is not all that common anymore. Why? Who knows? Maybe it's just too tough. **Most people don't like normal squats, let alone some mutant variation for 20 reps!**

In this article, I'll touch on the history of this great exercise, give you some examples of early routines and give you a routine to follow based on this exercise.

The 20 rep squat is also known as "**breathing squats**", having its origin in **Mark Berry's Deep Knee Bend system, dating back to 1930**. This was a simple, 4-5 exercise full body routine based around squats - but not yet 20 rep squats. J.C. Hise is perhaps the most dramatic example of Berry's routine, having great success with it. **Peary Rader, founder of Ironman magazine, with the help of people like Hise, is generally credited with coming up with the first 20 rep, breathing style squat routine.**

Breathing squats for those who don't know, are squats done for 20 reps with a weight you usually do 10 reps with, each time you hit failure, you take 3-5 deep breaths and continue until you get to 20(a full description will be given later) while I have seen lighter weight 20 and even 25 rep versions, this one is most common.

The original Ironman routine looked like this:

Press Behind Neck - 3 sets of 8
Squats superset with straight arm pullovers - 3 sets of 20 reps
Bench press - 3 sets of 8
Curls - 3 sets of 8

Quite a simple routine that came along with a "formula for growth".

Now, much of the "formula" to this program, is the idea of doing the breathing squats, eating a lot of food and drinking a lot of whole milk. This is, in fact, how this routine is defined by most proponents, including a book claiming you can gain 30 lbs of muscle following this routine.

A big part of this gain is fat weight instead of muscle mass, largely because these early versions pushed high fat whole milk - as in a gallon or so per day - so much.

The routine has evolved over time to more recently one like this:

Press behind the neck - 3 sets of 10
Bent over rows - 3 sets of 12
Curls - 2 sets of 15
Squats - 1 set of 20 super-setted with
Pullovers - 1 set of 20
Dead lifts - 1 set of 20 super-setted with
Pullovers - 1 set of 15 reps
Calf raises - 3 sets of 20 reps

A shorter variation of this routine is:

Bench press - 2 sets of 12
Squat - 1 set of 20 super-setted with
Pullovers - 1 set of 20
Bent rows - 2 sets of 15

So you see how these early routines were set up, **very basic full body routines, done three times a week.** Most current variations of this exercise include it on leg day as part of a split routine. While I can see value in full body style routines, I think a split routine is the only way to go for a serious bodybuilder. I also believe this exercise, when added to a good split routine, will add considerable muscle. **I think modern supplement standards have moved us out of the "whole milk" days, so a good supplement stack will really enhance this exercise's effectiveness (I'll suggest one later).**

This would be a good time to review the proper performance of this exercise: Pick a weight you would usually fail with at about 10 reps. At failure, pause and take several deep breaths, continue doing as many reps as you can, maybe one, may be two is all you'll get. Pause again, take 3-5 deep breaths, and go again. Keep doing this until you hit twenty reps. Make no mistake, this ain't easy, and you will want to quit before you hit twenty, but keep going. **This is as much mental as it is anything else.** If you've done the set correctly, when it's over you should pretty much hit the floor. **If you feel like you can do more, you did something wrong,** add weight and work harder next time! **Once done with your set, crawl over to a flat bench and do a set of light dumbbell pullovers for twenty reps.** This is, really, **a variation on rest pause style training,** which is enjoying new popularity under a variety of training program monikers.

Done in this fashion, this exercise is going to do a lot to promote not only leg growth but also overall growth - it's been said that squats can increase upper body size by 10-15%.

Here's why: squats are known to promote a lot of natural hormone release (igf-1, gh and testosterone) causing overall growth,

they target the legs like no other exercise but also involve most muscles of the body either directly or indirectly, and **the deep breathing combined with pullovers promote rib cage expansion, leading to increased chest size,** although this has a lot to do with age: the younger you are, the more pliable your rib-cage is and the more you should be able to expand it with this type of superset.

Following is a great routine based around 20 rep squats. I also added two variations to the basic routine. In these variations, the exercises are the same, but the rest days and body part split changes. This gives people with different schedules and lifestyle obligations something to work with and provides different recovery options. Since 20 rep squats are really a lot like rest pause type training, and are certainly a high intensity technique, we'll make this routine high intensity. After several weeks we'll follow it with a power type routine.

Routine:

Day 1 - Legs, abs
Squats - 2-3 warm up sets, start with a light weight for 15 easy reps, add weight and drop the reps to 12, add a little more weight and drop the reps to 10.
1 working set - breathing squats - 10rm for 20 breathing style reps, super set with 1 set - dumbbell pullovers - use a moderate weight, get a good stretch on these.
Rest 2-3 minutes
Leg curls - 1-2 working sets, 8-10 reps
Calf raises - 1-2 warm up sets, 3-4 working sets, alternating slow, full range reps with faster explosive reps, done over 3/4 range of motion.
Crunch - 3 sets of 50

Day 2 - rest

Day 3 - Chest, delts, tris, abs
Bench press - 3 warm up sets, done the same way as your warm ups for squats.
3 working sets, each set to failure, r/p after a 10 count, rep out, r/p after a 10 count, rep out
3 working sets incline press, same as bench press.
2 working sets incline flys, drop set style (3 drops) by going to a lighter set of dumb bells each drop.
Military press - 3 working sets, r/p style as in bench press
Side/rear laterals - superset and use r/p as in bench press
Close grip bench press - 2 working sets, use the same r/p technique
Triceps press downs - 1-2 working sets, using the same rest pause technique
Crunch - 3 sets of 50

Day 4 - off

Day 5 - Back, biceps, forearms, abs
Dead lifts, 2-3 warm up sets done the same way as with squats

3 working sets, each set to failure, r/p as with bench presses - keep an eye on your form, if it breaks down, stop the set.
Also watch your grip, that'll likely give out before your back does.
Bent rows - 3 working sets, same r/p style
Chins to failure, then go right into negative only chins
EZ curls - 3 working sets, using r/p
Hammer curls - 2 working sets, use r/p
Crunch - 3 sets of 50

I don't usually talk about rest time between sets but I've been getting questions about it from readers of my past articles (on other sites)- I usually rest no more than one minute, even when lifting heavy, but you have to be able to recover fast enough to warrant this. **Some extreme power lifting routines call for up to 5 minutes rest between sets.** I feel this is a somewhat individual thing, as you have to be recovered enough to do your next set justice, and the time needed to do that can vary depending on your conditioning level among other factors but you also don't want to start losing your pump and focus.

So I suggest no more than 1- 3 minutes.

Day 6 - off
Day 7 - off

If you are new to this type of training, you may want to ease into it by only using rest pause on 1 set of each exercise, and then gradually work up to the recommended sets. Remember to use a tough weight on every working set, don't make it easy. Rep performance: I tend to prefer explosive up and slow and controlled down. However, I alternate this style with more of a continuous tension, non-lockout style. One workout, do it explosively, the next, change it to more of a continuous tension approach.

Routine variation # 1
Day 1 - legs, abs
Days 2 and 3- rest
Day 4 - chest, delts, tris, abs
Day 5 - rest
Day 6 - back, bis, forearms, abs
Day 7 - rest

Routine variation # 2

Day 1 - legs, abs
Day 2 - rest
Day 3 - chest, tris, abs
Day 4 - rest
Day 5 - back, bi's, forearms, abs
Day 6 - rest
Day 7 - delts, abs

This is my favorite because I've always felt putting both delts and tris with back compromises intensity. Many people, however, just don't have time for four workouts in one week.

With this routine, **after 3 weeks, it's time for something new. A nice variation to a routine of this type is to switch to a power type routine, lower reps (5), straight sets, heavy weights and basic movements.** Also, we'll bring in a new exercise: **power cleans, one of the great forgotten exercises.** Regarding rest time between sets, some people like to rest 2-3 minutes on a power routine to enhance between set recovery for more strength on their next set.

Here is an example of a good routine along these lines:

Day 1 Legs, abs
Squats - 3 warm up sets done as in the routine above
5 working sets, reverse pyramid style - your first set is your heaviest for 5 reps, drop weight with each sets but stay at 5 reps, drop only enough weight to allow 5 reps.
Stiff legged dead lifts - 3 sets, 5 reps
Calf raises - 4-5 sets, 20-25 reps
Crunch - 5 sets of 50 reps

Day 2 - rest

Day 3 - Chest, tris, abs
Bench press - 2-3 warm up sets, 5 sets of 5 reps as with squats
Close grip bench press - 3 sets of 5 reps
EZ ext. - 3 sets of 5 reps
Reverse crunch - 5 sets of 25 reps

Day 4 - rest

Day 5 - Back, bis, abs
Dead lifts (always do deads!) 3 warm up sets, 4 sets of 5 reps

Low cable rows - 3 sets of 5 reps
Chins - 50 reps, then do 5 negative reps
EZ curls - 3 sets of 5 reps
Incline dumb bell curls - 3 sets of 5 reps
Reverse crunch - 3 sets of 25 reps
Twisting crunch - 3 sets of 25 reps

Day 6 - rest

Day 7 - Delts, traps, abs
Power Clean and Press - 3 warm up sets, 3 sets of 5-6 reps
Wide grip Upright Rows - 3 sets of 6 reps
Heavy partial side laterals - 2 sets of 8 reps, you should use a weight that allows for a range of motion of only an inch or two.
Haney Shrugs - 3 sets of 6-8 reps, these are **done behind the back, it's important to pull as high as you can on these**. Crunch - 2 sets of 50

I have always set my split routines up this way - legs **on their own day since they require a lot of energy and are very taxing to train, "pushing" muscles on their own day and "pulling" muscles on their own day.** This is logical as these muscles naturally work together. However, to mix things up, it's not a bad idea to change up the order of body parts - training chest and back together on their own day is common, for example. If you want to add a fourth training day, training delts on their own day is another good option.

Spend 6-8 weeks on this type of routine to build some meaningful strength before switching back to something else. It's **a good idea to have 3-5 good but different routines to use in an on going cycle like this, rotating each one, in most cases, after 3 weeks** but when going after strength, take longer. This helps keep variety in your training and promotes continued progress.

Variety is one of the main keys to progress but you have to keep it progressive. While this can be done in a number of ways, continual work on core movements like squats make a lot of sense.

Supplements and Nutrition:

First off, keep **your protein intake high, at least 1 gram of protein per lb. of body weight**, evenly divided throughout the day. **Don't be afraid of carbs, they are essential for energy for this type of routine.** Choose complex carbs, such as oatmeal, brown rice, sweet potatoes and whole grain products, and **shoot for 1 1/2 to 2 grams per lb. of body weight**. Some simple carbs are good as part of your pre and post workout shakes however: 60 grams simple carbs (fruit and/or fruit juice) to 40 grams protein make a good pre and post workout shake. You can, as part of your supplement stack, use a pre workout drink with caffeine, in which case you have to time its use correctly with your carb/protein drink.

Here's a great stack for use with the 20 rep squat routine:

Protein
Multi vitamin
a pre workout drink, e.g. No-Explode by BSN, or SuperPump250 by Gaspari Nutrition

Creatine Monohydrate
Nitric oxide
Glutamine
A good testosterone booster or prohormone, e.g. Anabolic-Matrix Rx or 1-Andro Rx by IronMag-Labs

End article

Author's note the above article was written more to the bodybuilding crowd than those into pure power or strength, so just keep this in mind.

Chapter Twelve

Hepburn & Harry

Another Player

Another contemporary of Anderson's was **Doug Hepburn**, another large man that lifted and did well in the Olympic lifting & powerlifting arenas

Though he was born cross eyed and with a club foot, he became quite a successful lifter and with a co-author penned "**Hepburn's Law**", which described the routine and exercises he did to propel him to greatness. Like the others in this book, he did much experimenting and kept diligent records on all that he did and how different exercises, repetition schemes and routines affected his progress. **Of course, the squat was integral to Doug's program at all times, despite the fact that the calf that was on the same side as was his clubbed foot was unusually small and under developed.** The rest of his program was very basic and consisted of a limited number of movements.

Doug claimed that the strength of his ultimately arrived on system was in its simplicity.

Doug Hepburn hefting a heavy Dumbbell

Hepburn penned a few articles for the old Iron Man magazine, including one titled

"The Deep Knee bend".

In his opening paragraph for this article, he says that if he were forced to choose only 2 exercises to build strength, bulk and power, he would choose the squat and the bench press. He said that these 2 movements had the influence on the most muscles of any of the standard exercises.

Doug was not apparently a huge fan of partial squats, but he did feel that standard, full squats were the key lower body exercise, and that they should be the first exercise done in such a routine. Doug liked a wide grip on the squat, suggesting a close one would throw one's balance forward. Hepburn was a very large man, and most men his size would opt for such a grip.

Doug talks about proper breathing during the squat, insisting that one hold the breath at least until one has almost completely ascended from the bottom position on heavy single repetitions. When doing higher reps, one must develop his own breathing pattern, but he advises that excessive oxygen intake may lead to dizziness. Doug suggests squatting with a wide stance, saying it enables one to "lock" into the bottom position with the tops of the thighs meeting the abdomen just at the proper position this way, and also putting less strain on the lower back. He also likes the idea of pointing the feet outward during the squat as opposed to straight ahead. Doug advised a controlled descent as opposed to a fast descent with a bounce off the bottom. He mentioned that some trainees presume that there is an advantage to doing this, but this is not at all true, and in fact can be harmful. He was not a big fan of ATG squats or going much below parallel. He said you could get more weight by just going to parallel, which is all that is required in a meet. (Really you must break parallel, if only just barely). He suggests squatting in front of a mirror in order to learn where proper depth is. A more modern approach would be to videotape yourself, and there are even devices you can strap to your leg that will beep to let you know when depth is good. Doug suggested walking for a short time while catching your breath after doing a rep set of squats, but not after heavy singles, and he also said that completely relaxing for at least an hour after a tough squat session is not a bad idea. Hepburn was fond of the push-pull idea; training upper body and lower body on alternate days so that both sets of body parts could be worked properly and fully.

Doug liked **deadlifts and high pulls as assistance movements** for squatting, but advised moderation in the volume of these, and cautioned they were to be kept secondary to the squat movement. Doug was not into high rep training, never going past 5 reps in anything beyond warm up weights. The gist of his squat routine was to warm up to 5-8 sets of singles, followed 5 sets of 3 to 5 reps. On the first workout, go for 5 singles you can get without quite going all out (leaving a little in the tank, Doug said). On the next, go for 6, then work your way to 8 with the same weight over next few workouts. When you reach 8, add weight and back to 5's again. Similarly, start reps with 5 sets of 3 reps, building up to 5x5, then add weight and start with 5 sets of 3 again.

On the assistance moves, Doug suggested 4 sets of 2 with a given weight on the high pulls, working to 4 sets of 3, add weight, etc. With deadlifts, follow the same rep scheme. This entire workout was to be done every third day.

Harry Paschall

Harry Paschall at work

Another contemporary of Rader's was **Harry Paschall**, who actually **gained notoriety as a student of Alan Calvert and his strength magazine.** It is funny that both Calvert and Henry got "the lifting bug" after having personally witnessed **Sandow** in action. In Paschall's book, which he penned when he was about 51 years old **"Muscle Moulding"**, Henry tells about his early encounters with weight training and how Calvert was basically the American guru of weights and weight training at that time (pre world war 1).

It was customary for Calvert to solicit pictures and success stories from pupils and purchasers of his barbell sets which would then be printed in his magazine. It was one of these stories that launched the career of Mr. Paschall.

He received letters from hundreds of other readers who were interested in his methods. Henry competed in a couple of the first real sanctioned weight lifting meets in the country in 1925 and 1926, winning the middle weight titles in both of these events.

He was one of 2 or 3 men of that weight to snatch 200 or more at that time, but beyond his lifting prowess, he was also a writer and an artist and he became famous for the muscle bound cartoon character that was somewhat Henry's alter ego; **BOSCO.**

Bosco became a regular feature in Strength and Health magazine in the early 1930's and was a staple for years. Being a student of Calvert and of course, the Milo First Course in Bodybuilding that we have already spoken of previously, Henry used a list of about 12 exercises from that course as his bread & butter basics.

His "dirty dozen" consisted of

Curls, Press, Squat, Pullover, Rowing, Shrugs, Side Bends, Sit-ups, The Straddle Lift, Deadlift, Calf Raise and Dumbbell Press.

Again, there is nothing tremendously special or unusual here. In his "Muscle Moulding" book, Harry decries the tendency of bodybuilders of the era after world war 2 "over doing it" in terms of time spent training and perhaps going astray from the old school basics that had served him and so many others in the early days so well.

He said that we should try to see how little we needed to train as opposed to how much we could take.

Harry also advocated the **double progression system** espoused by the Milo set, which was simply to progressively and systematically add repetitions up to a certain high limit, at which time weight was added and the repetitions lowered, re- starting the sequence and continuing on in this fashion.

Of course, progression on this system was assured for the novice and even kept one going well into the intermediate phase, but ultimately there would come a time when one reached that horribly ugly nemesis known as a plateau. There have been less affectionate terms, such as hitting a brick wall, which is more what it really feels like when you just cannot seem to make any gains no matter how much you try.

Harry was largely writing to people in that group, as am I, and as were Rader, Anderson, and the others who all got very creative about finding ways to break through that wall to start making solid gains again. We are all very different and some of the methods employed by these gents will not only not work for all of us, they could actually be detrimental to some. **We must all ultimately "find our own way" as we become more advanced in the strength training game.**

Harry was fortunate enough to have actually trained with **Mark Berry, at Sieg Klein's gym in New York,** and saw him squatting with copious weight there. He mentions **Steinborn** and his way of shouldering a barbell in order to get it in squat position which became known as the Steinborn lift.

He witnessed this being performed and talked about its dangers, saying that if the bar came down wrong, you could actually be paralyzed. I don't know that such a thing ever actually happened, but there is no doubt that the squat rack was a very welcome addition to the gyms of that era.

He also mentions that **Berry had a drawing of a crude type of squat rack** of some sort in the magazine Strength which he had become the Editor of after Calvert was ousted from Milo in its later years.

Berry had observed Steinborn doing his crazy lift and squatting in the neighborhood of 500 pounds in this manner, but must have decided there needed to be a better way, thus the invention of the squat rack. This was in the 1930's, so perhaps this preceded Bob People's rack which we spoke of as the first power rack earlier. It is not clear whether these were one and the same or Bob's was more advanced or exactly what the timing of either was.

Stands for deep knee bending which have served for many years in the York Bar Bell Gym.

Here is an early squat rack, possibly like that used by Berry in the early days

Paschall, while giving some small praise to Berry, was apparently not a huge fan of the **squats and milk program** that was all the rage in the 30's bodybuilding world. His main "beef" with the system was in its dietary recommendations, and I would have to agree with his thinking on that aspect.

Claims of folks gaining 20-30 pounds of muscle in a very short period, especially in a time when steroids were non-existent, were obviously something to be taken with a grain of salt, and Henry had his shaker at the ready. While many trainees may have indeed gained that much weight in a short period is not so much in question, but **whether that weight consisted of muscle was definitely questionable**.

Waistlines were expanding more than chest measurements according to Paschall, and he actually had some pretty funny comments about the whole thing in his Muscle Moulding book. To be completely fair, Henry had been a competitor in the 148 and 165 weight classes and never carried a great deal of muscle mass, though his strength was very good and he had a pretty good physique at his size.

The smaller boned folks often tend to be more critical of their larger brethren, and while much of his criticisms were perhaps well deserved, there may have been just a wee bit of jealousy underlying some of his rants against the behemoths of his era. He also spoke about cheating and partial movements with noticeable disdain, which may well have been directed at folks such as **JC Hise and Mr. Boon** whom was mentioned elsewhere. These were two of the larger specimens at the time. In fact, he talks about a sort of negative progression from doing correct and complete movements, to doing smaller and smaller ranges of motion until finally one just gets under a heavily loaded bar and moves the shoulders up and down while huffing and puffing like a locomotive. I could be mistaken, but that sure sounded like a blast at **Hise's Shrug** which had become broadly proclaimed as a wonder exercise back in the day.

To be sure, there were men then and there are men now who would sacrifice a 6 pack abdominal region and perhaps even their own well being in order to defy gravity. Bodybuilding purists will never understand this mind set, I suppose.

One thing that Harry and I could certainly agree on was that squats were a very beneficial and vital exercise and the popularity explosion of the exercise coupled with the invention of the squat rack and power racks was something absolutely revolutionary in the strength and bodybuilding worlds.

He states that it is maybe the best single exercise going, one that done properly **jars the entire metabolism into a new state of being**. One that not only builds leg strength, while it is the best exercise for doing just that, but also expands the chest cavity and builds the back and the internal organs.

As I mentioned earlier after Rader's sections on cheating and forced reps, I can relate also to what he(Paschall) said about cheating, in that it is often way over done and has become far too common in the routines of rookies and trainees who are really just kidding themselves and robbing themselves of the benefits of properly executed exercises. I have seen too many young trainees loading up a bar with more weight than they can do for even one or two quality reps, and relying on a partner to help them complete 6-8 reps. It is giving more benefit to the training partner, who is really doing a form of bent-over rowing on these silly sets. It is a good thing when used in moderation, and can help you move more weight, but should only be done in conjunction with or in addition to some quality, strictly done movements in the same exercises. Even **Earle Liederman** had a pet peeve about this and talked about how he went through a phase in which he thought he was making great progress when in fact he had simply been finding ways to make a particular exercise easier. This often disguises itself as progress, but it obviously is not TRUE progress. Earle spoke of the idea that we often avoid an exercise because we find it particularly uncomfortable or difficult, when **the reality is we should be embracing this kind of exercise in order to repair a weakness which makes it so hard on us.**

He (Paschall) talks about super sets becoming popular in the 40's, and claims that this method was great for a quick pump, but questions its overall value, and at the other end of the spectrum, **he talks about the rest-pause system.**

This is the one commonly used by Olympic style lifters, he tells readers, which entails doing a series of single reps with a near maximum effort weight until completing an extended "Set" of 10 reps or thereabouts. He said this was fine **for raw strength and building the ligaments**, but did little to add girth to a muscle.

Unlike many bodybuilding purists, Harry had a pretty well rounded idea of what he thought would represent the "**perfect man**". He shared the same ideas that Calvert emphasized on this subject.

Calvert said that a man should have true, useable strength and not just have the appearance of strength. Beyond even that, he should be able to walk, run or swim for miles without becoming greatly exhausted, be able to leap over a 5 ft fence in a single bound and be able to beat any man who was involved in menial labor at his own game at any time.

Author's note:

As a side note, there is no evidence that Calvert himself ever came close to this ideal himself

This was no small standard and we must question if such a man really even exists or has ever existed, for that matter.. **John Grimek** was said to have the physique and the strength components of this ideal, at least. Grimek was the new standard of bodybuilding in the 40s and was a bit larger than the Sandow-esque models put forth by Calvert earlier on.

I do like that the standard exists, at least as a theoretical ideal. We tend to see **extremes** in the real world; men of incredible strength but having seriously unenviable proportions, and even worse "organic health" as Paschall called it. We see men with huge muscles and carrying low levels of body fat, but being pumped up with all manner of potentially harmful substances and possessing questionable health.

Paschall was fond of some "**combination exercises**" and I was not familiar with all of these before. The first one, which I have seen is **the squat and press behind neck combo**. The **odd part about his description of this one is that he suggests pressing the weight while descending in the squat**, and letting the bar fall back (controlled) to the shoulders as you came up to the erect position. **This is the opposite way of how I have seen it done, and it seems as if it would require a bit of practice to get the coordination down correctly, which he admits**. The next one he talks about is **a combination of the stiff-legged deadlift, the shrug, and a sort of rowing motion put together**.

You start with a conventional style stiff-legged deadlift, but as you come erect, you shrug the shoulders up and back, and then spread & "lock" the lats. Keeping the lats in this spread condition, you lower the bar, allowing it to swing out into the typical rowing motion groove, and slowly lower as you **really concentrate on the weight pulling on the lats while lowering**. This is a new one on me, but I will have to try it as it sounds very interesting indeed.

See pg 144 drawings for depiction of exercise above

At the time when he was writing his Muscle Moulding book, incline benches were becoming a fixture, Swingbars and iron boots were popular and these items were used extensively by the bodybuilding crowd, but perhaps not as much by the weight lifter/powerlifter crew. Paschall talked about being questioned by countless trainees who just did not seem to be able to progress well.

His answer to most was to stop training for a full month, and then come back with his basic program 3 times a week, try to get an extra hour of sleep, and **learn to relax**.

Most folks were over-training in terms of volume, and or were under nourished or not getting enough rest. I would say this is still very much the case in our present day.

Most folks that are really interested in getting big and strong tend to bite off more than they can chew.

More is not necessarily better and this is a lesson many find hard to learn. If you are trying to gain solid muscle mass and strength, you would do well to follow Harry's advice in this regard.

Harry even went so far as to say that taking a full week off in between 6 week programs was advisable. That is something you won't often find suggested these days, and while I think that may be a bit too often to take a week off; I do think a week off after a somewhat longer cycle is a great idea. Even a week off every 6 weeks I'm sure would not be detrimental as long as you don't live in an all you can eat buffet restaurant during that week.

Here is a humorous cartoon with a quote from H.P:

CONCLUDING REMARKS 57

All I can do is humbly to remind you that STRENGTH is a priceless possession. When you acquire it, guard it well and use it gently, for it is quite likely the most precious single thing you will ever own.

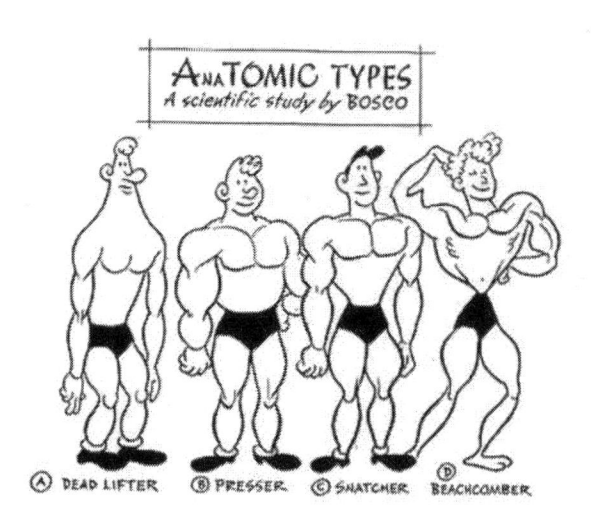

AnaTOMIC TYPES — A scientific study by BOSCO

(A) DEAD LIFTER (B) PRESSER (C) SNATCHER (D) BEACHCOMBER

Harry on the "Isolation Craze"

I seek to offer a number of strategies and methods for you to have at your disposal; in your **"toolbox"** as I like to put it, so that you can try some new and different things, experiment and discover what works for you. To get on a soap box and tout all the miraculous benefits of a certain program, rep scheme or particular way of doing things is pointless, I think. The body is or at least it should be in a constant state of change and is constantly adapting to the stimulus which it is dealt.

The program or scheme that gave you the best gains of your life a few months ago or a few years ago may not work worth a hoot next week.

Many modern gurus like Louie Simmons and friends will espouse the "**conjugate method**", which sounds a bit more complex than it really is. It is simply about constantly cycling in different exercises or ways of doing the old standbys that keep the body's responses from going stale and eventually ceasing to respond at all.

Some folks, in my humble opinion, have missed the boat with this concept and have strayed too far afield from the basic movements and their variations. One of the trends in bodybuilding that Paschall spoke of and that is still going strong in our present day is **the isolation craze.**

There are machines that isolate every individual muscle, hitting it from every possible angle. While there may be a time and a place for this, it is way over done.

One of the current trends in strength training is the growth of "**strongmanism**"**,** which is a trend I love to see happening, frankly. It is a movement towards **more functional and less "specialized"** training, and it has become integral to many hybrid programs. Perhaps this has been spurred on by the popularity of the televised "**Worlds Strongest Man**" competitions that many of us enjoy watching. Realistically, the weights moved and the feats performed by the super athletes in these events is beyond what most are capable of, but **the movements themselves are very sound and very productive, and can be appropriately scaled down for the masses, I think.**

The movements build not only raw power and strength, but also contain a strong cardio component and endurance training is also involved. The athletes with **power, speed, agility and endurance are the ones who dominate these events**, as opposed to being some kind of "one lift wonders". I have been incorporating some of these moves into my routine and will continue to build on this as much as possible. I feel it adds a valuable training component that can be enjoyable, especially considering that you can **train outdoors** when the weather allows it.

Much like the basic, compound weight training movements, the **strongman exercises** get the whole body or at least several parts at a time involved, which is really how the body is designed to function. Thus we have the term **"functional"** training.

One sort of "poor man's" strongman training is **Sandbag training**, which is another exercise mode that has found a niche and a following of late, with videos, books and programs singing its praises. They are cheap to buy or make yourself, and are an extremely versatile piece of training equipment. You can do pretty much any exercise with them as you can with a barbell or you can simulate strongman type events like loading them onto a platform at shoulder height, ala atlas stone loading. **Buying weight in the form of sand from your local home supply store or landscaping supply is a far cheaper proposition than purchasing barbell plates from a sporting goods or weight training specialty store. Fifty pounds of sand only costs a few dollars!**

You will find football and wrestling teams these days employing innovative methods involving the above types of training, and **sled training** has become very popular as well, which is really a strongman type of exercise as well.

It is without hesitation that I would point you towards these more difficult yet very fruitful training protocols as opposed to working your way around a circuit of machines that isolate all the different muscles. This is not to say that these machines have no value; they do. But they should be used as **supplemental items** to the basic movements; they should not become replacements for them! Sometimes, isolating a specific muscle because it has been established as a "weak Link" can be very helpful, but just keep in mind that these types of exercises should be supplemental to the basics. The machines can also be beneficial in therapeutic and rehabilitative work.

 Since we are focusing on the **basic exercises and most especially the squat** in this manual, I thought this section taken from **bodybuilding.com's** Q & A section relating to **Mark Rippetoe's** book **"Starting Strength"** would be beneficial for everyone, but especially those not familiar with the many variations of the squat and it's execution:

Chapter Thirteen
Starting Strength Squat Q&A session

The Squat

The Squat, Part 1

Question - How do I properly perform a squat?

The basics:

1) Get under the bar with your chest high and your upper and lower back tight.

2) Ensure your position is balanced from left to right, grip the bar, ensuring your grip is balanced from left to right.

3) Grip the bar as close to your head as possible. This will test your shoulder, elbow and wrist joint flexibility.

The closer your hands are (within reason, your hands shouldn't touch your ears), the tighter your upper back will be, and the better the bar will sit on your back. Use a thumbless grip. You aren't' supporting the bar with your hands. You're **holding the bar DOWN against your back**. Your wrist should NOT bend in either direction.

Here are a couple of unusual squats from our friend Harry Paschall, not discussed in the article at hand, but interesting ideas.

4) Place the bar on your back across the low portion of the traps and rear delts (low bar position). Elevate your elbows as high behind you as possible, while keeping your chest upright. If your pectorals are sore, you will feel this as a deep stretch in the pectorals and possibly delts.

5) Inhale as deeply as possible, ensure your back is tight, bend down a bit and squat the bar out of the rack. **DO NOT LEAN FORWARD** and perform a good morning to get the bar out of the rack. You will lose tightness this way and, as a novice, expose yourself to injury.

6) Stand fully upright with the bar across your lower traps and rear delts, and clear the bar from the rack in 3 steps: ** Take 1 step backward with one foot to clear the rack ** Take 1 step backward with the other (trail) foot so that your feet are even ** Take 1 step sideways with the trail foot so that you get your heels to proper stance width.

Do NOT perform a "backward walk" with the bar. No more than 3 steps are necessary, total. Fidgeting with a few hundred pounds on your shoulders gets tiring. Squats are difficult enough as it is, no need to tire yourself needlessly prior to exercise execution with needless steps.

7) Make necessary adjustments so that stance width is proper, i.e. heels at ~ shoulder width, feet pointed in a "neutral" manner, ~30° outward. ~30° is "neutral" because as you widen your stance, your toes need to point outward in order to maintain proper patellar alignment with the thigh bones. When your heels are at approximately shoulder width, your toes will need to be pointed ~30° outward.

8) Keep your chest high and the bar balanced above the midfoot, take a deep breath, hold it, and squat down all the way. Do not look up, do not look down, do not look side to side. Keep your eyes focused on a point that is ~ 6-10' ahead of you on the floor, or if you have a wall close enough, focus on a point a few feet above the floor along the wall.

9) 4 basics of execution: ** Sit back (**stick your butt out!**) ** Squat down (bending/flexing the knees) ** Balance the weight by keeping your chest and shoulders upright while your upper body leans forward **slightly** to keep the bar above the midfoot ** "Keep knees tight" - i.e. don't relax your quads and simply "drop" into the bottom position,

keep your thigh muscles tight throughout the motion

10) Once you have squatted down all the way into "the hole", without pausing or bouncing (more on this later), stand back up.

MUSCLE MOULDING EXERCISES 67

FIGURE 11

STIFF LEGGED DEAD LIFT + SHRUG

FIGURE 12

"LOCK OUT" LATISSIMUS

FIGURE 13

FORWARD BEND WITH LATISSIMUS SPREAD

Above is the special combo exercise described by Paschall in the previous section

11) As you raise out of "the hole", you will be doing 3 basic things almost at the same time.

* **You will be pushing your butt upward** ** You will be pushing your shoulders upward ** You will be extending your knees ** **You will be forcefully contracting your upper and lower back muscles isometrically to maintain tightness in your torso**

Do not begin to exhale (blow out) until you are near to completion of the repetition. This will cause you to lose tightness.

Question - What kind of squat should I do? ATG? (At the ground) Olympic? Front? What stance should I use?

The "back squat"

This term is a general one and it refers to any of the standard squats in which the lifter has the bar placed across the back or rear deltoids or trapezius muscles and then performs a "deep knee bend"

The **athletic squat** is a back squat performed with the **feet at a width that is generally just slightly wider than the shoulders. The feet are angled out in line with the knees.** This foot positioning will be the one with the most carryover to the majority of athletic endeavors, and does the best job at ensuring full thigh development, both in the front of the thigh (the quadriceps) and the rear of the thigh (the hamstrings and glutes). **It is the squat variation this is performed in the basic Starting Strength program.**

The **Olympic squat** is a back squat where the foot positioning is closer than shoulder width and the toes typically point nearly straight forward. **These tend to be more quadriceps-dominant,** and are very useful for Olympic lifters (hence the name). This is an excellent exercise as well, but it will not be used until the trainee advances further and chooses to specialize in Olympic lifting or physique competition.

The **powerlifting squat** refers to the extremely wide "sumo" stance that powerlifters favor while performing the squat. It generally allows them to use more weight, but this is due to mechanical advantage rather than even, overall muscular stimulation of the thighs. This variation is not used in the program.

***Author's Note"*
Keep in mind that this squat description is rendered by a bodybuilder, and while somewhat accurate, is a bit miss-leading. One of the key components to what is commonly called a power style squat is the bar positioning on the back, which is typically lower than an Olympic style squat's bar placement. Feet positioning is almost always wider than the very close stance used in Olympic style squats, but can vary from shoulder width to the extremely wide "sumo stance" mentioned above. The idea is to use every possible muscle available to do the lifting, as the goal is to lift the maximum amount of weight in a legal fashion, not to simply train any particular muscle group.

In the photo above you see Rickey Dale Crain, one of the best powerlifting squatters ever. Note the high bar position he uses here, an exception to the rule.

The box squat is a phenomenal exercise for an aspiring powerlifter. It is not a key exercise in the "Starting Strength" program, however, as it is considered a more advanced exercise.

The ATG squat (ATG = ass to grass/ground) makes reference to ANY of the above squat variations whereby **the trainee lowers his body as low as he possibly can.** This can be either advantageous or dangerous, depending upon the individual. Generally, hamstring flexibility will limit the absolute depth because, in the lowest portion (the "hole") of the squat, the hamstrings get stretched hard, and will pull the hips under the body, which can cause severe strain to the lumbar area. That being said, **you should ALWAYS go as low as you can without causing that hip rounding to take place, because this will stimulate the best overall gains.**

Author's Note Peary Rader, Paul Anderson, Milo Steinborn, John Grimek,etc., all suggested going as deeply as possible for best gains, but the safety considerations addressed above are pertitent*

"ATG" is a term that will be different for each person due to hamstring flexibility and structure, as well as overall musculature. **Endeavor to stretch your hamstrings frequently to avoid lower back injury,** and to allow for the most complete ROM (range of motion). Also note that some people say they do "ATG squats", when in reality, they barely hit parallel. At the opposite end of the spectrum are those that go incredibly deep as **an excuse for using very light weight.**

The **front squat** is an outstanding variation of the squat, except that it is performed with the barbell resting across the FRONT of the shoulders, in front of the neck. It is a variation **which will maximally stress the quadriceps, but can be very difficult to perform from a mechanical perspective.**

The **athletic squat** is a basic, medium-stance squat that will be used in this program for a few reasons.

1) It tends to do the best job of developing the entire thigh (quad, hammie and the "little thigh muscles") evenly and in proportion. **Front and Olympic squats tend to be a bit quad-dominant,** powerlifting and especially box squats tend to be more ham/glute dominant

2) The medium-stance "athletic" squat has the most natural carryover to athletics and sports. Rarely will you purposely use a stance that is extremely wide or close while playing any type of sport.

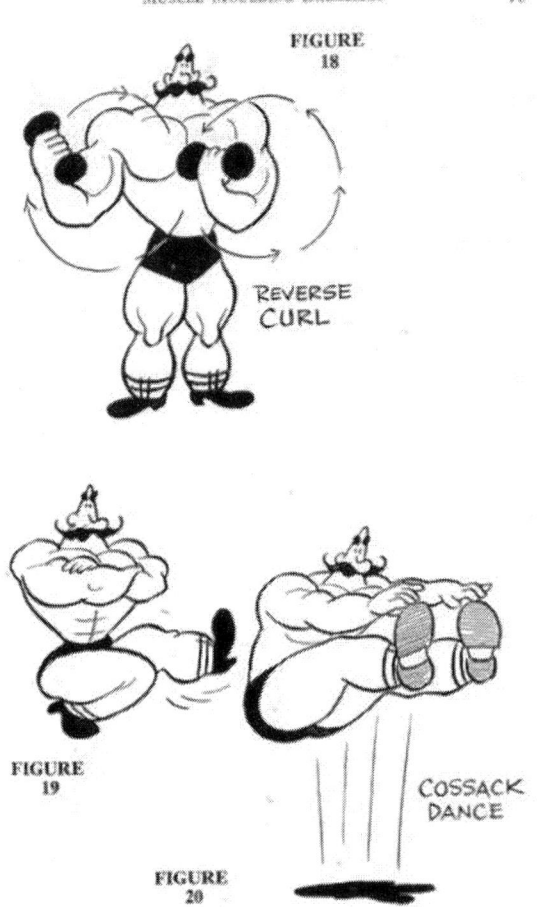

Here are a couple more of the unusual movements you don't see much these days, from Harry Paschal/s book discussed in the previous section.

3) The medium-stance "athletic" squat will give you the most "bang for your buck" as far as overall strength development. You might be able to lift more with a powerlifting style stance, but that is due to physics, not additional muscle involvement (in fact, one could say it involves a reduction in muscular involvement)

So there you have it. The stance should be approximately shoulder width, give or take an inch or three.

Author's Note

Using the "athletic style squat is fine for most when starting out or are considered an "intermediate lifter" Later on, you can experiment with bar position, foot position, etc in order to develop more power or to emphasize one muscle area over another

The Squat, Part 2

Question - Do I really need to squat if my legs are already big?

First off, 3/4 of the people who ask this question are punks. **Don't be afraid of the squat. Learn to embrace it.**

Having said that, I'll give you the benefit of the doubt and we'll assume you are part of the 1/4 that isn't afraid of the squat. Determine what your goals are. **If you want to get as big as possible, all over, then you will most definitely want to become a master of the squat.**

Your physical structure might not be ideal for the squat. You may have zero aspirations of becoming a powerlifting squat champion. You might not really give a flying fig how much you squat.

But if you SERIOUSLY want to be as large as you possibly can, all over, then yes, you will squat, even if you already have big legs.

There is simply no other exercise, and certainly no machine, that produces the level of central nervous system activity, improved balance and coordination, skeletal loading and bone density, muscular stimulation and growth, connective tissue stress and strength, psychological demand on toughness, and overall systemic conditioning as the correctly performed full squat. **Squats spur full body growth when combined with full body training much better than full body training without squats.**

If you want to look like some Abercrombie model, then find another program and enjoy your nice, easy training style.

If you are serious about adding muscle to your frame, then get under the damn bar and make it happen.

Question - What about the **leg press**?

The leg press restrict(s) movement in body segments that normally adjust position during the squat, thus restricting the expression of normal biomechanics (it) is particularly heinous in that it allows the use of huge weights, and therefore facilitates unwarranted bragging. Please slap the next person that tells you he leg-pressed a thousand pounds. A 1000-lb. leg press is as irrelevant as a 500 lb. quarter-squat. The leg press is an excellent tool for an intermediate or advanced physique athlete to use for quad and/or glute and/or hamstring development. However, it has NO place in the routine of a novice trainee.

Question - Can I use a **manta ray** when squatting?

Above is a depiction of the **Manta Ray** in use

Above is a close up of the Manta Ray itself. Note the slot through which the bar goes. It is designed to hold the bar in place without putting undue stress on the shoulders or elbows to do so.

If you have had shoulder problems, the manta ray can be a pretty useful piece of equipment. **It's use is certainly not advised unless absolutely necessary,** because it lengthens the lever arm between the weight and the rotation point (i.e. the barbell and the hips), which can cause problems with the lower back. **It can also "wobble around" atop the shoulders causing a load shift affect,** which also can cause problems with the lower back.

However, if you are experienced enough with the weights to know you NEED a manta ray, then by all means, it is better to squat with one than to NOT squat without one.

If, however, you simply want to use a manta ray for comfort's sake, then don't bother squatting at all. The amount of pain tolerance from a hard, heavy set of squats will be too much for you if you can't take a little bar sitting across your shoulders. Perhaps you should take up a different hobby...knitting, for example.

Question - **Can I use a safety squat bar or a buffalo bar while squatting?**

Assuming you have had an injury of some sort, or you have shoulder joint flexibility problems for whatever reason, then absolutely.

The buffalo bar and safety squat are outstanding pieces of equipment.

The Curved **Buffalo bar** in use

Imagine the accidental cambered bar mentioned in the section on J.C.Hise

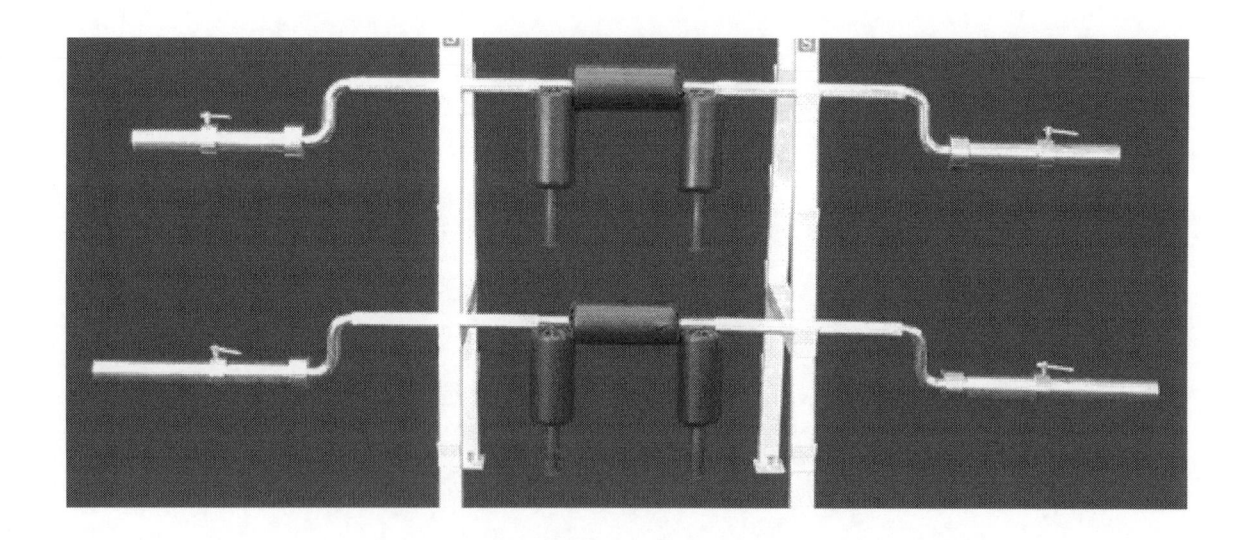

2 slightly different configurations of the safety squat bar shown above

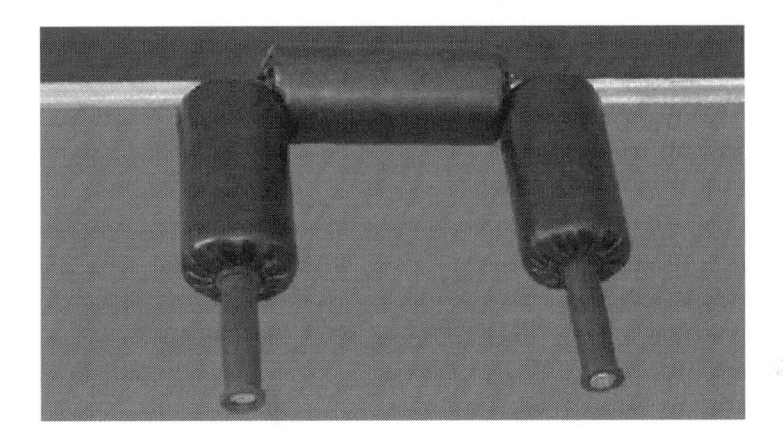

You can get a better look at the thick padding for the neck and shoulders in this photo

Here is Dave Draper's squat bar concept (the Top Squat) that he came up with to alleviate shoulder issues while squatting

They are great for the lifter who has had shoulder problems *raises hand and points to self*. **They certainly can create a different training affect than squatting with a conventional bar setup**, but the training affect can be quite beneficial, especially for those with shoulder injuries who cannot squat otherwise.

Understand, however, that **the novice trainee should NOT choose these devices over the basic barbell back squat**. Their use should be limited to those who have injuries and cannot perform a barbell squat.

The Squat, Part 3

Question - **Are deep squats bad for the knees?**

Deep, controlled squats not only are NOT "bad for the knees", they are, in fact, **good for the knees.**

Properly performed, they evenly and proportionately strengthen all muscles which stabilize and control the knee (in addition to strengthening the muscles of the hip and posterior chain, upper back, shoulder girdle etc). When the hips are lowered in a controlled fashion below the level of the top of the patella, full hip flexion has occurred, and **this will activate the hamstrings and glutes.** In doing so, the hamstrings are stretched at the bottom of the motion and they pull the tibia backwards (toward da' butt) which counteracts the forward-pulling force the quadriceps apply during the motion. **As a result, the stress on the knee tendons is lessened since the hamstrings assist the patellar tendon in stabilization of the knee. A muscle supporting a tendon which supports the kneecap is going to be better than the tendon having to take up the entirety of the strain by itself.**

Think about Olympic lifters. They squat VERY deep (almost ridiculously deep) all the time, frequently 5 or 6 times weekly, with very heavy weight. If deep squats were so bad for their knees, they wouldn't be able to squat that deep, that often, and that heavy.

Author's note:

The section later on about the great Tom Platz will drive this point home, I think

Partial squats, however, will NOT activate the hamstrings, and the amount of shearing force on the patellar tendon increases exponentially. What WILL happen if you do partial squats is that your quadriceps will become disproportionately strong as compared to your hamstrings, and the following are likely results:

1) In partial squats, the hamstrings aren't activated, which means the patellar tendon takes up all the strain/stress/pull during squats. As a result, fatigue and damage to the tendon can accumulate because tendons recover MUCH slower than muscles.

Author's note:

We will hear from another great squatter, Fred Hatfield expounding on this issue later on

Any type of action involving knee bend can then cause further stress and strain during daily activity. This is asking for trouble. **If the hamstring is strong, it drastically reduces the amount of stress on the patellar tendon.** Full squats make the hamstrings strong. Partial squats allow the hamstrings to become weak. Weak hamstrings are bad.

2) **Partial squats develop the quads and neglect the hamstrings.** Weak hamstrings coupled with strong quads result in hamstring pulls while sprinting, starting or stopping suddenly, playing sports, etc.. They frequently occur as the result of muscular imbalances across the knee joint.

3) Strong quadriceps and weaker hamstrings result in a knee joint that is unstable during rapid acceleration and slowing, and the hamstrings are unable to counteract the powerful forces that occur during sudden stops and starts. In other words, you do a sprint with extra-strong quads and weak hammies, and you are begging for a pulled hamstring because your hamstring isn't as strong as it needs to be to handle the amount of stress on the patellar tendon. **Full squats make the hamstrings strong. Partial squats allow the hamstrings to become weak. Weak hamstrings are bad.**

Author's note:

Perhaps the statements above have something to do with partial squats, as touted by Anderson, Rader, et al, falling into dis-favor in many circles these days.

3) In sports, your acceleration will be weak, as will your jumping ability, as a result of underdeveloped hamstrings and hips. Poor speed/acceleration = poor performance

4) You will end up using stupidly heavy weights in the partial squat due to the mechanical advantage afforded by partial squats, and you put your back and even shoulder girdle at risk due to the extreme loading of the spine.

If it's too heavy to squat below parallel, it's too heavy to have on the back. *

Author's Note

The above statement is directed towards novice trainees. Partial squats are advocated by both the old school trainers we have talked about and newer generation power gurus. Keep in mind that their use should be limited and that they should never totally replace full squats, but they can be used to provide an overload as much more weight can be handled with partial movements

As mentioned, however, not all the experts agree on this matter.

I prefer to offer both sides of the argument or discussion, and let you decide for yourself on such matters.

Try this one out for size

Question - **Can I use a back pad while squatting?**

Meow.

No. Don't use the "puss pad".

If your back hurts excessively while squatting, then **chances are good you aren't flexing your upper back muscles sufficiently to "pad" your skeleton.** When you grip the bar, you must keep your hands in toward the body as closely as possible while gripping the bar BEFORE you unrack the bar and start squatting.

In other words, get under the bar, bring your hands in as closely as possible along the bar, grip the bar with a thumbless grip, lift your elbows back and up, and step under the weight.

By keeping your hands close and your elbows back and up, the muscles of your entire shoulder girdle, as well as your trapezius muscles, will all "bunch/hunch up", which will provide significant padding for the bar. Ensure the bar is kept in the "low bar position" at the lower-rear portion of your traps and rear deltoids, and you should be fine.

The **main problem** with the pad, in addition to making you look like a wuss, is that **it tends to throw the center of gravity off.** For an experienced trainee, this won't be a problem, they can compensate (and they probably wouldn't ask to use a pad anyway). For a novice trainee, this can be VERY detrimental to proper technique and balance development inherent in the learning process of the squat. So, all joking aside, the pad might help your upper shoulders "feel better" while squatting, but **once you get to heavy weight, that little pad won't do jack squat, except for throw off your technique!** If you have a shoulder injury, then the pad won't help at all. Look into using a Buffalo Bar, a Safety Squat Bar, or a Manta Ray

The Squat, Part 4

Question - **Should I use a block under my heels while squatting?**

No. I say no for a variety of reasons.

When you raise the heel substantially during a squat, you shift the weight of your body forward, and as a result, **your knees can end up taking a disproportionate share of the load.**

Experienced physique athletes sometimes do this so they can get better development in their quads, although they generally will not perform squats this way for long. The average joe does this because they lack the flexibility in their hamstrings to perform a squat to depth without rounding their lower back, and by keeping their heels on a block, they are able to reduce the stretch in their hamstrings.

Here's a little test for you...if you have lower back pain when you try to do deep squats wearing a flat soled shoe (i.e. Chuck Taylor's or wrestling shoes), and you DON'T suffer this same lower back pain when you wear work boots (with a heavy heel) or you squat with your heels up on a block, then guess what?

Your hamstrings are too tight. Don't use a block. Stretch your hamstrings instead. Your knees will thank you in the end. By using a block, you merely mask the symptoms without treating the cause.

Question - Should I be leaning forward a little bit during the squat, or do I try to stand straight up and down?

Some amount of forward lean is natural, and in fact, is necessary. It is impossible, with a free weight barbell, to keep your upper body at a 90 degree angle to the floor. You cannot maintain any form of balance this way and if you try, you will fall onto your rump.

The bar, as it rests on your back, must remain above the midfoot area throughout the range of motion. It is common for a new trainee to lean back too far or, more commonly, lean forward too far. However, some amount of forward lean IS NECESSARY in order to keep the bar over your midfoot. **The lower on your back you hold the bar, the more forward lean will be necessary.**

The problem is that people have a tendency to lean so far forward that their heels come off the ground, or they end up putting far too much stress on the glutes and lower back and their squat turns into an impromptu good morning. Keep the bar tracking above the midfoot area, and you will be fine, as long as you don't round your back.

1) Work on calf and hamstring flexibility 2) Do NOT go up on your tiptoes 3) Stretch your hamstrings 4) Do a better job of warming up 5) Stretch your hamstrings.

Your lower back is rounding because your hamstrings are inflexible and your lumbar spine is weak. Maybe only one is true, but for most new trainees, both are true.

Your heels came off the ground because you allowed the weight to pull you forward. Again, weak spinal erectors and tight hamstrings are the most frequent culprits.

Sometimes, you simply lose your balance. Until you can correct these issues, don't add weight to the bar. Stretch your hamstrings.

A good and necessary stretch will be to start in a full squat position with your hands flat on the ground about 2 feet in front of you. Straighten your knees while keeping your hands flat on the ground. You should feel a VERY powerful stretch in your hamstrings. Keeping your knees straight, walk your hands inward toward your feet until you are able to touch your palms to the ground without bending your knees.

Question - Should my knees stay in, or should I push them outward as I squat down?

Most people will need to think about forcing their knees to stay outward during the up and down motion of the squat. It almost feels unnatural for the novice trainee to keep his knees tracking along the proper "groove" when the motion is very new. **Your knees, technically, should track at the same angle that your toes do.** Yes, powerlifters, you keep your legs wide and point your toes forward because this tightens your hips on the way down and up from the hole, but we're not talking about that.

(End excerpt)☺

I think the above section had some good instructions about squatting, in general, and especially for those new to the game.

Another great point about Rippetoe's system is that he has rookies squatting 3 times per week, and this is the **anchor exercise of the program.**

The program was designed for younger trainees that are involved in football and other sports programs, and are trying to build muscle mass and strength.

Older trainees will most likely find that squatting that often will not be possible or beneficial, but **squats are still keys to any sound strength system**, so simply cutting down the frequency could be the answer.

What is the relevance of Rippetoe's program to this book? Mark Rippetoe is a very well respected trainer whose methods are followed by many strength training coaches to this day.

His training ideas were most likely strongly influenced by old school trainers such as we have covered here, but also have been backed up and **fine tuned through tons of hands-on experience with actual student trainees.**

Much like some of the trainers previously discussed, **Mark developed a very concise and basic program using barbells and multi joint exercises like squats, deadlifts, presses and rows**. He was not a huge proponent of lots of bicep specialization training or things along those lines.

Another trainer who was popular in the 70's is **Bill Starr**, who also had a strong background in football related strength training.

Here is an interesting program excerpt from Bill I found:

Chapter Fourteen

Bill Starr's Strength Training Program: The Big Three

This post was submitted by StrongLifts.com reader Flying Fox.

This is a description of Bill Starr's strength training program described in The Strongest Shall Survive: Strength Training for Football (1976). I recommend reading Bill Starr's book, even if you're not a football player.

Bill Starr's program shows similarities with many other routines: Madcow's 5×5, Eclypse, Starting Strength, The Texas Method, Timed Total Tonnage, …

What Are The Big Three? The Big Three are the Squat, Bench Press & Power Clean. The reason Bill Starr chooses these movements is that **they build strength in all major muscle groups.**

Even though Bill Starr's program is designed for building overall strength and explosiveness in American Football players, **it can be used to build strength and explosiveness** in any other athlete.

Programming the Big Three. The Big Three are trained 3 times a week in a heavy/light/medium fashion. This means you don't train with maximum poundage every workout.

- Heavy Day: Work yourself up to one heavy set.
- Light Day: 80% of the heaviest set on Heavy Day.
- Medium Day: 90% of the heaviest set on Heavy Day.

Sets & Reps. 5×5 is used for The Big Three: 5 sets of 5 reps. The weight is increased on each successive set, the 5th set being your strongest set. The first 4 sets are used to warm-up to your heavy 5th set.

For the advanced trainee, a change of rep range is useful:

- **Presses.** Instead of doing 5×5, the trainee does 3×5 reps, 3×3 reps & 1 "back-off" set of 6-10 reps. Sets of 3 enable the trainee to handle heavier weights on the final set. The back-off set insures sufficient work. Back-off sets can also be applied to squats, but are less useful for pulls.
- **Squats**. Tens, fives and threes is another proven rep range. One would do 5×10 on Monday, 5×3 on Wednesday and 5×5 on Friday, increasing the weight each set. The difference with this routine is that a trainee goes to the maximum each workout. The program still follows the heavy / light / medium system, based on total tonnage. Even though the tens utilize the lightest weight, they produce the most total work load. The threes produce less workload and the fives something in between.

As you can see, a short list of very basic compound movements yet again is the core of the system. This is another system still commonly used by high school and other football coaches to this day, and with much success.

Here is a shot of Bill deadlifting in a competition

We are now **starting to see the common threads of the basic strength and mass building programs from the turn of the previous century through the 70s**. Though many inventions and pieces of new equipment have come down the pike, the basics are still the basics and strength training has not changed all that dramatically.

I would venture to say that the **dawn of the power rack** and squat racks in general, in addition to the addition of benches to perform the supine press on (bench press as we now call it) have been the most significant changes in the strength training world during the time frame we have been discussing up to this point.

While some might make claims about Nautilus machines changing the world, or the introduction of many other types of specialized machines doing that, I would tend to differ in my opinion, for what that is worth. So has anything earth shattering happened to the strength world in the last 40 years or so? Well, I guess it depends on what you would call earth shattering. **The 1970's was a golden era for the powerlifting game,** with numbers never before imagined being posted in all the major lifts. But at that time, the equipment being used had not changed dramatically. Of course, **steroids had become very popular** in all the strength related sports and were being used widely at this point.

Alexeev

In Olympic lifting, Russians and Bulgarians were dominating the sport, and **Vasily Alexeev** was breaking records in that field. **Russians and Bulgarians had quite a bit of influence** on the strength training world back then, and American lifters started to pay more attention to how things were being done over there.

Many made claims that they were using state of the art, advanced equipment and /or better types of steroids than everybody else and that these were the keys to their greatness, but this really was not the case.

For one thing, we were involved in a cold war with them at the time, and they took the Olympic sports very seriously, using them as propaganda method. They had top scientists observing the most talented crop of individuals they could find, observing the results of every exercise and every possible training scheme they could come up with, and they kept detailed records of everything that was done. They paid close attention to percentage of maximum weights being worked with, technique, speed of execution, frequency of workouts, etc. They found that the old school methods of periodization were not optimal in producing super human maximal 1 rep lifts. They developed various modes of periodization which have taken hold in the last few decades in the US and elsewhere. **Westside Barbell and Louie Simmons** is the best known teacher and strong advocate for this type of training, and they (Westside) have put their own stamp on it and modified it further with special equipment and special exercises along with pendulum waves, macro cycles, mezzo cycles and micro cycles.

They have done more to promote the use of **heavy band training** that anyone or anything else, I would say. They also have used chains attached to barbells, developed a piece of equipment called the **reverse hyperextension unit,** and commonly use the various types of squat bars we have previously mentioned, as well as some others.

They talk about using something called the "**conjugate method**", which essentially means cycling different versions of exercises and trying to hit personal bests on these, rather than doing standard squats ad infinitum, for example.

They use what they call a "**dynamic effort day**", and a "**max effort day**" with explosive, high speed reps being used on dynamic effort day, with a lower percentage of the one rep max being used here. The max effort day consists of working up to single reps at or very close to one's one rep max, but the key here is to use different variations of the key movement all the time. For example, in the squat, you might max out on box squats 1 workout, with a standard bar, and in the following workout use a **safety squat bar** at conventional legal depth. Perhaps the next workout you will use a super wide stance instead of your normal one, etc. You are hitting the same muscle groups, but making enough variation so that you don't get "burnt out" maxing out in the same exact movement continuously. Going back and forth between lower percentages at higher speeds and with more explosiveness and high percentages with max weights and slow speeds is the other key component of the system.

Since we are focused primarily on the squat, its variations and its role in the overall building of full body power, let's take a look at some of the more recent developments in power and leg strength from the New Westside Barbell perspective, in an excerpt from Louie's website: (www.westside-barbell.com) we will begin the next chapter, on the Westside influence, with this excerpt.

Chapter Fifteen
The Westside influence

We know that the **best way to squat is to box squat**, but what about building brute leg strength?

Author's note:

Keep in mind that not all the experts agree on this point

Belt Squatting: this requires a special belt-squat belt.

The weight hangs from the belt, **allowing only the lower body to do the work**. You may have seen our belt squat machine in our squat video. Belt squats can also be done on an incline; don't lock out your legs.
Incline Squats: do these with a Manta Ray or on a flat surface.
Safety Squat Bar: do these on an incline or on a flat surface.
Regular Barbell Squats
Front Squats - Free Squats: do these for high reps: 50-500 reps.
Hindu Squats: this is a variety of wrestling squat.
One-Legged Squat: do these with on leg supported behind you on a bench. This is also called a sprinter's squat. You can also hold on to a support for a little resistance. The hardest one-legged squat is done by balancing yourself unassisted.

Refer to the photos earlier, pages 94,95 on one legged squat variations.

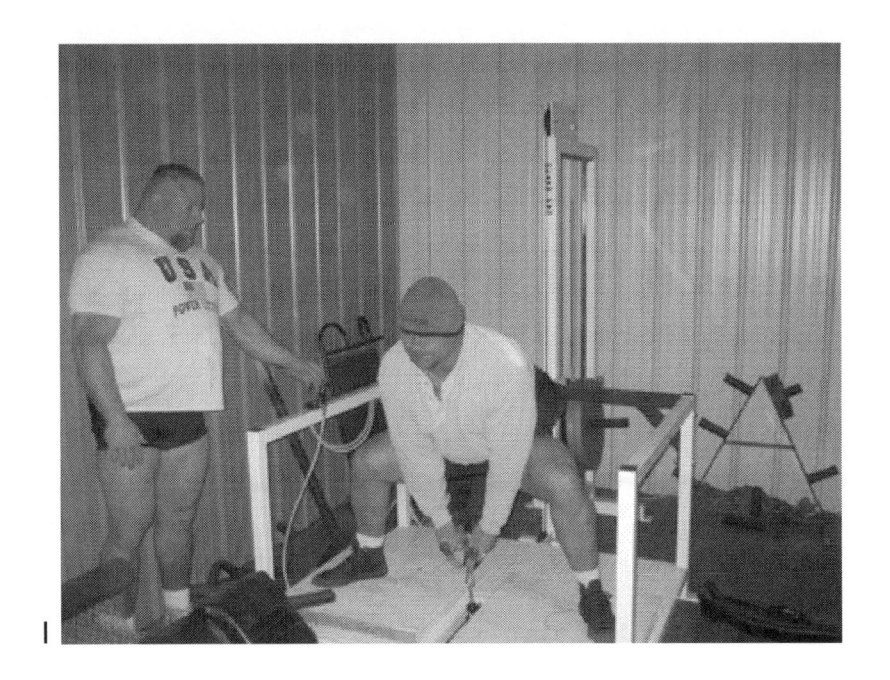

Here is the **belt squat machine**, hits only the lower body

When doing any type of squat, wear shoes with heels **occasionally**; this places the work more on the quads. Also squat as deep as possible. Depending on the amount of resistance, the reps are 5-12 per set. All of the above squats can be accomplished by holding a barbell or dumbbells.

One of these is **Zercher squats**. Their inventor, **Ed Zercher**, intended for the bar to be lifted off the floor in the crook of the elbows. At 181, I made 320 off the floor and an official deadlift of 670 in 1973. But at 198, I could no longer bend over far enough to hook the bar in my elbows. At that point, I placed the bar on the power rack pins and squatted from there. Squatting can also be done to develop flexibility.

Lateral Roll Squat. Start by squatting down as deep as possible. Next, roll your bodyweight to the right leg in a lunge position, then shift to the left leg, and stand up. Squat down again and repeat in reverse.
Frog Squat. Squat down with your hands over your head. Then place your hands between your legs and touch the floor.
Side-Stepping Squat. With a jump, step out laterally with both feet while descending. Stand up and repeat.
Uneven Squat. While squatting, place one foot on a box about 6 inches high and do full squatting.

The variety of squats presented here are intended for flexibility and agility. Something that most lifters are lacking. Many of these squats are illustrated in Twisted Conditioning by Bud Jeffries (1-866-strnger). This book has training tips for powerlifting, strongman competitions, and no holds-barred fighting such as Vale Tudo, of which I am a big fan.
Other leg developers are pushing cars forward or backward and walking with a heavy wheelbarrow. (Strongman movements) **Jesse Kellum** likes this type of training at certain times of the year and his legs are just about as strong as I have seen. At Westside we use sled pulling extensively.
Here are more **exercises for the posterior chain:**

- Walking Lunges: these can be done with a barbell or dumbbells.

- Glute/Ham Raises: we do hundreds of these at Westside.

- Reverse Hyper®5356,359 and 6,491,607b2 Machine: this builds the hamstrings, glutes, lower back and spinal erectors, plus acts as traction.

See a reverse hyper unit on following photo:

- **Inverse Curl**: this is a form of glute/ham raise. The glute/ham bench is elevated in the back by about 30 inches. Do a partial leg curl and a back extension at the same time. Hold at the top position (do not push with the toes). This exercise works the hamstrings at the hip and knee insertions simultaneously. A standard leg curl will not do the same.

- **Leg Curls** with Bands: do these seated on a bench in front of a power rack. Secure a band to the bottom of the rack, hook the band with the back of your ankles, and pull your fee under the bench.

- **Pull-throughs**: use a low-pulley machine with a single handle. Grab the handle with both hands facing away from the machine.

Walk out until there is tension and squat down. Let your hands go through your legs. Remember to keep your arms straight, then stand up and repeat. This is a great hamstring and glute builder. If done with straight legs, it will build incredible lower back strength.

- **Dimel Deadlifts**: use a shoulder-width stance and grab the bar with your hands outside your legs. First stand up with your back straight and arched. Maintain this position and drop the bar to just below knee level by squatting down. Quickly return to the top. Do 15-20 reps for 2 sets. These can be done up to 4 days a week, but only for 2 weeks at the most. These are named after my dear friend **Matt Dimel**. They pushed his 820 squat, which was stalled for over a year, to 1010 in 16 months. The same exercise raised Steve Wilson's deadlift to his all-time best of 865.

Author's Note: the above sounds similar to Peary Rader's Rebound training concept back on page 32

- **Deadlifts behind the Back:** this will build great leg strength for deadlifting. If you have large hamstrings, this exercise may be difficult. Ano, the great Finn, is experimenting with these to get some leg drive back into his deadlift.

- **Wall Squats**: Jesse Kellum suggested that I try these. This is **static squat** where you slide your back against a wall to an angle where you want to work you legs and hold from 15 to 60 seconds.

- **Plyometrics and Jumping**: Paul **Anderson was doing jumping exercises in the 1950's.** He would jump onto boxes of different heights to build explosive leg power. **Norb Schemanski, our great Olympic lifting champion, also did a lot of jumping**. He was reputedly able to jump onto a 4 foot high bar top at a local tavern.

The benefits of kinetic energy on the lowering phase is that it produces a phantom loading effect on the landing. I highly suggest you do a lot of research on plyometrics before using them in your training. They must be used correctly.

- I hope some of the exercises mentioned her can raise your squat and deadlift. **Some of the exercises are very old, and some are relatively new**, but all are proven to work. It's up to you or your coach to place them where they can do the most good.

☺☺☺

Power has a speed component. Physics laws tell us that the speed of acceleration is part of that equation, so that if we move x amount of weight over a certain distance in a shorter time period, **we have used more power** to do it. If you move a weight **explosively** through the range of motion on an exercise, as opposed to moving at a slow or moderate rate of speed, **you generate more power.** Experimentation with various rep schemes and percentages of maximum weight has shown that this explosiveness can only be achieved up to a certain percentage of max, which is somewhere below about 80 percent, give or take a wee bit between individuals. Therefore explosive training is typically done in the 60-75 percent range. Why not train at even lower percentages so higher speeds can be achieved then? At below 50 percent of 1 rep max effort, there is not enough tension produced to create the metabolic and cellular adaptations we seek.

What about the **slow, continuous tension methods** we hear about that bodybuilders often use? This may give a good pump and provide decent muscular stimulation, but **it is not a great strength and power builder.** The muscle fibers that move big weights are primarily the fast twitch fibers, and they are designed to work with the nervous system to create short, explosive bursts of energy, so slow repetitions do not give that system the stimulation it requires. When one is performing an all out, gut wrenching single rep on the squat, bench press or deadlift, there is some slow continuous tension going on, but only because inertia has ruled out the possibility of rapid acceleration in a relative sense. **One is still making every effort to accelerate the bar through the sticking point and on to the finish and lockout position,** but if it is a true max effort, it will be a slow grind to the top relative to the speed executed at 65 percent of max.

It has also been shown that working only 1 side of the equation is less effective than hitting the entire spectrum, at least in the power lifts which are slower movements than Olympic lifts.

Build explosiveness in the lower percentage ranges with dynamic work, and build raw strength with slower, max or near max efforts on max effort day.

Much of the older school power lifting routines were using what we call **linear progression**, starting with a low weight, doing high reps, gradually adding weight and cutting reps until one was at the 1 rep max single, which was hopefully at your competition time. More modern programs typically will show different types of periodization such as waves, with de-loading phases at certain points of the program.

Science has shown that the body responds well to a certain routine for about 3-4 weeks before adaptations make further gains on that same routine less effective. Using de-loading phases, varying percentages in a non-linear manner and using the conjugate method are ways of "beating the system" in a sense.

Here is an article from the well respected **Dave Tate,** a member of Westside, on the website **Elitefts.com**, which talks about The Westside program in some detail:

WESTSIDE BARBELL TRAINING PRINCIPLES

by Dave Tate. www.elitefts.com

You can always tell the members of the Westside Barbell power lifting team by the T-shirts with the Westside Barbell logo and the thickness of their physiques. They share more than just a name across their chest; they also share the recognition of being among the best, meet after meet and year after year.

Westside Barbell has produced twenty-three 800-pound squatters, six 900-pound squatters, thirty-six 500-pound benchers, eight 600-pound benchers, four 800-pound dead lifters and 47 Elite totals. An Elite in the sport of power lifting is the highest achievable level, the **gold standard of excellence.**

What is it that makes this group achieve standards others only dream of? What makes them known as The Best of the Best? This was the question I often asked myself before joining this elite group. I wanted to know what the magic bullet was. What were their secrets behind the numbers? What are they doing different? As I discovered, it has to do with a program that specializes in making a weak athlete strong, and a strong athlete stronger. The training behind Westside Barbell **ranges from increasing work capacity to increasing the level of preparedness.** The methods responsible for this are the max effort and dynamic effort methods structured under a conjugated method of periodization. These principles are responsible for creating a group of lifters who are confident, motivated, and inspired strength athletes.

At Westside, these attributes are developed year-round and have become known in power lifting circles as the Westside Methods.

Today's strength athletes can no longer rely on natural ability and strength derived from training using the progressive overload, Western method of periodization, or bodybuilding methods. **Today's strength athletes have to develop not only strength, but also explosive speed to progress to the next level. Strength is no longer enough.**

How did this all get started? Louis Simmons, the owner of the current Westside Barbell Club, chose the name in honor of the original Westside Barbell Club located in Culver City, California. This club was known for great athletes who include **Bill "Peanuts" West, George Frenn, Pat Casey, and superstar Billy Graham.** In Louie's opinion, this club was 30 years ahead of its time. This group of lifters was performing the **box squat and bench squats** long before Louie had ever considered the idea. It was from an article authored by Bill West and **George Frenn** that first introduced Louie to the idea. They would use the bench squat for what we refer to at Westside Barbell Club as a high box squat. The height of this bench was approximately 17 inches. They would also squat down to a 10 inch milk crate and this was called the low box squat. Louie has modified these two ideas and has come up with **the parallel box squat**, which has become a staple exercise at Westside Barbell.

Keep in mind; because change is one of the key components to success in the world of strength training, Louie did not always train under the methods used today. He used to train with the progressive overload approach that many still use.

In 1973 Louie suffered his first serious injury. He had totaled 1655 in the 181-pound class and felt like he was on top of the world. While performing a set of bent-over good mornings, he displaced his L-5 vertebra. Over the next 10 months, he received cortisone shots and walked with crutches. Severe pain prevented him from straightening out his legs completely. The doctor suggested traction for three weeks, however, Louie chose to see a chiropractor instead. After a few visits, he began to retain most of his back strength, but lost a great deal of flexibility in the back and hip region.

In 1978 he posted the fifth highest total in the country with a 710 deadlift. Once again, he was on top of the world, until the 1979 senior nationals when he tore his bicep. Two out of three doctors recommended surgery, but Louie opted to listen to the third. Six months after this injury, he won the Y nationals with a 1950 total, 50 pounds more than he had ever done. During the meet he pulled a 705 dead lift, which was 28 pounds more than he did prior to the torn bicep. During the course of the Y nationals, Louie received two tears in his lower abdominal region. This injury forced him to take six months off training.

Once he began to compete again, he succeeded in squatting 775 and deadlifting 722 in the 220-pound class. Once again in 1983, the lower back pain returned. He had decided to train through it and found himself unable to clear 500 pounds from the floor. This sent him back to the orthopedic surgeon who examined him and found a fractured L-5 vertebra, two compressed discs, and a bone spur! The doctor wanted to remove the two discs and the bone spur, but would offer no guarantee of reducing the pain or regaining flexibility. Louie decided against surgery and took 17 weeks off training. Amazingly, after five training sessions, he decided to enter a meet just to see where he was. He was able to lift a 683 squat and a 551 deadlift due to the lack of flexibility and strength in his lower back.

For most athletes, injuries are an excuse. However for Louie, it was a motivation. The injuries led him to look for better ways to train. His motivation, combined with his research into **Russian strength training methods**, brought him to the evolving system that is known today as the "Westside Method." Louie Simmons is a member of and oversees the most sophisticated strength performance team in the country.

So what are these training principles and methods that have propelled Westside Barbell into powerlifting greatness? The **periodization scheme used at Westside is known as conjugated periodization.** This simply means that there are several abilities being coupled together during the same cycles. These methods are the max effort method and dynamic effort method. There are two days per week scheduled for both methods.

Two days per week for the bench, and two days for the squat. The training week is listed below:

Monday: Max Effort Squat
Wednesday: Max Effort Bench
Friday: Dynamic Effort Squat
Sunday: Dynamic Effort Bench

Mondays are devoted to maximal strength development of the **squat and .deadlift** This is accomplished through the use of the maximal effort method.

This can be simply defined as **picking an exercise related to the squat and deadlift and working up to a one-rep max**. This method of training is one of the best ways of developing strength, but has its limitations. **One of these limitations is that you can't train above 90% for more than three weeks at a time, or your body will begin to shut down because of the high demands being placed on it.** Since the maximal effort method involves working up to one-rep, your training capacity is up to 100%. **We avoid the high demands and potential for overtraining by switching the max effort exercise every 1 to 3 weeks**. It is also important to warm up using small increases of weight when working up to your one-rep max. For those who squat above 500 pounds, use an average of 50 pound jumps, and for those under 500 pounds, use an average of 20 * 30 pound increases.

The exercises of choice for Westside are **Good Mornings, Box Squats, and Deadlifts.**

Box Squat: The benefits of this exercise are numerous. It **develops eccentric and concentric power by breaking the eccentric-concentric chain.** Box squats are a form of overload and isolation. The box squat is the best way to teach proper form of the squat because it is easy to sit way back while pushing your knees out. To take the bar out of the rack, the hands must be evenly placed on the bar. Secure the bar on the back where it feels the most comfortable. To lift the bar out of the rack, one must push evenly with the legs, arch the back, push your abs out against the belt, and lift the chest up while driving the head back. A high chest will ensure the bar rests as far back as possible. Slide one-foot back then the other, to assume a position to squat. Set your feet up in a wide-stance position. Point your toes straight ahead or slightly outward. Also keep your elbows pulled under the bar. When ready for the decent, make sure to keep the same arched back position. Pull your shoulders together and push your abs out. To begin the decent, push your hips back first. As you sit back, push your knees out to the sides to ensure maximum hip involvement. Once you reach the box, you need to sit on the box and **release the hip flexors.**

Keep the back arched and abs pushed out while driving your knees out to the side.

 To begin the ascent, push out on the belt, arch the back as much as possible, and drive the head, chest, and shoulders to the rear. **Keep in mind, if you push with the legs first, your buttocks will raise first, forcing the bar over the knees, as in a good morning, causing stress to the lower back and knees and diminishing the power of the squat.**

Good Morning: This is one of the most popular max effort squat exercises at Westside Barbell Club. This exercise is performed in one way or another on 70% of all max effort workouts. This is because **it works the posterior chain like no other exercise**. Done properly, this exercise will work everything between your traps to your calves. Begin this exercise by un-racking a barbell the same as you would a squat. Set up with your feet slightly wider than shoulder-width. Get into a tight position (arched back, shoulder blades pulled together, knees slightly bent, abdominal pushed out against your belt). This is the starting position. Slowly bend forward at the waist until your torso is slightly above parallel with the floor, then reverse the movement to return to the starting position.

Author's note:

You may want to refer back to Paul Anderson's discussion on these on pgs. 105-107, with photos

Conventional Deadlifts: This max effort exercise is designed to test overall body strength. It is normally advised to use a close grip, hands touching the smooth part of the bar. You will be pulling the bar a shorter distance, by rolling the shoulders forward as you rotate the scapula. This works fine for smaller lifters, but thick large men will do better by using a wider than shoulder grip. This allows room for the stomach to descend between the thighs, which are naturally set wider because of their girth. Most small men should keep their feet close together to use mostly back muscles to lift with, whereas big men use a lot of leg drive to start the lift. Pull the bar up to a standing position.

Sumo Style Dead Lift: Use a moderate stance and a close hand grip. To start the lift, you will rock into the bar, and the hips come up fast toward the bar. This requires a strong back because the legs lock out long before the bar is completely locked. The most common style is with the feet very wide, out to the plates. The lifter should not lower the hips any more than necessary. The back must be arched to the extreme. Most important is to push your feet out to the sides, not down. Why? By pushing down with a sumo or wide stance, your knees will come together, which is the most common mistake in the sumo. By pushing the knees out forcefully, the hips will come toward the bar fast making for a favorable leverage, placing most of the work on the hips, legs, and glutes. TIP: **Don't stay down too long. It will destroy the stretch reflex.**

There are hundreds of variations of each movement that can be chosen, with the most important group being the good morning-type movement, which are used on 70 percent of all max effort Mondays.

Monday's second movement is for the **hamstrings**. This is usually a very weak and under developed muscle in most lifters and is extremely important in the squat and deadlift. **Leg curls will not do!** You need to work the hamstrings from both origin and insertion at the same time. In other words, work the hamstrings from both ends. The best exercises for this are **Glute Ham Raises, Stiff-Leg Deadlifts, and Romanian Deadlifts**. The sets and reps for this exercise are left up to the individual. We are all different and what works for one will not always work for another. A great example of this is the development of the glutes and hamstrings of Eastern block weightlifters. According to many, they would not have been able to achieve this level of development with the use of 3 to 5 sets with 8 to 12 repetitions. The interesting thing is they seldom performed more than 3 reps per set! By leaving the sets and reps up to the lifter, the results will be better because more times than not, **the lifter knows what works for them.**

The third and fourth exercises for Monday's workouts are for **the core.** The **lower back and abs are probably the most important muscles in powerlifting**. Without them there will be very little transfer of power through the body to the bar. The most effective and most popular lower back exercise at Westside is the **reverse hyperextension machine.** We live and die by reverse hypers! After hyperextensions, we finish up with some abdominal work. The abdominal work consists of heavy leg raises, incline sit ups, Roman Chair sit ups, spread-eagle sit ups and standing crunches with a lat machine. **The key to abs is to train them heavy if you are interested in developing maximum strength!**

Wednesday's workout is designed to increase the maximal strength of the **bench press**. The same max effort is used as on Monday, but the exercises are now geared toward bench pressing. Some of these exercises include:

Bench Press: The bench press should be performed with the shoulder blades pulled together and driven into the bench. The elbows should be in a tucked position. The bar should hit you in the lower chest area. **The bar must be pushed in a straight line, not back over the face.**

Board Press: This is a special max effort exercise designed to help strengthen the lockout of the bench press. It is also very effective in increasing triceps strength. This exercise is performed exactly the same as the bench press except you pause the barbell on a board that is placed on your chest. The boards for this workout will be two, 2 by 4 boards about 12 inches in length.

Make sure to pause the barbell on the boards before the ascent.

Close-Grip Board Press: This max effort exercise is performed the same as the board press, except your grip will be closer. It is recommended to place one or two fingers on the smooth part of the bar.

Close Grip Incline Press: This is a max effort exercise designed to isolate the upper middle regions of the pectoral minor as well as the triceps. To begin this exercise, lay with your back on an incline bench and grasp the bar with one or two fingers on the smooth part of the bar. Unrack the weight so the arms are fully extended. Lower the barbell with your elbows in a tucked position to the upper chest region. Press the bar back to the starting position.

Floor Press: This is a special max effort exercise **designed to help strengthen the midpoint of the bench press**. It is also very effective in increasing triceps strength. This exercise is performed exactly the same as the bench press except you lay on the ground instead of a bench. Make sure to pause in the bottom of the movement before the ascent. This exercise has been used with much success at Westside Barbell Club for the past seven years.

The second exercise on Wednesday's workout is always **for the triceps**. The triceps are, without a doubt, **the most important muscle for bench pressing**. The exercises of choice are laying extensions and presses. Save the pushdowns and overhead extensions for pre/rehabilitation work or the beach. Once again, the sets and reps are up to you.

The third movement is **for the lats.** Against popular belief, if the bar gets stuck on your chest or right off it by 2 or 3 inches, it is your lats holding you back, not your chest. The primary responsibility of the chest muscles is arm adduction, or pulling you arm across your body. This is why the pec deck and crossovers work so well to isolate the chest. Most all pressing is performed by triceps extension and shoulder rotation. Shoulder rotation is the result or the implementation of the muscles of the upper back, known as the rotator cuff muscles. These muscles together with the lats act to stabilize and move the bar through the proper groove, which happens to be a straight line, not a "J" (pushing back toward the rack), as advocated by many. What is the shortest distance between two points, a straight line or a J? **The best exercise for the lats are those that work on a horizontal plane. We all bench on a horizontal plane so the lats should be trained the same way.** These exercises include any type of rows such as dumbbell rows, barbell rows, and chest-supported rows. After the lats, finish up with some light shoulder work and get out of the gym!

Friday's workout is designed to increase the **explosive strength of the squat**. This is performed with the utilization of the Dynamic Effort Method. **The Dynamic Effort method** is simply defined as training with sub-maximal weights in an explosive fashion. This style of training **will teach the central nervous system to explode through sticking points.** Sticking points are also known as "min-maxes" because this is usually the point where failure sets in and the barbell stops. What we try to achieve with this method is to **blast trough the sticking point.** You can always knock someone back further with a running start. There **is more force generated through acceleration**. More acceleration equals more force and therefore, no sticking point! The box squat is always trained on this day using 8 sets of 2 reps with **a four-week wave** starting with 60% and waving up to 70%. This most important aspect of this movement is the barbell speed, not the percent being used. Start with 60 percent and increase over a four-week period. Increase the weight each week as long as you can maintain the same barbell speed you had with 60%. After the Dynamic effort box squats, follow the same guidelines for supplemental work as on Mondays.

The Sunday workout is for the development of **explosive and dynamic bench press strength.** Use the same dynamic methods described in the Friday workout. The bench press is **trained with 8 sets of 3 reps using approximately 50% of your one-rep max**. We also use **three different grips when training the bench press and all of them are within the rings.**

After the Dynamic Effort bench, follow the same guidelines for supplemental work as on Wednesdays.

This is the basic format or template used by Westside Barbell Club. A summary is provided below:

Monday: Max Effort Squat Day Format:

One Max Effort Exercise: Good Mornings 70%, Low Box Squatting 20%, Deadlifting 10%: Increase weight in small increments for sets of three. When three reps become difficult, drop to singles until a one-rep max is reached.
Supplemental Exercise: Hamstrings: Glute Ham Raises, Stiff Leg Deadlifts, Romanian Deadlifts: Sets and reps are up to the lifter.
Accessory Exercise: Reverse Hypers: Sets and reps up to the lifter.
Accessory Exercise: Abs
Wednesday: Max Effort Bench Day Format:

One Max Effort Exercise: Floor, Board, Close Grip, Incline Presses: Increase weight in small increments for sets of three. When three reps become difficult, drop to singles until a one-rep max is reached.
Supplemental Exercise: Triceps: Lying extensions and presses: Sets and reps are up to the lifter.
Accessory Exercise: Lats: any type of rows.
Accessory Exercise: Shoulders and extra triceps.
Friday: Dynamic Effort Squat Day Format:

Box Squats: 8 sets of 2 reps using the Dynamic Effort Method.
Supplemental Exercise: Hamstrings: Glute Ham Raises, Stiff Leg Deadlifts, Romanian Deadlifts: Sets and reps are up to the lifter.
Accessory Exercise: Reverse Hypers: Sets and reps up to the lifter.
Accessory Exercise: Abs
Sunday: Dynamic Effort Bench Day Format:

Bench Press: 8 sets of 3 reps using the Dynamic Effort Method.
Supplemental Exercise: Triceps: lying extensions or presses: Sets and reps are up to the lifter.
Accessory Exercise: Lats: any type of rows.
Accessory Exercise: Shoulders and extra triceps.
The Conjugated Periodization method, utilizing the maximal effort, and dynamic effort methods have propelled Westside Barbell Club into strength greatness. The special exercises used by Westside have also had a great impact on the progress and success of its lifters. By applying these methods to your training program, you will see dramatic differences in maximal strength levels. I should know because I have been a member for the last 10 years and have seen my lifts go from a 750 squat to a 935, a 500 bench to a 585, and a 680 deadlift to a 740.

_____

We all have our challenges. What makes us who we are is how we rise to them.

I like Dave's explanations of the WS methods as they are simple and concise

☺

Even in the old school methods, we saw innovative trainees using their own versions of some of these ideas, but they may not have completely understood the science behind what they were doing. We saw programs that mixed up light and heavy training periods, or even light, medium and heavy training periods. We saw Harry Paschall suggesting taking a full week off from training after each 6 week training cycle, which was a form of de-loading, though he didn't call it that. We saw advanced men using partial movements with massive weights, using eccentrics, plyometrics, cheat reps, super sets and forced reps interspersed with the full range of motion movements, which was a form of the conjugate method. What was done by instinct and refined through self experimentation by the old school men has become a more scientifically validated and regimented training system used by today's top level lifters. Now, like back then, people are individuals and have different responses to similar stimuli, so shrewd trainees "**listen to their bodies**" and make sometimes subtle and sometimes not so subtle adjustments to the prevailing systems to make them work for themselves. It is this that makes some of the top level lifter's programs hard to pin down, or seem like they are being elusive or secretive when asked about what they do or how they train to obtain their power. **Their programs are in a constant state of flux and refinement.**

You have probably heard the phrase stating that the definition of insanity is to continue to do the same things over and over while expecting a different set of results. This is true in the strength training realm as it is in every other area of our lives.

We have also seen the wisest trainers over the years tell us that more is not always the answer. We have a tendency to think that if our program is not yielding results anymore, we need to do more sets or more exercises to "kick it up a notch", and this is often not true, and is just as often actually counter-productive. In one of my earlier books, (**Forgotten Secrets of the Old time Strongmen**) I talked about **Earle Liederman**'s dialogue on this point.
 Earle said that it was common to see young trainees who start off ready to set the world on fire, make steady progress for a few months or so and finally hit the inevitable plateau. They had staked out a plan based on the early phases of progression that most trainees experience, with an endless upward progression that would eventually lead them to breaking world records. Then, reality rears its ugly head and progression ceases fairly abruptly.

The trainee surmises that he is not training often enough or hard enough, so he redoubles his efforts. Now, not only does he not start to make gains again, but he is constantly sore, tired and is actually starting to go backwards with his training. He becomes depressed and decides there is no real use in continuing, so he stops training altogether. After a week or two, he begins to feel a bit better, with color coming back to the cheeks. In yet another week or two, he feels better yet, and decides that maybe he even feels good enough to start training a little bit. He begins to train again, and gradually starts again to make some progress, until again he reaches that wall where further progress becomes impossible and he quits again. After 2 or 3 cycles such as this, the would-be superman will quit for good, throwing all his aspirations for greatness under the bus. This is very unfortunate and unnecessary, and simply does not have to be the case, stated Liederman, and **I agree whole heartedly.**

Chapter Sixteen
Jumpstretch COO Interview

One of the more recent pieces of equipment that has been revolutionary in changing how strength athletes in particular and the general sports field trains is the **stretch band**, invented by football coach **Dick Hartzell**. He started the **Jumpstretch Company,** and the COO of the company was kind enough to do an interview for my website **Christianiron.com** a while back.

Here are some interesting excerpts from that interview that are pertinent to our subject:

Carl LaRosa is Chief Operating Officer for Jump Stretch, Inc. in Youngstown, Ohio. In 1997 he helped his father-in-law FlexBand inventor **Coach Dick Hartzell** to open the Jump Stretch Fitness Center. The two are considered the leading authorities in **rubber band strength training worldwide,** and had the privilege of **training the Navy SEALS in band techniques in September of 2002.**

Athletes in all sports train at Jump Stretch, starting at age 10 and continuing right on through to the college and professional levels. Carl has trained and designed exercise programs for male & female athletes who compete professionally in bodybuilding, powerlifting, football, baseball, basketball, track, soccer, dance and more, including John Simon at Ohio State University and
Brad Smith, with the **New York Jets.**

As the instructor for the FlexBand Training Seminar (a program that he also designed), Carl is responsible for instructing coaches, trainers, and other professionals in Jump Stretch techniques.
He is instrumental in helping other companies to incorporate "band rooms" into their own facilities.

The FlexBands are used by college and professional teams including the Atlanta Braves, Boston RedSox, Buffalo Bills, Cleveland Cavaliers, Dallas Cowboys, , LA Angels of Anaheim, New England Patriots, New York Giants, New York Yankees, Pittsburgh Steelers, University of Michigan, Mississippi State University, Mount Union College, Ohio State University, Thiel College, West Virginia University, and many more.

Carl LaRosa of the Jumpstretch Company

Here is Carl working out with some bands

I asked Carl about how things got started with the bands

Please tell us, Carl, when your father in law invented the flex bands, what led up to it, and was it a long process?

He was a football coach and he believed that strength had to be built through speed, so he padded a barbell and had his lifters do squats fast. After a couple of low-back injuries, he was frustrated and thought "Why couldn't this be done on rubber bands?" At that time the name "**Jump Stretch**" popped into his head, but the product didn't exist anywhere but his own mind. The 2nd chapter of Daniel says that God reveals secrets…it took a few years to get things going, and then **much longer to get this type of training accepted.**

When your father-in –law invented them, was it more or less for using with his students primarily or did he have a business plan right from the start?

There was no business plan at all. He had the idea to make squatting more sport-specific for football. We have a saying at Jump Stretch "Train quick to be quick. Train slow to be slow." He set out to change the way people looked at strength training and once the products were developed his goal was to impact the world, which I think has been done!

When they were first introduced, what reactions were seen?

People had a hard time believing that strength could be built on bands. Then Youngstown State University went to multiple National Championships using nothing but FlexBands for on-season lower extremity training. We also stretch with the bands, doing what we call dynamic stretching. At the time when he first developed the bands, static stretching was the only accepted stretching method. Now most of the pro and college teams are integrating dynamic stretches in with their programs. It makes more sense, because the game they play is not static in nature. This is another area in which we've made a big impact.

You instruct coaches and athletes in flex band seminars; do you teach students how to train using weights with bands, like the **Westside Barbell methods**, or more exclusively just band training without weights?

The training seminars we offer are focused on teaching our system of band training (without weights) to professionals
I have had health care professionals from all over the world come and learn our techniques. God has certainly blessed us to put such awesome people in our lives. One of the guys who got certified in the past couple of years is **Tom Gill** who you previously did a Q & A with for

Christianiron.com. He's a great guy & we've continued our relationship with him as we have with the majority of the people who take this course with us. As for Westside Barbell, we really can't give **Louie Simmons** enough credit for how his vision of combining weights with the bands has impacted our company.

The series of articles he wrote for Powerlifting USA in 1997 about the bands amounted to the turning point for Jump Stretch as far as being accepted with strength coaches on a wide scale.

On that subject, can one build strength & power using just combinations of the bands, platforms, etc without using barbells and such?

Absolutely! We had two guys known as the "Watson Bros." Stan & Ross Watson both had over 35" vertical jumps and played for Mount Union College, who ended up winning consecutive National Championships. They had never really trained with weights for their lower extremities. I can attest that they were great athletes. **We can be much more sport-specific with a band then we could with a barbell.**

Can personal trainers & fitness instructors get certified in band techniques?

Yes, we teach them the basics of our techniques, as well as how to implement them into their individual programs.
 This is an additional level of training that looks good on a resume, and we often get calls from coaches looking to hire someone who is well-versed in our techniques. Our course is approved for .7 CEUs (Continuing Education Units) through the National Strength & Conditioning Coaches Association.

For people who want to take this training to the next level and actually run a Jump Stretch facility themselves, we offer additional training in conjunction with a marketing agreement so they can even use our name and logo.

What is new and exciting on the horizon in relation to Jumpstretch equipment and training methods?

As I mentioned earlier, we are working on marketing agreements to get gyms to carry the name and properly implement the techniques. Also, many therapists are using the bands to treat injuries. The Red Cross is doing a regional test on our injury prevention and treatment program for ankle sprains, and if all goes well, this will expand across the country.

Are there any special benefits to using bands in physical therapy, rehab, and pain management?

Yes, there is a special technique for tractioning ankles that have been sprained that dramatically reduces downtime.
 I have literally seen our therapist work on someone in with a Grade II (2) ankle sprain and have them running drills in less than an hour. Our bands are a lot stronger than the thin bands you see at most doctors' offices, plus the fact that they are a continuous loop provides a wider range of options for the therapist.

☺☺☺

We thank Carl for helping us out with that interview!

The applications to powerlifting movements using bands are multiple and varied. One of the terms frequently used by the Westside crowd is **"accommodating resistance"**. This is accomplished using both bands and chains, and I will provide a brief excerpt from the man himself, **Louie Simmons,** taken from the website **deepsquatter.com**

By: Louie Simmons

Chains and Bands

There are many keys to success, but two invaluable ones are accelerating strength training and **accommodating resistance by adding chains or bands or sometimes both**.

Chains and bands are used in all of our training, be it the dynamic method for speed strength and acceleration or the maximum effort day to develop absolute strength.

In the bench press, bands and chains have helped 17 of our lifters achieve 550 or more and 7 lifters have done 600 or more. When I talk about bench training, I am referring to my lifters with a 550 bench or better; that's who we experiment with.

On speed day for the bench, while doing the 8-10 sets of 3 reps, the chains are attached in the following manner. Loop a 1/4-inch-link chain with a hook around the bar sleeve to regulate the height of the 5/8-inch-link chain (5 feet long). Run the 5/8 chain through the metal loop and adjust it so that half of the 5/8 chain is lying on the floor while the bars in the rack. Use 60% of a no-shirt max on the bar. For example, if your max is 500, put 300 pounds on the bar. When the bar is on your chest, only the weight of the bar should be on your chest; that is, all the 5/8 chain should be on the floor.

If your best bench is 250 pounds or less, use one pair of 1/2-inch-link chains; these weigh 23 pounds a set, so you are locking out an extra 11.5 pounds. A 350 or more bencher should use one pair of 5/8-inch-link chain. By doing this, you will be locking out an extra 20 pounds. (They weigh 20 pounds each, but half is on the floor at lockout.) A 500 pound bencher can use both the 5/8 and 1/2 inch chains for a combined added weight of 31 pounds.

A 600 bencher uses two 5/8 chains and sometimes adds a 1/2 inch chain, for 40 or 51 added pounds at lock-out.

You can experiment on your own, but remember this process is to build bar speed and acceleration. It also teaches you to launch the bar off your chest.

A special note: Lower the bar fast and try to catch and reverse the weight as fast as possible. Never pause.

On max effort day, warm up to 315, then do a single. Next, add a 5/8 inch chain on each side and do a single. On the next set, use two sets of chain, then three sets, and so forth. This is similar to how a bench shirt works: the weight is less at the bottom and much greater at the top. The chains build not only acceleration but also a fast start and a strong lock-out.

For floor pressing, simply drape the 5/8 inch chain over the sleeve of the bar and you're ready. J.M. Blakley and George Halbert do a lot of floor presses like this. George will use 200 pounds of chain (5 sets of chain) and works up to a single. His best at a bodyweight of 220 is 440 plus 200 pounds of chain, which is 640 at the top.

J.M. uses a different combination of weight and chains. ,J.M.s best is 400 pounds on the bar with 7 sets of chains, for a combined weight of 680 at lockout. Try any weight-to-chain ratio. Feel free to experiment. **A cambered bar** can be used as well.

These are a few methods to add to your max effort day.

Bands are a little tough for some on speed day because of the **added eccentric properties they create**. Also **the weight resistance is much more radical at different positions:** much less at the bottom, but much greater at the top. Remember, the bands are literally pulling down on you.

There are three bands with different strengths: pink is the least strong, for 300 pound benchers and below; green for 300-450 pound benchers; and blue for 500 pound benchers and above (shirtless max).

When using bands, be careful not to overdue it. **The bands produce a large amount of eccentric overloading** and can cause excessive soreness, but they are more than worth it. **They build the lockout as well as the start**. One realizes very fast that you have to outrun the bands, so you develop a fast start to enable you to lock out a heavy weight.

The most popular methods using the bands are as follows. On max effort day, do board presses with four 2 x 6's. Loop the bands through the bottom supports of the bench and then around the sleeve of the bar. When using four boards, the tension is never released. Be-cause of this, a quick start is impossible and locking out a heavyweight is really tough. To make it even tougher, use a cambered bar. 'J.M. presses' with bands are very popular at Westside. To make it as tough as possible, use several bands. Lower the bar straight down, aiming between the nipples and chin, stop 4-5 inches off the chest, and press back up. Use a close grip.

Bands and chains are often used for triceps extensions.

This will radically change the strength curve of the movement by accommodating resistance (lifts are usually easier at the top).

A Westside supporter who constantly bugs me with some of the craziest ideas actually came up with an exercise that really works. So thanks to Doug Ebert for the following band exercise. Attach a blue band to the bar and start with 95 or 135 pounds because this is tough.

Then take a pink or green band, depending on your strength, twist it once, and place it around your upper back so the tension is pulling back your hands. Now lie down on the bench, stretch the band to grab the bar, and start benching. This 'double' tension is unreal.

Also try the 'lightened' method, **recommended by Carl of Jump-Stretch.** Attach a set of blue bands to the top of the power rack with a slip knot. Load the bar to 135. It should be almost weightless at the chest. This way you can bench 135 pounds more than normal. **This builds tremendous power at lockout,** which is perfect for bench shirts.

Bands and chains have helped to increase our list of 550 benchers at Westside to 17. George Halbert recently benched 688 at 235 to capture the world record at 242. George also holds the 220 world record. Only two people can claim to hold a world record bench in two weight classes: George Halbert and Dave Waterman.

Now on to squatting. With an army of 800+ squatters, 22 to be exact, when we experiment and establish results, they are sound and proven. We also have a 755 squatter at 165 and a 782 squatter at 181. **They all use chains and bands**. Here's how.

First use a set of 1/4-inch-link chains that attach to the bar sleeves. We suspend a metal ring from the 1/4 inch chains, which regulates height of the 5/8 chain from the floor. Loop the 5/8 inch chain through the metal ring so about three chain links are lying on the floor when you are standing. When you are sitting on the box, slightly below parallel, half of the chain will be unloaded onto the floor.

How much chain should you use? If you squat 350 or less, use one set of 5/8 inch chain, equaling 40 pounds at the top. If you squat about 600 pounds, use about 60 or 70 pounds of chain at the top. If you squat 800 pounds, use 80~120 pounds of chain at the top. As you can see, about 10% of your squat weight should be added with chain. If you are doing sets with 400 on the bar, you will be standing up with 520.

An 800 squatter whose top training weight is 480, or 60%, will add 80-120 pounds of chain to the bar, equaling 600 at the top.

To use bands for squatting, if you squat 650 or less, use green bands. If you squat more than 650, use blue bands. Here are two examples of 900+ squatters. Billy Masters and Dave Barno used a top weight of 500 pounds and 150 pounds of tension with blue bands. Billy did 909 and Dave did a perfect 925. Neither train at Westside, but they use our methods.

When squatting, **wave** your training weights from 50% to 60% in a 3 or 4 week cycle. Do mostly 8 sets of 2 reps with 45 seconds rest between sets.

For max effort work, one can choose a bar weight of, say, 400 or 500 pounds. Do a single and then add a set of chains. Keep doing singles and adding a second and third set of chains until you break a PR or miss. You can do the same with Flex bands. Good mornings are a great exercise to do with chains and bands. High pulls with the pink or green bands are also great.

I have seen one of our lifters with a 600 deadlift go to 670 in 6 months by using bands on the deadlift. Bob Young would use 275-315 on the bar, with about 200 pounds of tension from the bands. We use the platform that Jump-Stretch sells with their bands to do this exercise.

If you want to excel at powerlifting or any sport, then **you must develop speed strength, increase acceleration, and gain absolute strength. Bands and chains can be instrumental in developing these aspects of strength.**
I highly recommend that you try them as soon as possible. For chains, call **Topper's Supply at 614-444-1187. For bands, call JumpStretch at 1-800-344-3539.**

You noticed Louie mentioning the 3-4 week wave concept that I spoke of earlier. Louie has reams of info available on these concepts and has a recent training manual describing just about all of the Westside methods.

Chapter Seventeen
The original Westside Barbell

So, you may be wondering how **Westside Barbell** came about. Actually, the original Westside Barbell was started by **Bill "Peanuts" West**, yet another throwback to the old school methods and legends. Let's take a look at an interesting article presented by **Earle Liederman** on Bill:

Bill "Peanuts" West
by Earle Liederman (1961)

When Bill West succeeds in attaining his goal of a 600-pound squat, he will be one of the smallest men in the world to accomplish this rare feat of strength. This 460 went easy.

Here is a photo of Bill from the time frame of this article

The story of Bill West, the California strongman, is **a revelation of what a special diet combined with weightlifting can make out of a thin weakling**. Bill weighed but 102 pounds when his hands first touched a barbell; and after a few years this bodyweight soared to 218 pounds due to progressive lifting and living chiefly on **peanuts**. But let me go back to the time he began.

When Bill was 15½ years old in 1952, he associated with Gene Wells, who lived near him in Pennsylvania. Wells, at the time, held the physique title of Mr. Pennsylvania. And Bill at the time had never heard of health foods, vitamins, proteins or rightful living. Neither had he ever given a thought to lifting a dumbbell or any sort of weight. He was just a thin kid who looked *at* sports rather than being one of the players. It was Gene Wells who prompted Bill West to try some weight training and to build up his scrawny body, and so Gene got him started with very light bells. Bill gives Gene Wells much credit for his start in the iron game.

In July of 1952 they both became very interested in a copy of ***Strength & Health* magazine** and were fascinated by an article about "**Muscle House by the Sea**" at Santa Monica, California. Both of them immediately decided to get to the West Coast pronto! They did, and right to this Muscle House they went!

Now, this famous abode is owned and operated by a lovely lady, **Fleurette Crettaz**, who is also known around her loyal following as "**Joy**". This is undoubtedly due to her friendly and optimistic disposition, as she is ever striving to help everyone along healthful avenues and rightful ways of living. Her large house is always filled with musclemen and health enthusiasts and is strictly vegetarian. This lady looks after her flock of muscle boys just as though they were her own children. A great many of the past Mr. Americas and other prize winners have lived there, as have numerous noted lifters. Bill West and Gene Wells felt right at home when they first entered her door.

The nickname "Peanuts" was bestowed upon Bill because he was given a rigid diet at Muscle House of proteins, chiefly peanuts. He ate one pound of *raw* peanuts daily, also a half-cup of peanut butter each day as well as six spoonfuls of raw peanut oil every 24 hours. Of course, in addition to this entire peanut intake he had numerous protein drinks and **raw milk** as well as many assorted fruit juices.

Within 60 days he leaped from that 102 lb. mark to 132 lbs. bodyweight. At the end of the first year he went to 155 and kept right on devouring the peanut variations. **He had also settled deeply into weight training.**

His experiences during the second year with weights and peanuts were a trifle discouraging to Bill as he only went to 165 lbs. Perhaps he had expected too much. But during his third year of training he increased to the 180 lb. mark through heavier lifting.

It was now 1955. He became interested in lifting events.

In his initial local experience Bill took second place in the Muscle Beach lifting meet and third in the odd lift meet. He was a novice, yet he managed a 230 press, a 205 snatch and a 280 clean & jerk. In that same year he won an A.A.U. odd lift meet with a 330 bench press and a 420 squat. But he was far from satisfied, and aimed at higher goals and greater power.

At this point Bill went on **a heavy squat and press program** and chanced to meet Ike Berger, who advised him to increase his bodyweight to 198 lbs. He then trained with Berger and Dave Ashman, lifting heavier and heavier poundage as well as increasing his peanut-based diet intake. He could almost see himself enlarging weekly at this point. Bill's aim was to get heavier, so he went on a more severe lifting program, until one day when chancing to weigh himself he was amazed to find the scales showing 218 pounds!
It revealed the benefits derived from heavier training and greater food intake; but Bill was actually far too heavy. He recalled how Ike Berger suggested an increase to that 198 lb. mark, and now Bill was 20 lbs. over the mark! But he felt powerful. Nonetheless, he decided to reduce.

His next step was to eliminate excessive peanut eating and milk drinking. By controlling his protein diet and eating less, he began to reduce. It wasn't long before he was down to that desired 198 lb. class, and he has stayed there ever since.

"**Peanuts**" has absolutely no desire to train for muscular effect. His entire interest lies with lifting exclusively, and he especially enjoys the odd lifts. He is now performing in training, and with reps - **435 lb. bench presses; 525 lb. squats; and 175 lb. strict barbell curls.** He can easily power clean 305, push-jerk 330, and that's without training for these latter lifts. Bill also presses 145 lb. dumbbells at an 85 degree angle, and does 3 sets of 10 reps in presses with 100 lb. bells; presses 242½ lbs. behind the neck, collar to collar grip.
He has also done **bench squats** from a 19" high bench with 770 lbs.

He likes everyone and everyone likes Bill West. I have found Bill to be a swash-buckling openhearted fellow with one of the most electrified dispositions I have encountered in years. He seems a mass of energy. One grand thing in his favor is his honesty and truthfulness. He speaks with authority and relates facts, especially about his lifting poundage. Bill's sense of humor is immense. Once I chanced to catch him standing and talking in the midst of a group of seven or eight fellows. Bill was gesticulating and smiling as he talked, and all the other guys were continuously enjoying a prolonged spell of laughter. He's a quick thinker and a very rapid talker; and yet remains true to himself, and that's really saying something.

One example of his appreciation for what others have done for him was expressed when he emphatically requested that I kindly give full credit to **Gene Wells and Ike Berger** for his earlier progress, and also to mention the healthful and helpful benefits he obtained while living at Muscle House be the Sea.

Bill is a hearty eater, yet lives on but two meals a day. He trains every day, with the alternate system, performing all upper body work one day and all leg work the next. He tells me that he takes about three hours for his upper body training and one-and-one-half for his leg work. Bill has eliminated all milk from his diet at present in order to hold down his weight at that 198 lb. mark, and he only drinks water during his training period, not otherwise.

He prefers home training and finds he can secure better concentration than he could by working out in a crowded gymnasium. Bill has his own training quarters in the garage in back of his home, where he and a couple of friends have their enthusiastic power workouts.

His ambition at present is to make a 600 lb. squat and a 500 lb. bench press in strict style at his present bodyweight of 198 lbs. Will he do it? I'll wager he will! Bill has learned that if anyone wants strength he must use strength to get it. And I am sure you will be reading and hearing more about "Peanuts" each year as he progresses with his odd lifts and attains his goals.

Bill is a shining example of how a once weak and skinny youth can transform himself into a full-fledged heavyweight with a body packed full of power through heavy weight training and the right diet. However, that peanut diet adds food for thought also.

My own personal opinion regarding such a forced, extremely heavy protein diet is that it should be supervised by someone who thoroughly understands the complete functioning of the organic system, and then also outlined as adaptable to each particular individual. Otherwise a beginner might overstuff himself with far too much "oily" protein and possibly have an unfavorable reaction. And yet again, there always remains something in life to contradict logic. If Bill West's experiences with such a peanut diet combined with heavy lifting can produce a body packed with power and filled with energy, well then it is worth acquiring by such methods. **All barbells and other weights have been tried and proven through the years;** therefore few "new" suggestions are realized concerning their usage. I merely caution a beginner against too oily a diet for long periods of time unless given under expert supervision.

Anyway, this frank and open account of Bill "Peanuts" West has given me great pleasure to impart to you. But let me repeat and make this clear: everyone likes Bill West and Bill West likes everyone. Such a combination is bound to make this world a happier place for all.

☺☺☺

Ok, so that was Bill West's story. Or at least it was part of it. **So how did the Westside Barbell we now know come about?** Well, here is a brief paragraph from Louie Simmons from his website, which was pretty much his autobiography:

Bill "Peanuts" West in the early days

No fewer than 13 dead stop bench presses with 320 pounds were performed by Bill West on the day these photos were made. His best single is around the 400 mark.

Bill benching

As you can see, Bill was no slouch in the deadlift, either

No one knew anything about powerlifting. One day I picked up a **Muscle Power Builder**, which **later became Muscle and Fitness**. In that magazine, there was a powerlifting article about the **Westside Barbell Club of Culver City, California**. It was about **box squatting**. I had never heard of this, but with nothing to lose, I gave it a try. To my amazement, the **box squats** worked to the point that I later made top 10 squats in five weight classes.

Here is a 1968 cover shot of Muscle Builder/Power magazine featuring the great bodybuilder of the time, Dave Draper, who is still training these days, by the way.

Bill West, George Frenn, and the guys, through those articles, got me started on the right foot. I was never able to visit Westside in Culver City due to work, which I regret to this day.
After getting out of the Army in 1969, **1 built a power rack, got some weights, and started training full time using what I learned from the articles.** They were my only training partners.

After Bill West died, I referred to my place as Westside Barbell, but never publicly until 1986. Westside Barbell is a trademarked name (and so is Louie Simmons).

In another article on Louie's website, he talked about his influences from the original Westside a bit more:

Training Strong Legs for World Records

By: Louie Simmons

It was around 1970, and I was reading **Muscle Power Builder and articles by members of Westside Barbell in Culver City, CA. George Frenn** was discussing how important strong legs were to breaking squat records. He recommended several exercises and methods that he and Bill "Peanuts" West had developed over the years. They pushed box squatting on different height boxes, good mornings, and even calf work to develop their immense back strength. They were responsible for the first 800 pound squat, by **Pat Casey.** I realized they knew what they were doing. An old friend, **Roger Estep**, made the trip to Culver City and gained priceless knowledge. He brought back what he learned and shared it with a West Virginia group, later known **as the Wild Bunch: Luke Iams, Jack Wilson, Chuckie Dunbar, and the rest of the guys in New Martinsville, WV.** After talking to Roger, I was convinced.

About 30 years later, we at Westside in Columbus, OH, continue to improve on what Bill West's boys were doing **by adding science and technology to the system.**

☺

Chapter Eighteen
George Frenn

Since we saw George Frenn mentioned by both Louie and Dave Tate, I thought I'd throw in this little tidbit for good measure, a nice little gem found online:

Here is Frenn's training schedule and comments from the April 1972 issue of Strength & Health. Weights are in pounds.

"I train only on Tuesdays and Saturday with the weights and I throw the hammer and run on Mondays, Wednesdays, Thursdays, and Saturdays. When I train for the Powerlifts I do the bench press: otherwise I never do any pressing movements as it hurts the hammer throw."

Tuesday
Bench Press
Bench Squats (20 inch bench)
Low Box Squats (14 inch bench) 4 sets x 1 rep
Lat PullDowns: 3 sets x 5 reps heavy as I can go.
Good Mornings: 3 sets x 5 reps 135, 225, 315, sometimes 425
Power Cleans 5 sets x 5,4,3,2,1
Triceps Extensions: 3 sets x 10 reps heavy as you can go.

For the bench press and bench squat, do 12 sets. Low Box follows bench squats.

BENCH PRESS

135 X 10
225 X 10
315 X 8
390 X 3-4
425 X 1-2
460 X 1
485 X 1 X 4 sets
405 x 6-10 close grip
375 x 10 regular grip

BENCH SQUAT

225 x 10
335 x 5
425 x 5
535 x 5
625 x 5
715 x 3-4
805 x 2-4
855 x 1-3
900 x 1-3
955 x 1-2

LOW BOX

445 x 1
535 x 1
625 x 1
715 x 1
625 x 5
445 x 10

POWER CLEANS
225 x 5
275 x 4
305 x 3
330 x 2
345 x 1

DEADLIFT
225 x 5
315 x 5
425 x 3
535 x 2
625 x 1
700 x 1 x 2 sets
650 x 5

"As for Saturday's training, I do only the bench press, full squat, and deadlift. For the bench press schedule, follow the one I use on Tuesdays. Use the bench squat schedule for your full squats. The sets are the same but the poundages are not quite that heavy. During the hammer throwing season, I do not bench press, so I substitute the power clean and snatch for the bench press. Follow the power clean schedule for these two exercises."

Here is a shot of George on the cover of Weightlifting Journal, taken from Dave Draper's website

Chapter Nineteen
A Bodybuilder's perspective:

Here is an awesome Ironman interview with Tom Platz, one of the greatest squatting bodybuilders of all time:

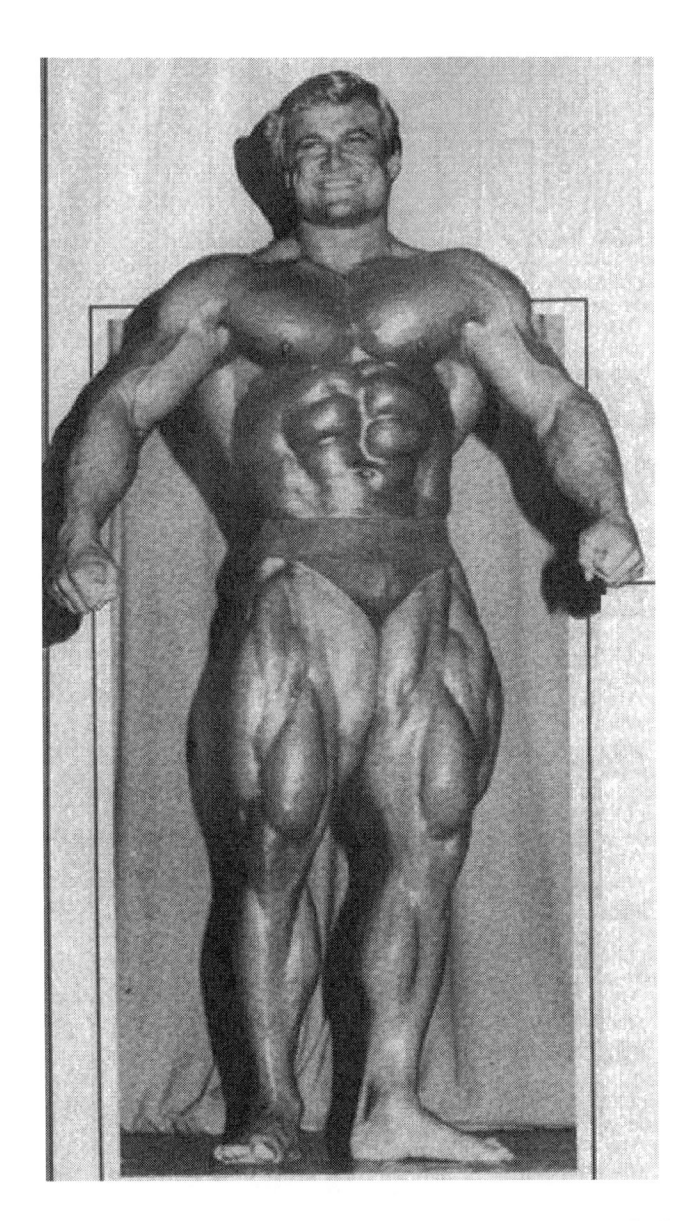

Ironman: Tom, to start at the very beginning, when did you first get the idea that you wanted to do this – weight training? And when did you actually start bodybuilding?

Tom Platz: When I was ten years old, probably closer to 9 ½, I looked at a muscle magazine and saw that picture of **Dave Draper** on the beach with Betty Weider on one arm and two girls on each leg and another on the other arm. He was holding the Weider Crusher in his hands, and in the background were the waves and the surfboard stuck in the sand.

This photo was the deciding factor and inspired me to become a bodybuilder.

I looked at that picture, and it was like, "God! I don't believe this." **It was an incredible transformational moment which changed my life forever**.

That photo just motivated me and inspired me and said something to me –

about the physicality of California, about lifting weights and having muscles of iron. I was just totally moved by that; it was like becoming a priest, having a calling from God at that young age. That's what I had to do with my life. I knew that at the time. In fact, **when I was 11, I was dead set on becoming Mr. Universe. And I knew it was going to happen; I had rehearsed it many, many times in my own mind.**

On the facing page of the magazine I remember a picture of Arnold drinking protein out of a blender, and it was almost like his biceps were hanging out when he was doing that. I showed both of those pictures to my dad and I said, "That's what I want to do for a living." Somehow I fully expected money to be involved in the sport, although there wasn't at that time. I was assuming there would be business opportunity in bodybuilding, and eventually there was for me many years later.

IM: So you actually started training when?

TP: When I **was 9 ½.**

IM: And what was the nature of your training at that time? Did you actually do a full training routine?

TP: When I was 9 ½, I can remember doing bench presses on the cellar floor after dinner. My father would take my brother and sister and myself downstairs to the basement, to the cellar – they have cellars back East – and I would lay on the floor, and he would read the Weider instructional manual to me.

My brother and sister were just learning to count at that time, and they would learn how to count by counting my reps. I remember my elbows would always hit the cement floor, and I couldn't figure out how to do this thing called the bench press. It seemed like such a stupid exercise, and I couldn't figure out why it wasn't working right (laughs). Later I learned that there was such a thing as a bench you could lay on so your elbows could go below the level of the bench and you could do the exercise properly.
I also did curls. You know, I did just the very, very basics – just learning what the muscles were, learning what the exercises were and how they could be applied, learning the **very basics of human movement or kinesiology applied to bodybuilding.**

As Mr. Universe, Arnold brought down the house with his 21½-inch arms... the most massively-muscular ever seen!

Towel tug o' war between Arnold and John Maldonado before contest helps blow up the biceps, delts and pecs.

Joe Weider warmly congratulates Arnold on his brilliant showing, and agrees to supervise his training in California.

Arnold's happiest U.S. discovery was Weider food supplements. Look at the mighty oak gulping down a stein of Super-Pro 101!

IM: and did you do some work for the legs at that time as well?

TP: No, I never did any leg work back then. I think I tried a couple of sets of squats, but my father wasn't sure how to do squats. And some of the friends I had later on in life up until the age of 15 told me that squats weren't good for you, that they would make your butt big or they were bad for your back.

*I also had a back problem when I was a child – I was born with some kind of deformity in my lower back where something wasn't fused together. Squats bothered it, so I didn't squat, but I continued to do upper-body exercises at that time.**

Author's Note

Can you imagine that this guy had a lower back deformity as a youngster?!?

IM: I take it your father wasn't really an experienced person with weights or athletics.

TP: No, he wasn't. You know, he was very much a military person, very much a corporate executive, and he wasn't an athlete. But he was able to lift the entire bar over his head, which was 135 pounds at that time, all the weights that I had, and I was completely mesmerized by that act (laughs).

IM: When did you adopt a more formal training program, and when did you actually start training your legs?

TP: When we moved to Kansas City, I was (pauses), well, I was always big for my age. I was a big kid. I think at age 15 I was like 165 pounds. I was training and I had a big chest, and I always looked like I trained. I drove my motorcycle down to the health spa, and I applied for a position as an instructor.

I was very young at that time – in fact, too young to legally be employed. And I think the manager of that particular health spa, which was called the European Health Spa, sensed a great deal of passion and excitement in my voice for the practice of weight training, and he hired me!

He hired me at age 15, and I was able to drive my motorcycle down each day to the plaza to work after school, to instruct people.

I think the manager probably felt that my excitement and passion for weight training would be a useful tool in obtaining or signing up future members. Which it was! I was really into bodybuilding and excited about it, and I would talk about it to new people coming into the gym. Bodybuilding was a passion of mine, and that passion translated into gross sales.

I worked there, I think, for a couple of years – from age 15 to 16 or 17.

And **I just started doing squats because there were a couple of serious lifters there and somebody showed me how to do squats. I tried it one day; my first workout was 95 pounds for what felt like a very hard set of 10. I really didn't like the exercise that much.** I mean, I sort of just did it to do it. I did three sets of 10 eventually just because it was leg day supposedly, and leg day was my 15 minute workout, whereas chest and back and arms were my big days. **Legs were trivial. That was my attitude.**

IM: So at age 15 you started doing leg work for the first time, and the workout would consist simply of squats?

TP: Yes, 95 pounds – never more than 105 pounds – for sets of 10.

IM: How long did you actually stay with this one-exercise beginner routine?

TP: Well, I trained for about two years like that – just sort of making my leg day an easy day. I think I did some abs that same day and some other things. It was a day I would go into the gym more or less to recuperate and to talk to some of my friends, never really applying the energy necessary to legs that I did to other body parts. In fact, **I was known in high school as having, you know, twig legs and a huge upper body.**

IM: That's rather surprising. Most people who know about your bodybuilding accomplishments might just assume that you started working legs right from the very beginning and your leg development just took off.

TP: No, it was completely the opposite. In fact, a lot of my high school buddies would say to me years later, "Oh, my God, in high school you never had legs. In fact you were known for having skinny legs."

It wasn't until we moved to Detroit and I went to a place called Armento's Gym, which is still there, that I really got into leg training.

I think I was in the 12th grade, and there were a lot of serious Olympic lifters in that gym. In Detroit it seemed everyone worked for the automobile industry. Just like everyone in Los Angeles seems to work for the studios or on films or production of some kind, everyone in Detroit works for GM or Ford (laughs). And a lot of the people who were working at those car factories were very serious lifters. **Norb Schemansky**, the **famous Olympic weightlifter**, used to train at Armento's Gym. A lot of his students, a lot of his training partners were my initial teachers for the squat. And there's another guy from Michigan State, Freddie Lowe, who inspired me to squat. He was a great Olympic lifter.

When you've been taught to squat by an Olympic lifter, it's a very serious thing. I mean the **bar real high** on your neck. You know, the very strict squat performance – **our butt touching the ground. They taught me to develop ankle flexibility, which was a prerequisite to being a great squatter.** And I did what they told me. You know, I was a young kid – maybe 165 pounds – and these guys were 240 to 300 pounds. I was like, "Whatever you say, I'll do" (chuckles). And they showed me how to squat. I think they saw that **I had the genetic predisposition for leg strength or leg size**. And as they showed me and planned my workouts for me, I gained strength and size very rapidly.

They would actually write my workouts up for me, these Olympic lifters. Especially one guy – his name was Bob Morris – who would really work with me. He would put the weight on the bar for me, him and his partners. **They wouldn't let me leave the gym until I adequately squatted and met all their requirements according to proper squatting protocol**. Being a 16 or 17 year old kid, I was very inspired.

So, rather than adopting bad form, **I adopted perfect form**. And since I had the genetic predisposition for squatting ability – such as a high degree of ankle flexion, low center of gravity, and correct muscle attachment sites for the necessary and proper kinesiological function in relation to my anatomical structure – well, they noticed all those things. And they would actually tell me what to do, when, how much to do, how many reps to do, and they were often amazed! Because at the end of the workout once a week they would say to me, "Well, Tom, now that you did your heavy weights, I want you to do a set of 10 with a lighter weight.

Just a warm down set." **So we'd sometimes put 310 or 315 pounds on the bar to warm down with – this is when I'd been squatting for a few years; this wasn't the first day – and rather than doing 10 reps, I'd do like 25 or 30. And, you know, they were blown away by the reps I could do with heavy weights.**

They taught me how to squat very strict and very true to the Olympic style. They would not allow me to train like a powerlifter or to squat like a powerlifter. Nor did I want to.

IM: For people who aren't familiar with the respective techniques here, what's the difference between powerlifting and Olympic squatting?

TP: **In powerlifting squatting the bar is real low on your back, and you use your butt and your lower back almost exclusively.** Your legs are just a leverage piece of equipment basically (laughs). The stress isn't on your legs – well, it is to some degree. But you're using your butt and your lower back to push yourself up. And the **angle at which you squat is sort of a forward lean rather than an up-and-down angle.**

The upper body is leaning forward, your knees stay in front of your toes.
In Olympic squatting your knees are in front of your toes, the bar is very high on your back, and you go down to the point where your butt is touching the ground or your heels.
Olympic-squatting technique is more of a straight up-and-down movement in which the stress is directly on the quadriceps. If you think about it, **in bodybuilding you try to make the exercise as hard as you can make it. It's: How hard can you make the exercise and how productive can you make the muscle response in reference to that?**
In powerlifting the objective is: How easy can you make the exercise so that you can lift the most weight? Powerlifting is not an easy sport, not by any means, but the point of it is:

 How do you get the most weight up and establish the best possible leverage, whereas in bodybuilding the objective is to make the exercise hard. I liked Olympic lifting for that strict protocol involved. And every Olympic lifter knew that I had great leg development.
In fact, bodybuilders back then never squatted. I first came out to L.A. in '77, and the squat rack at Gold's Gym was way in the back behind all the old equipment. Nobody ever used it. **The bodybuilders were all doing leg extensions, hack squats and lunges.**
I came out to Los Angeles, started doing squats, and people were going, "**What is he doing? Is he crazy? It makes your waist big. It makes your butt big.**" But after a while that all died down, and I like to think that I was somewhat instrumental in making the squat a popular exercise to train legs again. A lot of the guys joined in with me.

IM: When you lived in Detroit, were you still doing only one exercise?

TP: Well, I would do squats with the Olympic lifters, but I was fascinated by this one bodybuilder whose name was Farrel. That was his first name; I don't even know what his last name was. He trained in the Detroit gym – Armento's Gym – and he was a thin guy, a little thin bodybuilder, but he had tremendous leg separation and tremendous leg shape; more so than the Olympic lifters. Not the same size, not the same denseness and quality of musculature that the Olympic lifters had. But he had tremendous shape and tremendous separation, which I wanted to have in addition to the size of the Olympic lifters.

So I watched him train, and he taught me how to do **hack squats** – how to put my heels together. The platform that we had back then was just an itty-bitty platform, and, you know, you **had to put your heels close together.** But he taught me to put my heels close together and point my feet out like a duck. And **his theory was it would develop the lateral section of your thigh, which it did – and it does!**
So we did hack squats on both of my squat days back then. I would go, oh, usually about five sets. I would generally work up in weight as a warm up, and then I'd work down.

But **this became my second most useful exercise in leg development.**

IM: And how long did you stay with that routine?

TP: Well, my late high school days and all through my college days I stayed with that routine. In fact, I even followed that routine up to my competitive years, and **I really didn't start doing leg extensions until before a contest.**

IM*: So squats and hack squats were the combination that laid the foundation for your thigh development.*

TP: **<u>Absolutely. Beyond any question</u>**.*

Author's Note

Imagine that!!

IM: Can we get an idea here of the sets and reps and the kinds of weights you were handling? I take it the weights you were using gradually increased with time.

TP: Well, I can remember training through various weight barriers during the course of the years. **I can remember the first time I did 315 for reps in the squat – three plates on each side. It was a big accomplishment.** I mean, that's what the big guys did, and I was able to do that for a set of three to four reps. I was totally mesmerized and excited and passionate about the exercise. It felt perfect – **it felt like a piston inside a cylinder. That's the way I sort of visualized myself doing the exercise.***

Author's Note

Tom plays some mind games on himself... fascinating stuff!

I developed little techniques back then – like wearing high socks. If I wore high socks, I would look shorter in the mirror. And if you're real short, you don't have that far down to go. At least that's what the mind perceives.

So I developed these little mental strategies to really train myself to handle bigger weights. Nobody taught me; I just developed those things on my own.

The Olympic lifters also taught me things like looking up high, looking at an imaginary spot on the wall or the ceiling to allow you to perform perfect squats. And I have my own little things that I worked in there as far as mental training was concerned, but now I'm getting away from the question you asked me.

You wanted to know about reps and sets and weights I was using. Like I was saying, I hit various barriers at different times. I remember doing 405 for the first time in my career. I remember doing 505 for the first time in my career. And so on. I mean, **505 for 15 reps was a tremendous accomplishment for me.**

But back then, during the early days of the intermediate stage of my leg training, 315 for two or three reps was a normal heavy day for me in the squat. And I would never do more than 10 sets of squats, counting the warm ups.

Here's the way I set up my leg training. **One day would be my heavy day in the squat.**

That heavy day would consist of anywhere from doubles, two reps, up to, say, six reps, maybe as high as eight. Two to eight reps would be a heavy day; depending upon how I was structuring my training at that particular time – whether I was peaking to handle heavy weights or just training prior to that point.

Then in **my other squat workout for the week I would train for reps**. On the rep day I would do **two sets of reps only**. I did that because it felt right at that time. It just felt right for me. In fact, the Olympic lifters had a similar program where they would lift various percentages on different days. And I followed suit according to their protocols and their training strategies.

On the rep day the reps would be somewhat higher, obviously. (Usually between 15 and 20.)

IM: And you said you did only two sets on the rep day?

TP: Only two sets. But when I say two sets, I'm not counting the two or three warm ups. And when I say 10 sets on the heavy day, I'm including the four or five warm ups I would do to get to the heavier weights.

IM: And on the heavy day you would always, I take it, strive to move up to a heavier and heavier weight as time passed.

TP: Each workout I'd add five pounds to the bar on each side. I would start low enough in my training cycle so I could add two five pound plates to the bar each time. I wanted to add five pounds to each side if I could every workout on my heavy day. And a lot of times I was able to do that for a prolonged period of time.

IM: And you were also doing hack squats?

TP: Hack squats were done directly after the squat sessions.

IM: What was the sets-and-reps format with the hack squats?

TP: Usually I would warm up a little bit to get up to a heavy weight – maybe five 25's on each side – and then I would work down. It was a very difficult, old-fashioned hack squat machine. It wasn't very smooth at all. In fact, it was rusted, and it wouldn't slide very well.

One hundred pounds was like 500 pounds (laughs). **I trained in the dungeons in those days the old-fashioned, YMCA-style dungeons with no windows. And those are the gyms I loved and enjoyed.** In fact, I can tell you stories about that, too, but I won't.

Anyway, in the hack squat I'd start out by putting a plate on each side, two plates on each side, three plates on each side. Then I'd put five plates on each side and start my way down.

IM: How many sets would you typically do?

TP: Usually five sets, not including the warm up sets. And the reps would be somewhere between six and eight. I'd perhaps work down from maybe 500 pounds to a light weight.

IM: Were you doing low reps on the warm up sets in both squats and hack squats?

TP: I'd push maybe 10 reps, just to warm up.

IM: With something fairly light?

TP: Sure. But progressive enough to allow me to graduate to a heavier set, to a heavier weight the next set.

IM: Why were you working your way down in weight in the hack squats consistently like that?

TP: Well, I've trained all my life on instinct. **Fred Hatfield** watched me years later and said I was obviously much schooled in the acquisition of muscle and in muscle physiology. And I said to him, "Fred, I just do what feels right" (laughs). I was always the kind of bodybuilder who really followed his instincts – and my instincts led me to do things that were correct as far as muscle growth was concerned and what was effective specific to my body type and my fiber type.

IM: So this intermediate routine you've just described was what you followed until you started competing in bodybuilding contests?

TP: Yes, I'd say I followed this program for about four or five years – from age 17 to about 21 or 22. **I started competing as a powerlifter originally.** My first bodybuilding contest was in about 1973, so I actually started competing while I was still doing this intermediate routine. In fact, I stayed with this routine right up till the time I moved to California, in 1977. By that time I had already won the Mr. Michigan title at age 19, finished second in the Teenage Mr. America and placed high in the Mr. America contest. So I competed in quite a few contests while I was still on this routine, although I didn't compete that often, because I was busy studying for exams and working full-time as well – usually as a gym instructor and selling memberships. Then, after I moved to California, I switched to what you could call my advanced leg routine.

IM: Given the awesome leg development you ultimately achieved, something rather dramatic must have started happening immediately after you got into serious leg work.

TP: **It became almost a special sport to me – a different sport from bodybuilding. The squat rack became like the altar, where life and death would pass in front of your eyes, and you looked forward to that every squat workout.**

IM: So this was really, really tough training you were doing.

TP: Very tough, but I responded very well to very hard training, and I became motivated to train harder because the harder I trained, the more strength and leg development I attained. So it was like, "God, how hard can I train? How much do I want to grow?"

IM: You started your bodybuilding career and progressed to the national level when you were lifting back east. When did you move to California?

TP: In 1977 for the Mr. America contest, but I came out here to live in '78.

IM: At that point what contests had you won?

TP: Mr. Michigan. I had been second in the Teenage Mr. America . . . I competed in the Mr. America in '76, '77 and '78. and I never did win the Mr. America, although I won Best Legs almost all the time when they had that category. I usually came in first or second in my class – the Short Class back then. **Ron Teufel** was my biggest rival.

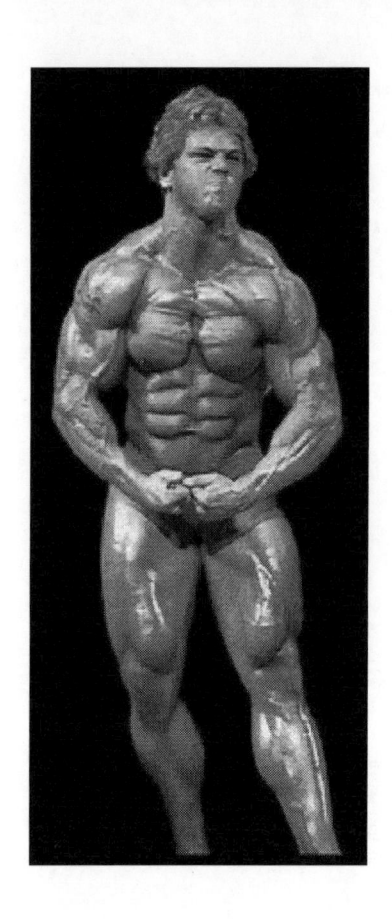

Ron Teufel

Prior to the '78 America, which was my last Mr. America, I trained a lot more to balance my upper body to my lower body because my legs had begun to over-shadow my upper body, and I almost won the America, but **Tony Pearson** was picked as the winner. Ten minutes later the judging panel changed, and we had the Mr. America pose-down to select who was going to go to the Universe to represent the United States. And I was able to win the Mr. America pose-down, beating Tony Pearson 10 minutes after he won the Mr. America.

IM: What would you say was the most significant change you made in your leg training when you moved to California?

TP: I trained my legs less frequently and no longer consistently did the low-rep workouts with maximal weights in the squat. So I trained less frequently and was able to up the intensity, but I did that by doing higher reps while still using heavy weights. And the less I emphasized leg training in terms of training frequency and doing low reps with maximal weights, the more vascular, the more separated, the more detailed and the more polished my legs became.
So starting in '78 I focused on not doing the real heavy leg work that I did previously, although I would still go heavy. I mean. back then I was still able to put 495 on the bar and do 15 reps in the squat. But I would concentrate on reps – I started concentrating more on reps, rather than maximum weight, in my leg training after '78.

IM: You said that in your intermediate routine, you would perhaps do 495 to 500 pounds for two or three reps in the squat.

TP: Right. That was intermediate. That was probably the best I could do during the intermediate stage.

IM: But later you were actually capable of doing 495 for something like 15 reps?

TP: Yeah All of a sudden I came out to California, and, you know, I walk in the gym in the morning, the sunlight was shooting in the gym, **Robby Robinson** was over in the corner doin' those little baby presses he does with a tiny barbell, lookin' unbelievable! You know, muscles hangin' out of his shirt. All those other big-name bodybuilders were there – **Arnold, Franco, Ken Waller, Danny Padilla**. And I was just so inspired and pumped up, it's like energy came from within. And pretty soon I was able to take a weight which was a very heavy double or triple during my intermediate days, and now I was able to do reps with that – 15 reps. It was unbelievable!

IM: You're saying that the ambience had such a dramatic effect on your strength, endurance and performance?

TP: Oh, yeah! And it still does. First of all, **there's energy here**. I knew I was supposed to be here before I moved out here. I somehow knew that it was my destiny. I love passion. I love excitement. I love feeling good about stuff and being plugged in. I love feeling in tune and in line and centered in that sense.

California gives that to me on a continual basis, and I was smacked in the face with it back in 1977 when I came here. I came out to California, walked in Gold's Gym and World Gym, and it was like – Wow! This is where I wanna be! I could just touch a weight and grow! **I was around the best in the world on a daily basis, rather than just reading about these characters.**

Author's note:

Perhaps this is also true of the Westside power club; just the atmosphere there with so many awesome lifters is very inspiring. I have always enjoyed lifting with or at least around guys that blew me away, lifting among your peers or being the strongest in a crowd does not get one jacked up to train harder.

Here I was training with Danny Padilla, Arnold, Robby Robinson, Dave Draper – I mean, it was extraordinarily energizing. Whether they knew it or not, **I just picked up on their energy.**

Danny Padilla

Robby Robinson

IM: So perhaps it was comparable to a baseball player reaching the major leagues after playing in the minors? Or playing in Yankee Stadium for the first time?

TP: There you go. To me it felt like, Oh, this is the epitome of what I've been thinking about all those years when it was snowing back in Detroit and I was training in the dungeons back there. I wanted to be in California, I knew I was supposed to be there, I could just smell success and taste success. Every weekend someone from the gym was winning a contest. And I just thought, "Well, my turn is coming up," and it sure as hell did, as you know.

IM: After moving to California, you did squats, hack squats and what other exercises for your legs?

TP: I would usually only add leg extensions before a contest. But as I developed more of an advanced routine, I decided I was only going to train legs once a week. I was trying to de-emphasize my leg girth, if you will, and put more energy into my upper body. **In fact, I squatted every other week – only twice a month – and I got progressively stronger in the squat, which was almost mind-boggling, scary. It's a mystery to me, and to most of my training partners to this day how that happened.**
As I began squatting twice a month, I would do reps on both days usually, instead of doing one heavy workout and one rep workout, as I was doing during the intermediate phase. And on the other leg day I would do leg extensions – my own specialized version – and hack squats. I also began using Nautilus machines for the first time on the leg curl.
During the advanced routine the workload was cut dramatically, but the intensity was increased in almost the same proportion. Consequently, the intensity went to the point where I could actually feel a muscle begin to tear from the bone, and I'd quit the set.

I was able to take intensity that far – you know, I was careful not to injure myself. I needed more recuperation time. Because the intensity level was so increased and at such a high level, I couldn't recuperate that fast. I couldn't squat and train legs every week or twice a week. And I developed that kind of attitude and understanding about my leg training.
During the height of my career as a far as the advanced level was concerned, **I did 635 for 15 below-parallel reps in the squat prior to the '86 Mr. Olympia. I mean, 15 perfect reps.**

IM: Wow!

TP: That was only weeks before a contest mind you. So I really wasn't training for strength at that time at all. But my ability and endurance factor went way up, my intensity went way up to the point where I can remember lying on the floor after a set of squats feeling like somebody was stabbing knives in my legs. It was extremely painful, but I always had a high pain threshold – or I probably should say I developed a high pain threshold over the years.
But again, the focus in my advanced leg training was not on workload; it was on intensity and on isolation and on instinct.

IM: So even though your thigh development had reached a maximum perhaps as far as sheer size or girth by the end of the intermediate phase of training, your leg training during the advanced stage was even more demanding. **You really took it to the outer limits.**

TP: Oh, yeah. Absolutely. I would go further than I ever had in the past. Sometimes after a set of rep-squats during the advanced routine I would lie on the floor gasping for air, and I would think to myself: Jeez, what if I don't make it back? What if I don't recover from this tremendous oxygen debt I'm in right now? And I knew I always would, but sometimes I felt like, my God, I could have a heart attack.

But to me it's like **I had to function within that red zone** – like a Porsche has to function at the higher RPMs. For me, to attain the higher, freaky levels of extreme leg development, I had to explore the realm of risk. And risk to me is associated with any successful venture.

Especially with exploration – where someone has never gone before.

IM: You never injured yourself?

TP: Oh, I injured little things here and there as far as the legs were concerned. I have torn my fascia, a thin sheath which covers the muscle underneath the skin, and I had to train around that. I have torn that numerous times. But I never tore a muscle, no, I may have you know, slightly jarred a little muscle in my leg biceps once, but never to the point where it was permanently damaged.

IM: You said earlier that you did leg extensions only before a contest. How long before a contest and why just before a contest?

TP: Well, I felt that by squatting continually, I was encouraging leg growth. The muscles were becoming larger; however, I could not produce the desired muscle separation and definition just by squatting. So I found that by not squatting for a number of weeks or even a couple of months, especially prior to a bodybuilding event, I could make my legs become much more refined, much more polished. You could see muscles you didn't you didn't see before. Of course, you have to squat to get there with your overall leg development, but I would conclude squatting anywhere from two weeks to two months prior to an event.

IM: And just do leg extensions?

TP: That would be about it, yeah. Sometimes hack squats but not usually.

IM: And this is the routine that you stayed with really for the rest of your competitive career until you . . .

TP: (finishes) **Retired from competition in '86, right.**

IM: Now let's get to the specifics. With squats, for instance, how many sets would you typically do?

TP: Let's take one month as an example. There are four weeks in a month. The first week and the third week I would do squats. And I would go into the gym on the first and the third week on a predetermined leg day, okay? And I would go in relying on my instincts really – I mean, I wouldn't go in to train with any specific weights, I would just do what felt right for that day. At one point that was, you know, 635 for 15 below-parallel reps. Other times it was **495 for 25 or even 30 reps. You know, I never counted reps – my partners usually did.**
But I would usually only do about two sets that we counted. I would work up in weight – I mean, to get to 495, obviously I wouldn't just come in the gym and put 495 on the bar. I'd do like 135 for a set of 15 reps, 225 for a set of 10, 315 for a set of 10, 405 for a set of five or six reps and then eventually 495. So it took me four sets to get to that one rep-set. And then after the rep-set I'd usually do another rep-set, which was four, five, six sets total.
But on the two rep-sets the attitude that I had back then was that my life had to pass in front of my eyes. I wanted to climb to that point.

And if I couldn't get to that point, I was disappointed and frustrated and extremely angry at myself, and I would make sure I got to that point every squat workout.
When I say your life passed before in front of your eyes, I mean you go to the point here you get 10 reps and then somehow you manage to get 15 or 20.

It's just conjuring up the deep-rooted emotions and the passion and the energy that you have within your body and your soul and your mind to push the weight up one more time and one more time and one more time. It's very demanding to so that with heavy weights, but I would endeavor to get to that point.

Author's note:

It seems as if Tom was the ultimate practitioner of the 20 rep squat concept started way back in the Mark Berry days, but took it even farther than any of those guys had

IM: That's hardcore stuff.

TP: I don't mean to be painting a picture that's not real – to me this was very real.

And to go to the gym that morning would be a very scary thing. **I'd be shaking going to the gym.** And I'd get there and **my heart was pounding**, I could barely breath normally. Sometimes I would concentrate on slowing my heart rate down and just try to relax. But once the workout was over, once I accommodated my expectancy and got to that point and went through a workout like that, I felt fulfilled. I had my training partner tell me about it because usually I wasn't aware of what was goin' on; it would be almost like I went somewhere. I went somewhere to like a special place. I explored a terrain or a feeling or a style of training that was never done before, and that's what I wanted to do.

IM: **It sounds like the intensity that you were generating was in a class by itself.**

TP: Well, I don't want to say that no one else is capable of that. I'm sure there are people who can do that and there are people who can do that now. I just want to say that that's what I was doing back then, and that's what was most important to me back then. And **it took me a lot of years to develop that kind of intensity**. It wasn't something that I read about in a bodybuilding magazine and just started doing right from the outset.

You know, I wasn't capable of actually pushing my body and my mind that far at the beginning of my career. It took 15 years for my body to be trained to that point, for my nervous system to really be trained to that point. **I mean, after a squat set like that, I can remember my back bleeding.**

The bar was real heavy and I think I had a heavy scab on my back from squatting previously and the scab broke open. I remember blood going down the shirt. I mean, it's crazy stuff we did, but was just the feeling . . .

And one time at Armento's Gym back in Detroit when I was doing an intermediate workout, I remember my nose started bleeding – there was blood all over the place – **but I kept on squatting.**

IM: Was the actual technique you used – i.e., the strict, up-and-down Olympic style of squatting – a major factor in the awesome leg development you achieved: As opposed to, say, if you'd been using the less strict, forward-leaning powerlifting-squat technique?

TP: I did use the straight, up-and-down, Olympic-style technique. I was taught how to squat by Olympic lifters and I definitely feel that my thigh development was achieved through the practice of strict, high-bar Olympic squats, not – repeat, NOT – powerlifting style.

I've tried to squat like a powerlifter on occasion just to find out what it was all about, to educate myself along the lines of that performance pattern. And there's definitely a lot more butt and lower back involvement in the movement.

Let me put it this way, powerlifting to me is like football, and what we do in bodybuilding is, we play basketball. In other words, they're two entirely different sports. And using the powerlifting squat style, in my mind, would never be conducive to developing great thighs, because the legs don't really come into play. In a power squat my back and my butt work substantially, and my legs just seem to be there for leverage.

IM: Obviously you would recommend that a bodybuilder adopt the strict, Olympic-style technique of squatting.

TP: Yes, beyond any shadow of a doubt.

I wholeheartedly suggest and encourage anybody reading this article to do high-bar, Olympic style squats.

IM: High-bar – in other words, with the bar high on your back?

TP: Yes. And not to squat like a powerlifter but to squat like an Olympic lifter. Or should I say squat like a bodybuilder, putting all the stress on the thighs.

Occasionally, I would walk in the gym and, you know, my instinct led me to do something different besides just the two rep-sets of squats. I can remember going into the gym occasionally on a squat day, and I would do, say, 585 for a set of 10, okay? And maybe squeeze out 12. Lower the weight to 495 and get as many reps as I could. Sometimes 25 to 30 reps. Lower the weight to 405 and get as many reps as I could – sometimes another 30. Lower the weight again after, you know, maybe four or five minutes rest, and with 315 do as many reps as I could. Lower the weight again to 225, **do reps until I couldn't move.** Finish up with 135 – I was barely able to stand up. That was one example of one workout I did.

But in doing squats that intensely, followed by leg curls and then calf work – I always finished every leg workout by training calves – **I couldn't even think about coming back in the gym and training legs for another 10 to 12 days.**

IM: You explained that you worked on the squat the first and third week of the month. I take it on the second and fourth week you did hack squats?

TP: Hack squats and leg extensions – and leg curls. Well, let me revamp that. On the squat day, after the squat workout I was usually so fatigued, I couldn't do hack squats.

I couldn't do leg extensions either. So I'd do some leg curls on the squat days. And for me to get on the old Nautilus leg curl machine and have my training partner give me negatives, isometrics, forced reps, positives, partial isometrics – my leg biceps would grow like crazy. The squat was elemental to my leg biceps growing as well. But the Nautilus leg curl machine, I could look at that machine and my leg biceps would grow. It was unbelievable.

IM: Could you explain what you meant when you said that the squat was elemental to your leg biceps growth?

TP: I'm saying there was a lot of influence to the leg biceps in doing the squat. What I'm getting at is that the strict, Olympic-style squat has been conducive to my total leg development, including the development of my calves and leg biceps.

There's definitely an influence on the leg biceps when you're squatting, especially at the depth to which I squat, so my butt almost touches the floor, okay? But without even addressing that point, there is some influence to your hamstring muscles as you flex the frontal-thigh muscles, or quadriceps. You can't bend down without getting some leg biceps involvement.

IM: Of course, to really work the hamstrings, or leg biceps, directly, you would do leg curls.

TP: Right. I would do that after squats on my advanced-level squat days. And on the leg curls you're looking at four to six sets.

IM: What number of reps?

TP: Reps were anywhere from seven to 20. But I might be doing the whole stack on one set and only five plates the next set. I was using a lot of techniques to make the exercise much harder. One set of leg curls would always include positives. One set would always include negatives. One set would always include forced negatives. One set would always include isometrics – someone holding down on the machine until I couldn't pull anymore. I'd train midrange, low range, the high range. I'd have someone actually push against the weight and give me extra resistance at different positions in the range of motion.
It wasn't just a matter of doing sets and reps. It was like making the muscle scream for mercy Leg curls were always performed in this way.
I would do the leg extensions on the leg extension machine Joe Gold had designed. Have you seen the old-fashioned one, the one in the middle room at Gold's Gym, Venice? I would start with reps, or course, and I would just do the extensions very slowly and very precisely – all the way up as high as I could and then lower it slowly.
But I was fortunate enough to be able to do leg extensions on this machine.

Joe Gold made this first machine. To me, it's still the best leg extension machine that exists to this point in time. I used it the other day, and my legs immediately felt a response. There's no leg extension machine in my opinion which comes close to Joe Gold's original creation. I mean, Arnold's fingerprints and Dave Draper's handprints are on this thing, okay?

So I would do leg extensions, usually about an hour. I didn't count the number, but it was usually an hour of sets. Sometimes 10, 20, 30 sets, where I would employ forced reps, isometrics, negatives, the same things I did in the leg curl. I had my old training partner Tony Martino stand in front of me and push the machine down and take it to different ranges of motion. I other words, I'd go to the top if the motion, and I'd say "Okay, now push!" and he'd push down as hard as he could and I'd fight back. I'd say, "Take it to the middle range," and he'd push down halfway in the middle range. Then we'd take it to the low range. I'd yell to him what to do as my instincts told me.

And this leg extension machine became one of the best leg exercises I ever did – and still do. I'm getting excited just thinking about it (laughs).

IM: And after the leg extensions, you moved to the hack squat.

TP: Yes, the hack squat. Usually at that time I was barely able to stand up; I was pretty well blitzed. So I'd have my partner take me through the range of motion in the hack squats. I would usually only do about three sets, with maybe two 45s on each side, and he would push me through the entire range to accomplish maybe 20 to 25 reps. But I would stand on my toes and push my hips forward, much like a sissy squat, sort of a sissy hack squat. And I would do that very strictly and intensively to gather . . . well, I always imagined that I was swimming in the ocean, looking for more and more fish, and I had to gather up as many fish as I could. That was a visualization I used. You know, I had to keep grabbing more and more fish, and pretty soon there weren't any fish left.

This vision was very important to me; it helped me train harder. Okay, when I first started the leg extensions, there were a lot of fish there, there was a lot of contractile strength there. As the contractile strength became less and less and less, it became harder to contract the muscle, and in my mind there were fewer and fewer fish left.

So as I went to the hack squats, you know, there were only a few fish left, and I could hardly contract the muscle at all at that point. In an effort to contract the muscle I had to have a training partner push me through the range of motion. Actually push the machine up and down to allow me to keep the muscle contracting. And he would take me to an even higher level of contraction at that point.

IM: So essentially you were doing forced reps in the hack squat.

TP: Exactly. And I wouldn't stop until I felt that one more rep would tear the muscle from the bone. And at that point I would yell, "That's it!"

IM: Again, how many reps and sets would you do on the hack squats?

TP: Three sets – roughly. Maybe 20 to 30 reps, and sometimes pausing. I'd finish the exercise, and I'd go halfway down and just pause – stay there without moving up or down. Or just move slightly. And have my partner help me do that.
The reps and the weights didn't really matter – although on the leg extension machine I'd have a 100-pound plate placed on top of the stack. I mean, as much weight as I could possibly put on the machine would be on the machine.

IM: So obviously you were very, very strong in these exercises.

TP: Yes, but to me it got to the point where I really wasn't concerned with reps or sets. I was concerned with contracting the muscle, and this fish visualization is something I made up in my own mind to help me contract the muscle. I had to become the muscle. My job was to grow. Any way I could put tension on the muscle, whether it be no reps, holding the weight at the top or the bottom of halfway, or anything to make the muscle respond and achieve more tension within the muscle, I would do.

IM: If you'd been pushed at the time to do one rep in a powerlifting squat, what do you think would have been your maximum?

TP: Well, I'd say with a little bit of training for a maximum lift I probably could have squatted just under a grand. And I wasn't really trained as a strength athlete. Although I did train with **Fred Hatfield last year, and I was able to do – what did I do? Eight plates (775 pounds) for a single. However, back then, if we're looking at those years, '85 to '86, I think realistically 800 to 900 pounds would have been a predictable single. With some training specificity.**

While it's on my mind, let me explain that sometimes I would not do leg extensions first or I would do hack squats first. In fact, I'd usually mix it up according to my instinct. In some workouts I'd go on the hack squat machine first, and I would start with some warm-up sets.

I can remember doing reps and sets and partials and isometrics and half-reps, with my partner there helping me, to the point where I'd actually go somewhere. **My mind would leave the gym.**
It was a strange experience. But the reps were always quite high and the weights were very heavy. At that point I was able to put five 45 pound plates on each side and do 30 or 40 reps.

IM: The sheer mental and physical intensity that you established in your leg work, did this idea also carry over to your training for the other body parts?

TP: It sure did. I usually trained each bodypart like that. It was a lot of stress, a lot of mental stress, but it was something that I enjoyed; however, by '86 I had to cut back and retire because I couldn't withstand the stress anymore. I mean, taking your body and pushing it that hard on a daily basis for, jeez, I don't know how many years that was, almost 10 years as a pro – there was a time when you wanted to explore other realms of life and living. It ultimately becomes counterproductive to put that much stress on your nervous system. I think the hardest thing about training that hard is your nervous system has to recover all the time. And it's very difficult to continue to do that for years on end. But that's how I trained, and if I had to do it all over again, I wouldn't do it any differently.

IM: Many bodybuilders believe in doing a tremendous variety of exercises, the idea being to hit a muscle from every conceivable angle. **Yet in your case you basically built those unbelievable thighs with only three exercises**. What is your philosophy on this point?

TP: Throughout my **career my training has always been centered on very few exercises**. But rather than change the exercises to accommodate different degrees of stress development or tension development, I would change the way I performed each exercise. One day I would do reps, one day I would do heavier weights. I could change the way I was holding the weights in my hands or the way I was squatting. I could change the position.

There are a lot of things you can do with one exercise that can make it like 15 exercises.
That's something people don't usually relate to.

They'd rather change the exercise. And sometimes it's more fun, depending upon your personality, to change the exercise rather than changing the technique or the style or the way in which you perform the exercise.

IM: In other words, there are really an endless number of variables in how you can do a given exercise.

TP: Exactly. The speed of the motion may change. Or the exact way you push the weight, turn the dumbbell or stand or that sort of thing.

IM: Is there anything else that we haven't covered here that's really germane to this topic?

TP: I think you've pretty well encapsulated it all in the last couple of questions you've asked me as far as the intensity and instinct being the important factors. But beyond that I have to add one more item – and that would be passion. **Having a clear-cut passion and a need, an innate need to explore that passion. That's what fuels your endeavor.**

What a set of legs!

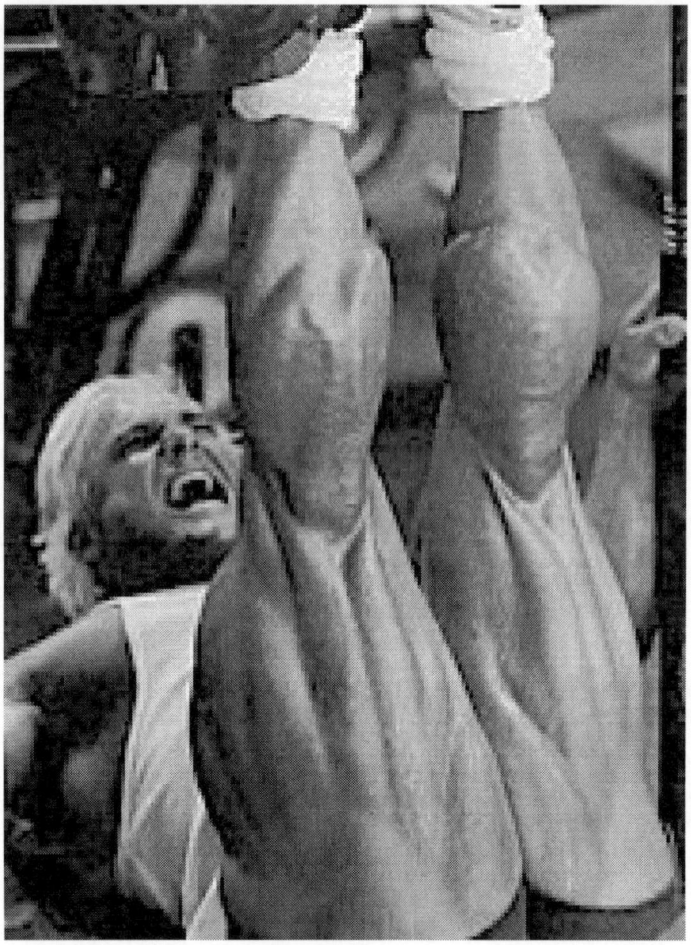

Chapter Twenty
Dr Fred Hatfield

We would certainly be remiss if we did not bring in the expertise and wisdom of the man commonly called "**Dr Squat**", one Mr. **Fred Hatfield.**

A point of interest here is that **Tom Platz and Fred Hatfield once had a little competition between them**, with one part consisting of a certain weight for as many reps as possible, and the other part being who could hit the highest 1 rep max single. Not too surprisingly, Tom beat Fred hands down in the rep department, but of course Fred prevailed in the max effort.

Searching on his very resource rich forum, (found on his website, http://drsquat.com/home) I came across this gem (**I know squat**) by the good dr. himself:

First, let's establish Fred's credentials;

Career Best Lifts	
Squat:	1014 pounds
Bench:	523 pounds
Deadlift:	766 pounds
Total:	2303
Snatch:	275 pounds
Clean and Jerk:	369 pounds
Olympic Lift Total:	645 pounds
Supertotal:	2948

Dr. Frederick C. Hatfield earned his doctorate in philosophy from Temple University with competency examinations taken in sport psychology, motor learning and sport sociology.

Dr. Hatfield is **President of the International Sports Sciences Association (ISSA)**, a major provider of continuing education and a certifying agency for sports training, fitness therapy and personal fitness trainer professionals. Under his direction, Fort Hood (Texas) has implemented an ISSA certifying protocol for the U.S. Army. He is frequently retained by law firms to serve as an expert witness in fitness and sports training-related litigation.

He has provided research and development and marketing consultation to several nutritional and fitness equipment manufacturers and other fitness-related corporations around the world. He has been both a principal in, and consultant to, numerous commercial enterprises involved in fitness, nutrition, publishing and education since 1970, and has been directly involved in establishing and consulting for numerous health and fitness clubs across the U.S. He has taught sports psychology, strength physiology, and physical education at the University of Wisconsin, Newark State College, Bowie State College, Temple University and the University of Illinois.

Early in his career he was cited in "*Who's Who in American Education*," and voted "*Outstanding Young Men in America*." He was a consultant to the U.S. Olympic Committee, the International Federation of Bodybuilders (IFBB), the West German Bodybuilding Federation, Australian Powerlifting Federation, FOX Network and CBS Sports. He was coach three times for the U.S. National Powerlifting team and a member of the executive committees of the U.S. Olympic Weightlifting Federation and U.S. Powerlifting Federation.

The founding editor of Sports Fitness magazine (now Men's Fitness), he has written more than 60 books and over 200 articles on sports fitness, weight training and athletic nutrition. He is a former standout college gymnast, *Mr. Teenage Connecticut, Mr. Atlantic Coast* and *Mr. Mid America* in bodybuilding, Wisconsin and Connecticut weightlifting champion, broken over 30 world records as a powerlifter competing in five different weight divisions, and won the World Championships in powerlifting three times in three different weight divisions.

In 1987, at the age of 45, Hatfield established a world record in the squat at 1014 pounds (255 body weight), the most anyone had ever lifted in the history of competition. His frequent world record-breaking performances have gained him the nickname of "**Dr. Squat**." He remained competitive in Masters Level Olympic Weightlifting until recently, having represented the USA in the 1998 World Masters Games in Oregon. In June of 2000, **Dr. Hatfield was inducted into the Powerlifting Hall of Fame, located in York, PA.**

OK, here is the article mentioned above:

I May Not Know Diddley... But I Know Squat!

by Frederick C. Hatfield, Ph.D., MSS

My youngest son, Beau, has a sign in his room which reads "Beau knows Squat." I like it! 'Course, it's a play off the ol' Bo Jackson thing, but I don't care. I know Beau, and I don't know Bo. And, Bo doesn't know Squat!

Humor me once more. See, I used to be pretty good at squatting. Eleven hundred pounds ain't a bad squat, no? You might say that I too -- ahem -- know squat!

Ok, ok! I'll spare you. Problem is, the doctors don't care, the coaches don't think, the athletes don't have time, the bodybuilders don't want to know, and the sports scientists writing about squatting don't have the in-the-trenches experience to really "know".

And I don't understand. Why someone just doesn't TELL them why **squatting is the one exercise that EVERYONE (bodybuilders, athletes, kids, your Mamma) ought to do.** I tried to do it once back in '85 with an article in Sports Fitness, a magazine that I launched for Joe Weider. That magazine metamorphosed into what is now known as Men's Fitness. In that ten year old article, I wrote about a few myths associated with squatting that seemed persistent back then:

- Squats are bad for the knees.
- Squats are bad for the spine.
- Squats are dangerous to the heart.
- Squats slow you down.

Well, **these four myths, it seems, are still somewhat alive.** However, others have arisen that are even more troublesome. And, you know what? This time, the sources and perpetuators of the myths are from the ranks of several muscle mags!

Well, it's a tough job, but I'm gonna give it my best shot. I'll tackle these myths -- and the old ones -- one by one. You pencil necks out there who disagree with me (anyone who disagrees with me on the issue of squatting has GOTTA be a pencil neck) on these squat issues, do me a favor. Put up or shut up. Let's see some science for a change, not just jabberwocky and claptrap.

And, please! Get this once and for all! Marketing fitness to the masses does NOT have to include making it palatable for the newly initiated by saying things like, "Beginners shouldn't do squats," or any of the other myths listed.

I know better. More importantly, the 42 ladies who participated in a 12 week research project I conducted all LOVED squats. All were chronically obese, 40-70 years old, and none had ever trained before in their lives. My son, Beau -- he's six -- loves to squat. Every athlete I've ever coached squatted and loved the outcomes. How come it is that elite weightlifters, powerlifters and shot putters -- all of whom squat -- vertical jump higher and run a 5 meter dash faster than any other class of athletes in any sport? Including high jumpers and sprinters?

Myth #1: Squats are bad for the knees.

Just as calluses build up on the hands with the application of stress, ligaments, tendons and other connective tissues thicken in response to the stress imposed upon the joints during weight training. Also, strengthening the muscles that move the knee joint improves its stability, and there's some evidence that even the portion of the bone into which the tendons insert becomes stronger, further improving the joint's integrity.

Relaxing the muscles while in a rock-bottom position is improper and hazardous. The relaxed muscles allow the knee joint to separate slightly, placing the ligaments and cartilage under stress that may exceed their tensile strength. While proper stress produces adaptation, overly stressful exercise can cause breakdown of bodily tissue.

Myth #2: Squats are bad for the spine.

If performed with a relatively straight back, the weight is borne directly over the spinal column, and torque as well as shearing force is minimized. Weight training is supposed to strengthen the supportive tissues of the body (bones, muscles and connective tissues). So wear a belt when the weight is heavy and reps are low, but stay away from such supportive devices otherwise.

Beginners often find squats uncomfortable for the neck (the cervical spine) because of the pressure of the bar resting there. You'll get used to it. In the meantime, it doesn't hurt to pad the bar with a towel or piece of rubber. Me? I prefer the padded yolk of the Safety Squat Bar. Ok, so I'm a whimp! I don't like unnecessary discomfort!

Myth #3: Squats are dangerous to the heart.

Many weight-training exercises restrict blood flow because of prolonged muscular contraction. The result is elevated blood pressure. The condition isn't dangerous and it's temporary. The heart, like every other muscle in the body, responds to stress by adapting to it. In time, the cardiovascular system is strengthened through weight training.

Squats can sometimes tax the heart to dangerous limits, however. My blood pressure rocketed to 220 over 130 or more during a set of squats. That can be rough on the ol' ticker if your ticker needs tinkering!

People suffering from coronary disease will find heavy squats more taxing than beneficial. In most cases in which a prior condition existed that would have precluded heavy training, a qualified sports physician could, with careful screening, prevent these kinds of accidents. All athletes as well as fitness enthusiasts who want to train with weights should see a good sports physician before embarking on a stressful training program.

Myth #4: Squats slow you down.

It's well known among exercise physiologists that the stronger the muscle is, the faster it contracts, particularly against resistance. An athlete's running and jumping ability can only be enhanced through the development of great leg strength.

There. That takes care of the old myths that I wrote about a decade ago. Look back, and you'll see that very little has changed in my rebuttals to these early myths. Some science is as good today as it was yesterday.

Here are some of the more recent "opinions" I read and hear about squats. The really funny thing is that many of them contradict one another! At least ten years ago perpetuators of myths were together in their belief that squats were bad for you. Nowadays, there are so many new "chiefs" (self-proclaimed gurus who, in fact, aren't qualified or well informed enough to hold an opinion on much of anything, let alone squatting!) that one wonders where all the Indians went!

New Myth #1: Only powerlifters need to do squats.

There are many forms of squatting, each having unique benefits and applications. The powerlifting style of squatting is the best way to lift limit tonnage. It's also the most dangerous because of the immense shearing forces placed on the lumbar spine. For your information, though, it's only dangerous for those powerlifters who never learned how to periodize their training. The ONLY time I ever did powerlifting style squats was right before a competition (6-8 weeks out). Otherwise, I did several of the other varieties of squats, depending upon where I was in my cycle and what my training objectives were at the time.

Here are the noteworthy variations to the squat movement that have been employed over the years:

SQUATTING VARIATIONS

Name of Technique	Comments	Uses
Powerlifting Squats	wide, intermediate or narrow stance – hip angle acute and knees near 90 degrees place stress on gluteals and hamstrings	ONLY for Powerlifting Competition (too stressful on the low back for other uses)
Olympic Squats	also called "High Bar Squats" or "Bodybuilding Squats" – hip angle near 90 degrees and knee angle acute place stress on quads	ONLY for bodybuilding training (too stressful on the knees for other uses)
Athletic Squats	Angle at hips and knees are equal, placing stress equally on gluteals, hamstrings and quads	If all you have is a bar, it's the best way to squat for most athletes and fitness trainers because stresses on knees and back are minimal (within the safety zone)
Manta Ray Squats	a device is clipped to bar distributing weight evenly across the shoulder girdle	RECOMMENDED if all you have is a bar.
Safety Squats	torque hold bar on shoulders, pads distribute weight across shoulder girdle	BEST way to squat for most athletes and fitness buffs alike, as all potentially damaging stress removed from knees and low back
Twisting Squats	ascending from lunge position, twist 90 degrees away from front leg	Sport-specific applications near end of training cycle
Lunge Squats	one leg front and the other back	Same as athletic squats, but one leg at a time
Side Lunge Squats	legs spread, lunge sidewards onto one leg	Same as athletic squats, but one leg at a time

Partial Squats	also called half squats	Useless and dangerous
Box Squats	touch box below you -- do not sit down	DANGER! Lots of lifters swear by them, but they're DAMNED dangerous when not done properly!
Jefferson Squats	bar between legs, one hand in front and other behind, lift toward crotch	Archaic
Hack Squats	Rails on an angle to floor, pad to lean against. Can be done with barbell (as originally designed by Hackenschmidt)	Archaic, although bodybuilders appear to like them
Leg Presses	angle of weight ascent ranging from 0 degrees to 90 degrees	Archaic and damaging to knees, although bodybuilders appear to like them
Overhead Squats	also called snatch grip squats	Sport-specific to Olympic weightlifters
Magic Circle Squats	also called Peary Rader squats, metal circle with shoulder harness, weights hung on circle	Archaic and somewhat dangerous, as circle swings
Sissy Squats	holding weight on chest with one hand, and holding upright with the other, lean back by bending knees, keeping upper legs in line with torso	Archaic, tough on knees
Front Squats	bar on front shoulders	Sport-specific to Olympic weightlifters, although bodybuilders appear to like them
Platform Squats	weight suspended from waist and goes through a hole in the platform	Leg workout without low back involvement

Zane Squats	hooks on bar hang over shoulders, bar sits against chest	Great for athletes and fitness enthusiasts...no spotter devices though (dangerous)
Platz Squats	Olympic squats done with a bent bar	Same as bodybuilder squats or athletic squats (bent bar "comfortable" says Platz)
Bear Squats Mini-Gym and other isokinetic devices	isokinetic machine – movement speed controlled	Isokinetic device "teaches" explosive strength by giving you more time to achieve max fiber recruitment...but machines all have inherent flaw, that being "unnatural" movement path
Front Harness Squats	Shoulder harness with hook holds bar against chest	Great for twisting squats (sport-specific to athletes who must twist while rising (as in throwing, hitting, etc.)
True Squats	lever machine -- squat is circular motion, leaning against a back pad chest	machines all have inherent flaw, that being "unnatural" movement path
Zercher Squats	cradling bar in bent arms	Archaic

All are good, all have their unique benefits, and at least one or two should ALWAYS be incorporated into all mesocycles of your leg training regimen, regardless of whether you're just an average Mrs. Jones looking for fitness or Quadzilla. It just depends upon what your objectives are.

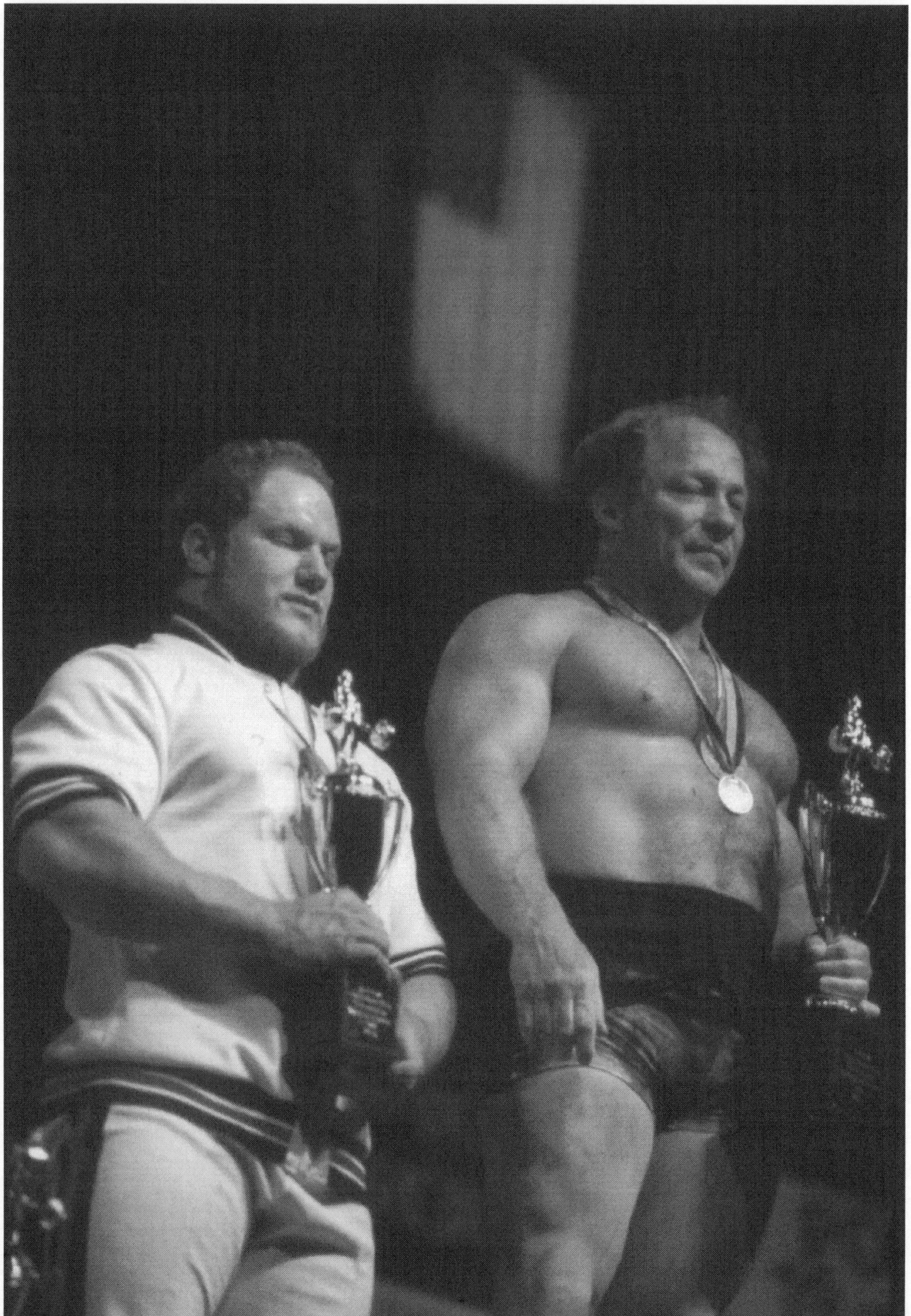

New Myth #2: Since no athlete in any sport moves vertically up and down with a load on their shoulders, there's no reason for athletes ever to do squats. They're just not "sport-specific."

Good observation, although not entirely logical. Any good strength coach knows that there is a general movement away from "general" movements to more "specific" movements as the competition season gets nearer and nearer. Straight up-and-down squats (preferably safety squats) are done in the off-season. They give way to lunge squats, side lunge squats, Bear squats and finally the ultimate form of squatting for most athletes -- twisting squats. Of course, front squats are generally best for Olympic lifters, and regular squats are best for powerlifters in their pre-competition cycle.)

Didn't know that? It doesn't surprise me. You don't know squat!

New Myth #3: Bodybuilders will get bigger, more cut quads with leg extensions, and they'll get bigger, more cut hams with leg curls. So they don't need squats.

I recognize the need for other leg exercises in a bodybuilders routine. Leg curls and leg extensions are great, but don't get the idea that they are how bodybuilders get cuts! DIET provides the cuts. As for squatting, well, let me give you words of wisdom from Jeff MADDOG Madden, the ISSA-certified strength coach for the Miami Dolphins. Actually, MADDOG didn't write this poem, Dale Clark did.

A young man was heard to say,
"No matter what I do, my legs won't grow!"
He tried leg extensions, leg curls, leg presses too.
Trying to cheat, these sissy workouts he'd do!
From the corner of the gym where the big guys train,
Through a cloud of chalk and the midst of pain,
Where the big iron rides high, and threatens lives,
Where the noise is made with big forty-fives,
A deep voice bellowed as he wrapped his knees,
A very big man with legs like trees,
Laughing as he snatched another plate from the stack,
Chalked his hands and monstrous back,
Said, "Boy, stop lying and don't say you've forgotten!
Trouble with you is you ain't been SQUATTIN'!"
'Nuff said.

New Myth #4: The ONLY way to get big legs is to squat.

Squatting provides the greatest amount of adaptive stress to the greatest number of major muscles in the upper leg. That simply means more bang for the buck. More effect for the effort. But don't get the idea that squatting is all you have to do to get big legs!

There are many other exercises (listed already), that are necessary, but they're **to be regarded as auxiliary to squatting!** Why? Read Maddog's poem again!

New Myth #5: Narrow stance for the vastus lateralis sweep.

While the inner and outer quads are activated via separate neural input, they function as a single unit for most intent because 1) the origin points of 3 of the quads are so close together, 2) they share a common insertion and 3) the quads span such a long bone. There may be a bit of differentiation possible through foot placement, but not so much that overall size takes a back seat to whatever meager shape changes you can effect.

Get big, and hope that the good Lord, in his infinite wisdom, gave you the genes necessary to have that pleasing "sweep" bodybuilders favor.

New Myth #6: Squats will give you a broad butt.

First, re-read my response to New Myth #5. Add to that bit of wisdom the fact that gluteal development is more often a genetic thing. Look at Tom Platz! No hammer there! Lots of guys and gals squat without getting big butts. Wide, intermediate or narrow, it doesn't really make that much difference.

On the other hand, no advantage is ever gained by going real wide (beyond, say, 24-36 inches wide) for anyone other than powerlifters. So keep your stance somewhere inside 24 inches or so, and you'll do great.

New Myth #7: Hack squat machines, Smith machines, leg press machines and the amazing plethora of other leg machines the past 30 years have witnessed are all safer than squats, and just as effective. So why even bother with the old fashioned squat?

Folks, squint your eyes and watch as someone does hack squats. Likewise for leg presses. Tell me what you see! Visualize that person standing on the floor and doing the precise same movement with the precise same body position. What do you see?

An unbelievably funky lookin' squat that isn't much good for much of anything.

Now, that's not to say that while in the machine (instead of standing on the floor doing the same movement) it's a worthless exercise! Hack squats have value. So do sissy squats. So do leg presses. Most you us who live in the trench know them all. But don't tell me that they can take the place of squats! They are to be considered auxiliary to squats. Only during injury are they ever to be considered replacements for squats.

Proper technique for the Bodybuilder's Squat:

- Position the bar on the squat racks at a height approximately three to five inches lower than your shoulders.
- With at least two spotters standing by (NEVER only one spotter), position your hands evenly on the bar and, with your feet squarely under the bar, lift it from the rack with the legs.
- Step back just enough to avoid bumping the rack during the exercise, and position feet at no more than a bit more than shoulder width.
- The weight should remain centered over the back half of the feet, not on the heels or toes.
- Slowly descend into a near-bottom position, keeping the torso and back erect so that the hips remain under the bar at all times. Do NOT allow the hips to drift backward or the torso to incline forward.
- A check on proper position is to ensure that the angles formed at the knee joint and hip joint are close to being equal. (Powerlifters almost always have more of an angle at the hips, and close to a right angle at the knees.)
- Do NOT relax or drop swiftly into a rock-bottom position. Keep the muscles contracted and stop just short of the bottom.
- Rise out of the squat position following the same path that you descended -- the torso and back remain erect and the hips remain under the bar throughout the ascent.
- Repeat the squat movement for the required number of reps.
- The use of supportive devices is not advised except in cases where the weight is extremely heavy.
- When returning the bar to the rack, have the two spotters carefully guide you in, being sure that the hands are not in the way of the bar or racks. Your fatigued state has diminished your control over the heavy weight.

Squatting Technique

In disproving the more persistent myths about squats, we've exposed some of the more important points off proper technique. For example, it's clear that there are several ways to perform the squat, but you must identify your training objectives for the cycle you're in before choosing the technique.

Powerlifters, for instance, use a technique during competition that in no way resembles the one that bodybuilders or athletes should use in training. But non-powerlifters are often guilty of mimicking that contest technique because more weight can be hoisted. The feet are spread beyond shoulder width, and the thighs barely break parallel when the lift is completed. The bar is carried as far down the back as rules permit, just below the deltoid muscles, and a considerable amount of forward lean is used to allow the legs to share the load with the gluteus and hamstring muscles. The weight distribution and better leverage afforded by the bar position and wider stance allow the powerlifter to squat with as much as 20 percent more weight than the upright technique allows.

Athletes have their own particular way of squatting, although the difference is not so much in position as it is in speed of movement. Athletes interested in developing explosive power (for jumping, running, kicking, tackling and the like) typically use explosive movements in their weight training, particularly in squatting.

This is referred to as **"compensatory acceleration"** training, and it requires that maximum effort be exerted against the bar throughout the entire range of motion. For example, near the top of a squat movement, the weight is easier to move because of improved leverage. Athletes **"compensate" for the improved leverage by accelerating the bar, thereby applying maximum overload in the full range of motion. Such explosiveness also leaves you with an amount of "learning"-- training explosively literally "teaches" the athlete to be more explosive.**

So what constitutes good squatting technique? This booklet sets down the important points of proper squatting form for athletes in all sports. But the theory behind the technique tips isn't all that simple. For example, what about the isolation principle? This important theory states that it will be easier to apply adaptive overload if a muscle is isolated. Implicit is the notion that a chain is only as strong as its weakest link. Relating this analogy to anatomical terms, if a group of muscles act to move a weight, the strength of the movement can be measured by the strength of the weakest muscle in the group. While the stronger muscles in the group may get some benefit, the overall gain to the group will be minimal.

This would appear to be a strong argument in favor of the leg curl and leg extension exercises over squats for overall leg development. But is it really? Because of the peculiar arrangement of the leg muscles' insertion and origin points (three of the quadriceps and 2 of the hamstrings span two joints, the hip and knee), it's impossible to get sufficient intensity of effort during maximum isolation movements, such as leg curls and leg extensions. **The leverages involved in squatting generate more intensity of effort than do the isolation movements, and overload is more easily achieved.** It takes both intensity and isolation to maximize the benefits of overload. The squat's efficient mix of isolation and intensity will yield improvements in both size as well as strength much faster than will any other leg exercises.

OFF-SEASON LEG TRAINING FOR MAXIMUM SQUATTING POWER

Despite the fact that they have been much maligned by (pencilneck) physicians who rarely have the opportunity to observe "healthy" people (they usually only see sick people), **squats are the single most effective leg exercise ever conceived.** This is true whether your training goals are those of a bodybuilder, power athlete, endurance athlete or fitness freak. For powerlifters, they're obviously an integral part of the sport.

In all honestly, however, and in deference to the good docs who eschew squats, **they have to be done VERY carefully.**

So, without disregarding those of you who squat for basic leg strength or size, I shall direct my attention to off-season squat training for my brothers and sisters of Irondom, the powerlifters.

High-Bar Squats

To work best -- with the utmost safety and effectiveness -- your off-season squats must be done with an upright torso, with knees not extending beyond your feet in order to protect the integrity of the tissues comprising your knee joint.

Despite what some of the purists among you may believe, I strongly advise you NOT to "bury" your off-season squats so deep that you inflict trauma to your knee joints rep after rep. Remember, your contest style squats are performed in such a way that your knee joints are as close to 90 degrees as possible. So why train beyond that during the off-season?

You should go to a depth necessary to stimulate maximum quadriceps contraction, but not so deep that 1) your knees are traumatized, or 2) hyperflexion of your lumbar spine exposes you to serious back injury. Descend to a depth where your thighs are approximately parallel to the floor.

Well before contest day -- around 6-8 weeks out -- you must turn to the more effective contest technique of distributing the weight to your hips, hams, back and quads.

Despite the fact that your off-season training requires them, conventional straight bar squats (called "Olympic" or "Bodybuilding" squats) have several inherent disadvantages:

1. The chance of leaning forward or rounding your back
2. under heavy loads is always a problem
3. Falling off balance forward or backward also jeopardizes your safety during heavy squatting
4. Your shoulder girdle, shoulders, wrists and elbows often take a beating holding the straight bar firmly in position
5. Missing a squat attempt is something which happens to all of us from time to time, often with dire consequences
6. Discomfort to the back of the neck (typically at the 7th cervical vertebra) where the bar sits is a problem we all shrug off as part of the game
7. Individual anatomical peculiarities often make it extremely difficult -- if not impossible -- to assume the most efficient stance in order to derive maximum benefit from squats
8. Not being able to squat because of the lack of competent spotters has been one of my personal gripes
9. Perhaps the most dangerous part of squatting is the need to take several steps backward to set up, and then return to the rack after squatting. This factor alone accounts for over 75 percent of all squatting-related injuries!

Despite these problems, all of us put up with them and get on with the business of learning good technique, taking proper precautions, and doing what we know is best for us. We squat no matter what, because, it has always been thought of as best to do so. That we've gotten by and made progress with conventional squats is due in no small measure to the fact that squats are a necessary part of our training. It's what we do.

Of course, the ubiquitous pencilnecks who suffer an injury will opt to completely eliminate squatting from their training. But impassioned powerlifters -- those of you with more than half a brain and more than your fair share of heart -- will find a way around whatever injuries you may have until the problem is solved. The best way around problems with squatting is to find other means of training your legs that eliminate trauma to the injured area.

Here are a few leg exercises (including some unique squatting techniques) which may provide both protection from and ways around injuries:

Lunge Squats

There are many variations to the squat movement. One extremely important one is the "lunge" squat. Lunge squats can be done to the left, right or forward, placing the weight on the lead leg. The quad muscles of the lead leg are targeted with both front and side lunges. Side lunges also target the groin muscles (especially the adductor gracilis of the opposite leg).

Twisting Squats

From a front lunge position, you can "twist" to the opposite side of your lead leg while ascending from the lunge position. This is an exercise which I had originally developed for athletes like down-linemen or shot putters who are required to explode laterally out of a lunge or squat position. Powerlifters benefit too, in that fuller leg development is achieved in the sartorius and adductor muscles of the upper leg.

"Twisting squats," as they're called, require a special harness to wear on your chest and shoulders to hold the short bar in place. DO NOT attempt to do twisting squats with a long bar, or with the bar placed on your shoulders! Loss of control in this exercise can mean groin, knee and low back injury.

Hack Squats and Leg Presses

Hack squat machines and leg press machines come in handy if 1) you haven't learned how to do squats properly yet, 2) you don't have a safety squat bar, 3) you don't have a spotter to help you do squats, or 4) if your back is tired or injured and you can't do regular squats. They're good substitutes for regular or safety squats, but NOT a replacement for them.

Hack squat machines come outfitted with a weighted sled that rolls up and down on tracks or slides on linear bearings, and shoulder pads so you can support the weight while squatting. Leg press machines' padded shoulder supports are stationary, on the other hand, and a sled device similar to those used on hack squat machines is pressed upward at varying angles, depending upon the design of the specific leg press machine.

Stiff Legged Deadlifts

A lot of powerlifters ill advisedly use stiff legged deadlifts to exercise their lower back.

Because your lower back is more efficiently and effectively developed with back extensions, there is no need to do any other off-season exercise for your lower back, and ESPECIALLY not stiff legged deadlifts!

However, stiff legged deadlifts are particularly effective for developing your hamstrings (the back of your upper legs).

The traditional way of performing this exercise is to lower the weighted bar all the way down to your bootstraps while standing on a platform or bench with stiff legs (or knees slightly bent). In this way, it's believed, you'll get maximum effect on your hams. This may be true to a degree, but you're also going to unnecessarily expose your lumbar spine to injury. Those intervertebral discs down there come loose all too easily!

I submit that there's a better way. With barbell in hand, poke both your butt and belly outward. In this position, you look kinda like one of the "Keystone Cops" you see in the 1920s movies. This variation of stiff legged deadlifts has thus become known as "Keystone Deadlifts"

This seemingly strange position will prestretch your hamstrings because of the forward tilt of your pelvis the position entails. Then, while maintaining this position, slowly lower the barbell to around your knees, keeping the bar close to your legs during the descent and ascent.

You must NOT go more than an inch or two below your knees. By the time you reach your (slightly unlocked) knees, your hip joints have fully flexed, and any further lowering of the bar is accomplished ONLY through eccentric hyperflexion of your spine -- a NO-NO!

You will feel a decided "burn" in your hams and glutes when keystones are done correctly. You should feel virtually no discomfort or stress in your lower back. If you do, experiment with the movement until you feel no discomfort at all. Invariably, a slight adjustment in your position will correct the problem.

The nice thing about doing stiff legged deadlifts this way is that you can use a far heavier weight, thereby getting better adaptive stress applied to the targeted hamstring muscles. All without any low back trauma at all!

One more important caution: NEVER do this exercise explosively! You'll risk pulling a hamstring or blowing out a lumbar disc.

Author's note:

This exercise is elsewhere called an RDL or Romanian deadlift.

Leg Extensions and Leg Curls

These two exercises are favorites of bodybuilders and fitness enthusiasts. While **they may be "ok" for them, they are decidedly useless for otherwise healthy powerlifters**. Eliminate them from your training except during times when, due to injury, they're the only movements you can perform safely and pain-free.

Squatting With the Manta Ray™

The Manta Ray™ is a shoulder girdle support manufactured from indestructible hi-tech molded plastic. It clips to a straight bar and completely eliminates the discomfort of the 1" round bar pressing on your 7th cervical vertebra, or the sharp knurling ripping your flesh. I personally LOVE this thing, and if I don't have a Safety Squat Bar™ (see below) to use, I ALWAYS have my Manta Ray™. In fact, it is a device I instruct all ISSA-certified personal fitness trainers to use for their clients. My belief is that ANYTHING that makes squats more comfortable is great because a perennial problem with squatting has always been that people just don't like them! They're uncomfortable to newcomers and ironheads alike! The Manta Ray™ solves this problem exquisitely.

Safety Squats

There's a training device called the "Safety Squat Bar™" (sometimes called the "Hatfield Bar") which can give you a new lease on effective off-season squat training. Some of you may have seen it collecting dust in the back of the squat platform. Pick it up! Put it on the rack and use it!

The exquisite isolation the Safety Squat Bar™ provides for your quads will be a truly unique experience, I assure you. Let's go over the good points of the Safety Squat Bar™ one by one.

Your hands are not holding the bar. This allows you to grasp the handles on the power rack. Because of the heavy loads involved in squatting, there is a tendency to "round" your back and place unnecessary stress on those easily displaceable intervertebral discs. This is avoided by exerting pressure against the power rack handles and thus maintaining a perfectly straight back throughout the entire squatting motion. Using your hands to spot yourself prevents you from falling forward or backward.

Squatting with a straight bar, you're forced to use a load that you can handle in the weakest position. This results in using an inadequate amount of weight in the strongest position of the squatting motion.

This problem is solved by use of the hands in the Safety Squat Bar™. When the "sticking point" is reached, the hands can be used to help you through it.

This unique feature allows you to work with heavier weights in the ranges of movement where you are strongest and gives you help when you are weakest. You are exerting closer to your maximum effort through the entire range of motion.

The padded yolk that the Safety Squat Bar™ is equipped with effectively eliminates neck and shoulder girdle discomfort. And the fact that you needn't use your hands to hold the bar on your shoulders eliminates wrist, shoulder and elbow discomfort.

By using your hands to regulate body position, your posture under the bar can be adapted to suit your own anatomical peculiarities so that you can literally "tailor" your squatting style to afford maximum overload.

Conventional squatting places the weight behind you, fully four inches behind your body's midline. That caused you to lean or bend forward for balance. With the Safety Squat Bar, the weight is distributed directly in line with your body's midline, and completely eliminates the need to lean forward.

Finally, because you are holding onto handles build onto the squat rack, you do not back up before squatting, and you are not obliged to walk back into the rack after squatting. This element alone has the potential of eliminating up to three quarters of all squatting-related injuries.

As a final note, remember that your off-season training is NEVER meant to be a time for impressing your training buddies by seeing how much weight you can squat with -- or "still" squat with after your long layoff, as the case may be. It is a time for establishing a solid foundation for the high-intensity pre-season training to follow. It is a time for eliminating weaknesses. It is a time for establishing a high degree of limit strength in all muscles of the body in preparation for the highly ballistic speed-strength training that must be incorporated into your pre contest preparation.

And remember this... Explosive strength, which can only be maximized by first establishing a supernormal level of limit strength in all of your synergistic and primary muscles, will give you your greatest squatting ability come contest day. There is no way that you can get away with being explosive before you've adequately prepared your body for the tremendous stress such training entails.

We can see here that Fred has some discrepancies with some of the other trainers we have been covering up to this point. Surprise, surprise!

There have been and always will be differences between even those considered to be the gurus of strength training, whether we talk about modern day contemporaries or old school contemporaries, or compare between these two sets.

Some of Louie Simmons favorite exercises are called "archaic" by Mr. Hatfield, such as Zercher squats. That may not necessarily mean that Fred thinks these are useless, please keep in mind.

Also note Fred's comments on box squatting, seemingly completely contradicting the advice of the Westside Barbell club's advice on the same topic.

While Westside considers them a vital component of their program, Fred does not seem to like them much at all. Fred also is not apparently too fond of partials according to his box diagrammed comments thereupon. In contrast, Paul Anderson and Peary Rader as well as Bob Peoples found these movements indispensible. My humble take on all this is that Fred has a more "scientific" approach and as a respected member of a personal training certification group (see his autobiography above), he will approach training with a more cautious and safety oriented viewpoint than perhaps the others mentioned might. I think Fred tries to eliminate exercises that are inherently more risky or dangerous to perform, even if they are potentially beneficial when done properly and carefully. It is the better safe than sorry approach, in my opinion. To be sure, some of the exercises and ways of doing them that we have discussed, both from the distant past and more modern ones, would make many well educated modern-day trainers cringe. Take the Bob Peoples deadlift technique, for example. If a novice lifter performed his first set of deadlifts that way in front of one of these guys, he would get a serious tongue –lashing or worse! Yet, it not only worked for Bob, it helped him set records in the 1940's that are still impressive even today.

I actually asked Fred about these subjects, and here is what he said;

Fred Hatfield

Contrary to popular belief, squatting above the parallel position -- knees at approximately 90 degrees flexion -- is actually more dangerous that going to parallel or below. There are two reasons for this. When you look at the structure of the knee, you... See More'll note that at about 90 degrees flexion, the tibia's sloped shape allows it to shear upwards and over the femur. This causes a lot of compressive force against the patella, and pulls forcefully against the posterior cruciate ligament. These potentially destructive forces become significantly less as you descend further into the squat postion, largely due to the fact that the tibia's surface isn't as sloped posteriorly, where it articulates with the femur. The second reason is that, because of better leverage while doing partials, you're obliged to use a far heavier weight in order to gain any sort of adaptive overload on the muscles involved -- dangerous to the entire shoulder girdle, neck, low back and knees.

As for box squats, I have seen waaay too many guys blow their backs out with box squats. Lee Moran was a perfect example. Further, I do not see any real science supporting this potentially dangerous exercise. And, since I have over a half century of personal experience with this lift, well, that's gotta count for something, no?

I thank Fred for his quick and honest response. I will let you readers decide for yourselves on these matters, as there are many such matters that each individual must consider and make evaluations about. There are some dangerous aspects to serious weight training, for sure. Many of the methods presented in this book come with a certain amount of risk. Lots of them are only suggested for the hardcore trainee that is seeking to reach the pinnacle of elite strength, or trying to bust through stubborn plateaus. These methods if used at all should be used with a great deal of caution, and Fred's idea of having multiple spotters on hand is a wise one.

Chapter Twenty one
Some other voices of experience

There are many great folks we could talk about and learn from, but I would at least like to add a few more here that I especially admire and respect, not to say that there are not many more qualified people out there.

Brooks Kubick

Brooks has written lots of articles, has his own website and perhaps is best known for his **"Dinosaur Training"** book which I have read.

He likes basic movements in the weight training arena, as do most we have been learning from here. He also is fond of training more in the strongman realm, lifting kegs, odd objects, etc. One of the ideas Brooks constantly harps on is the area of having a strong grip, and how this is often overlooked or at least under emphasized by many modern trainers.

He eschews the use of straps, hooks and other artificial aids, and in fact is fond of finding ways to make gripping something you are training with even more difficult than normal. He says that anyone wishing to obtain superior strength and power MUST have a strong grip, strong hands and wrists, as well as forearms.

Of course, as an advocate of the basics, he strongly believes in the squat as the central leg developing weight training exercise, and I found an article he wrote about the squat some years ago.

Like many we have covered, he defends the squat against the nay sayers and says that the majority of injuries and problems that are complained of are the result of improper form, and inflexibility, which of course are often closely related. If you have tight hamstrings or lower back area, your squat form will suffer.

Brooks suggests a period of stretching before embarking on a serious squat routine, if you have such flexibility issues .If you can't reach parallel without ending up leaning too far forward, as in a good morning position, the chances are pretty good that you have flexibility issues.

We have seen photos on past pages depicting squatting with raised heels. Brooks is not a fan of such squats, to put it mildly.

He says it will cause knee and back problems in the long haul. He also is not a fan of high bar squats as our friend Mr. Platz was. He says that the lower legs should be as close to the vertical as possible, the feet should be typically at least shoulder width apart, and that you should be looking straight ahead as opposed to up at the ceiling or down at the floor He says that if you are not having to make at least somewhat of an effort in keeping your elbows up to keep the bar in place, you are most likely positioning the bar too high. The bar should not be sitting atop the highest point of the deltoids, but an inch or two below that point.

One should be driving the heels into the ground throughout the lift, not the toes. This helps to keep the weight properly centered over the heels, and ascending in a straight line. The upper back must remain relatively flat and kept tensed and tight throughout the lift.

Like Dr. Squat and unlike Louie Simmons, Brooks does not espouse the box squat, for essentially the same reasons touted by the good Doctor. He prefers a parallel squat as opposed to a butt to the ground version as many of the old schoolers liked, and somewhat surprisingly, he says if your back typically starts to round when going all the way to the parallel position, it would be advised to cut it short by a couple of inches. He says there are a few trainees who just can't get parallel in good form and they should not push it. Unlike Doctor Squat, Brooks advises against padding of any sort on the bar, even for ectomorphic beginners for whom just having any kind of weight on the bar is very uncomfortable at first. He suggests toughing it out and says you will get used to it in time, and be far better for it. You could say that Brooks is more inclined towards a power style squat, in which you can perform with maximum weights, and the load is more distributed between hips, back, butt and legs as opposed to over emphasis on any one particular area. He mentions that some like to don wrist wraps to aid in keeping the lower bar in position, and speaks against the idea. He says "throw the wrist wraps away" and toughen up your wrists and forearms in the process.

Brooks kind of reminds me of a drill instructor in some ways, always advising one to toughen up, man-up, shy away from supportive aids and develop a can-do attitude.

He definitely has a certain appeal to the hard core among us. Some will find these qualities endearing; others may not.

He certainly will not stand by for a trainee or training partner slacking off in any way, shape or form, and in that regard, I'd love to train with him or anyone like-minded. Brooks has a very strong work ethic when it comes to training, and I think he does a pretty good job instilling this in others through his writing.

With that being said, I think some of his ideas may lead to over training because of their sheer severity. Workouts in which you find yourself puking or on the verge of blacking out, like the ones Platz talked about in earlier sections, seem to have been Brooks bread & butter. While I am no stranger to a "balls to the wall" workout, it can be overdone, especially for the mature lifter such as me and those older yet. If one engages in these types of workouts, the frequency of training needs to be adapted to accommodate it, in my opinion. Even Platz talked about seriously spacing out his heavy squat workouts when he was training at his most intense levels, and there is a man that was no stranger to pain and intense workouts, as you will recall from his previous dialogue.

A couple photos of Brooks in action

Larry Pacifico, one of the best squatters ever

Brooks advises squatting in a power rack with safety pins set a bit below the parallel point, and mentions that you don't want to hit the pins at the bottom, as this will throw off the natural groove, and I can personally attest to this fact as I have experienced just that. The other problem with doing that is that if you have a wide grip position, you may smash your fingers on the pins, which we obviously should avoid. He also speaks about the tendency of some squatters to drop very quickly while descending, to the point where you reach bottom before the bar does. What happens next in this scenario?

When the loaded bar catches up with you at the bottom, it jars you forward, throwing you out of the proper groove and adding stress to lower back and knees, while making the ascent more difficult than it should be. You may get more bounce effect from your supportive gear like a suit and knee wraps in this method, but Brooks is not big on support gear in the first place anyway.

One of Brooks' tips is something not often suggested by most; to wear something long sleeved in order to help keep the bar in position. If you wear no shirt or a sleeveless shirt, you may have sweat under the bar, which is not a good idea. Using chalk on the back where the bar sits is also advised.

Brooks is OK with using a cambered bar if you like, especially advisable for the large and heavily muscled upper body types. He also suggests that the feet should be angled slightly outwards, with the knees tracking directly out over the upper legs, not buckling in or swaying outward. On the same subject, he says that some bodybuilders will suggest different feet positions (straight or pointed in) to hit different aspects of the quadriceps muscles. He claims this to be a load of crap and ill-advised, leading to potential injury. He says to descend at a controlled pace, not actually counting, but remaining in control at all times and never bouncing, yet he does not suggest a pause at the bottom. He says one should immediately rise up upon hitting parallel position. Start in a firm, fully upright stance, and begin the descent by breaking the knees, and then breaking the hips once you are about one third of the way down. You should "**feel the bar**" all the way down during the descent phase, according to Mr. Kubick. I will close this section about Brooks with his own words in summarizing the squat, as follows:

Learn to be Aggressive!

Poor squatters are timid and tentative. A good squatter attacks the bar when he squats. I don't mean that he moves quickly, that he bounces up and down, or that he loses control when he lifts. A good squatter lifts with ferocious, white-hot concentration, a total absence of fear, tremendous intensity, and a burning determination to complete every rep that he is scheduled to perform.

Some readers complain that they feel they are being "crushed" as they squat. As a result, they either squat with light poundage, switch to inferior exercises, or cut their range of movement way down. This is a mistake.

I will let you in on a big secret. A heavy squat makes ANYONE feel like he is being crushed. A 500-lb. squatter feels just the same – "Wow, that's heavy!" – as does the novice struggling under the 90-lb. bar or the intermediate who can't get over the 250 mark because the bar "feels too heavy."

The difference between a good squatter and a poor one is two-fold. First, the good lifter uses proper technique. This allows him to control the weight and stay in the groove at all times. When you are properly positioned, it is much easier to fight to fight a heavy weight than when it has pushed you out of the groove. In fact, many lifters cannot squat heavy solely because poor technique causes them to lean forward as they descend, and as a result, they naturally feel that they are being "crushed."

The second difference between a good squatter and a bad squatter has to do with mental attitude. The good squatter is TOUGH. He knows that the lift will feel heavy, he knows it will hurt, he knows the bar will feel like it is crushing him – but he doesn't care. He is not going to let a minor thing like discomfort keep him from doing what he desires to do. In contrast, the poor squatter feels the bar on his back, panics, and convinces himself he cannot lift it. The good squatter uses to his advantage the sense of being "crushed." He reacts by driving upward as hard and forcefully as possible. The poor squatter lets the feeling overwhelm him.

I have a personal theory that the sense of being "crushed" by a heavy weight is a GOOD thing – a good thing when you squat, a good thing when you bench, and a good thing in any other heavy exercise. I believe that the fear of being crushed will trigger a harder muscular contraction solely as a result of your body's reaction to what is perceived as a dangerous situation. Remember, the mind, body and emotions are linked in ways that science can barely begin to unravel. If the bar feels heavy when you squat, WELCOME that feeling and use it to tap into some extra power. Use your emotions to help you, not hold you back.

The above paragraphs are a good representation of Kubick's mentality on training.

I happen to like it.

Comrade Pavel

Pavel Tsatsouline is a former fitness instructor for the Russian secret service, or so goes the rumor. Largely responsible for the great resurgence of **kettlebell training** both in America and the world, Pavel has made quite a name for himself in today's strength training circles. He is knowledgeable on old school methods, and he uses some, but with his own unique twists. We have mentioned him earlier in reference to the idea of "**greasing the groove**". Pavel has written a number of books and training manuals including **Power to the People** and **the Naked Warrior.**

He and **John Ducane** have put together quite an enterprise, centered around **Dragon Door Publications.** They provide certifications for high level kettlebell training protocols for personal trainers as well as offering various publications and media on physical fitness. Pavel has a good sense of humor that comes through in his manuals, even though he is a pretty serious dude when it comes to training. He is not known for being massive, but he possesses a very lean and mean, wiry & ripped physique.

He believes strongly in **addressing weak areas, flexibility issues and problems with mobility as precursors to trying to develop ultimate strength and power levels**. He reminds me a bit of **Sandow** in that regard.

He likes bodyweight training, calisthenics and kettlebell training but is also well versed in the traditional power and Olympic lifts, more so on power. He has a fairly well rounded approach to overall fitness and health, and addresses cardio type training and endurance issues rather than purely strength and power. Pavel spends a lot of time teaching about stretching and mobility and he conveys the idea that they are keys to strength gains. His **Naked Warrior** book is concerned with these issues as well as being a good bodyweight training manual for anyone. He has written a book called **Relax into Stretch** and another **called Pavel Superjoints,** so it should be obvious how important these areas are to him. He also penned **Bulletproof Abs,** and even has marketed an ab workout device he calls the Pavelizer. Pavel uses martial arts ideas and techniques thrown into his mix, and stands apart from many other modern day trainers in this regard.

He talks about **strength being a skill**, and accordingly that we should talk of training bouts as practice (as in practicing a skill) as opposed to calling them workouts. He goes into considerable detail on learning **to use muscle tension and control** as well as extreme focus and concentration. He tries to teach that the nerves are in control of the muscles and that the nerves are controlled ultimately by the brain.

His Naked Warrior book is no diatribe on why bodyweight exercises are superior, but rather how one should be well prepared to train that way if there are no weights or other such tools available. The **2 key exercises** are the **one armed push-up and the one-legged squat, also known as the Pistol** (we mentioned this earlier). Pavel is fond of routines consisting of very few or even only 2 exercises, provided each hits enough parts intensely enough. He claims that in the realm of bodyweight exercises, variations on the 2 exercises named will cover the bases pretty well. Also interesting in a bodyweight focused manual, Pavel claims it to be focused on **maximal strength building**. He offers ways of making the traditional BW exercises more difficult rather than adding reps upon reps of the standard movements, thus one legged and one armed movements become the focus. He also has a section on **martial arts based power breathing** in this book.

Pavel says that **respectable strength can only be built with high resistance, low repetition, high tension work**, which can be adapted to BW routines.

Tension generating skills are more important than sheer muscle mass building, and we can hardly argue this point when we see the power generated by a Bruce Lee or a 148 pound class powerlifter that can bench press 500 pounds. Pavel preaches very strongly **against the concept of training to failure,** and says we should always stop a set with a rep or 2 "in the bank".

Of course, he uses Russian lifters as examples of folks who train very often, but in the fashion of skill practice as in the concept called "**greasing the groove**" Westside barbell has adopted this idea in a fashion with their speed days, training **multiple sets of low reps with moderate percentages of a one rep max weight, as we have discussed previously.**

The **grease the groove** concept is simply a high volume, high frequency, low intensity one. Pavel quotes a Russian strength expert saying: "**do as much quality work as possible while being as fresh as possible**". Some of the core principles are never going to failure on a given set, and actually usually only doing about half the number of reps you might be capable of.

He offers many testimonials from trainees who have made great gains using this concept, usually involving new personal bests in the number of max reps in something like the pull-up. He speaks of instructing a friend trying to rebuild his rep numbers in the pull-up to do pull-ups numerous times throughout the day, every day, which flies in the face of "**conventional bodybuilding wisdom**".

If we think back to Bob Peoples deadlift training, he talked about training every day, on that particular lift. Earle Liederman also taught one of his pupils to build a better chest by training it every day, and I was just reading last night about one of the best lighter weight bench pressers of all time, **Rick Weil**, who said when he first started training at the age of 13, he benched every day, and did little else. This is food for thought.

One phrase you will hear at every power meet over and over again is "**stay tight**". Pavel is big on using this technique as well, and he has a few tricks for learning how to do this better. He mentions the idea that when one hand or leg exerts a force, the other arm or leg has a corresponding response.

Using this principle, he suggests tensing up the opposite fist while shaking someone's hand after doing it in the normal fashion. Ask the other guy if the second way felt stronger. It should. You can use this method when doing one legged push-ups and squats, too.

He also mentions **tightening the abs, not sucking them in, but bracing as if for a punch**.

Tightening the glutes, as in squeezing a coin between the cheeks is yet another bracing technique. **Tightening the grip, as in the tight fist, on any exercise will allow more power to be realized**. This is something our friend **Brooks Kubick** would agree on, I think. Good bench pressers will advise that you **squeeze the bar** as tightly as possible during the bench press, even trying to pull it apart, which sounds a lot like what Pavel calls the "**corkscrew technique**", in which you visualize screwing your arms into the shoulder sockets, 1 arm clockwise, the other counter-clockwise, while squeezing tightly all the while. (While doing pushups, for example) Pavel also talks about having a training partner "punch" you while you are engaged in one of the exercises, in order to teach you to keep muscles tensed up, another martial arts based idea. We can apply the tightening of grip, abs and glutes to the power or Olympic lifts, and Pavel suggests it highly.

Pavel is a strong promoter of gaining strength sans mass gains, which is not everyone's cup of tea, but is certainly of interest to those trying to stay in a weight class for their given sport, or who have blood pressure issues and for many other good reasons. Pavel says most of us only ever learn to fire 20- 30 percent of our available muscle fibers at a time in performing a lift. Maybe top lifters reach the 50 percent level. At the 100 percent level, muscles would rip from tendons and ligaments and other such not so desirable things would occur, so this is a bit more than we seek. **But what would happen if we got up to even 60 or 70 percent?**

While Pavel's "Naked Warrior" book focused on bodyweight training, his "**Power to the People**" focused on **weight training**, though he still went with the 2 exercise workout concept in PTP. The 2 exercises were **deadlifts and presses**. Pavel is fond of the idea that the deadlift is the best overall body strengthener you can do, and I would love to agree with him on this, as it is my best lift. I'm not quite sure I do, though, in all honesty. Pavel is not alone in this thinking. To be sure, the deadlift is a key, foundational strength exercise that may indeed be on a par with the squat. To neglect either in a serious strength program would be unwise, in my opinion. Does this mean I disagree with Pavel's program as laid out in PTP? Well, yes, sort of. For an intermediate lifter to do this program for a couple or three months would not be horrible, but I don't think such an abbreviated routine would benefit the advanced trainee in the long haul. Of course, everyone is different, and there are probably a few folks that would do very well on this regimen. It may well be worth a shot if you are in a rut.

Pavel quotes a lot of old school guys like Earle Liederman, Sandow and others, as well as more modern trainers such as Leistner and Simmons. I think he tends to "cherry pick" those quotes and excerpts from these gents that would support whatever point he is making at a given juncture in his writings, but that is not so unusual. I think we would find a lot of disparate ideology of training concepts and methods if we dug deeply into all of the folks mentioned above, much as we have seen throughout this manual. It is just the nature of the beast. One man's bread & butter is another's laughing stock.

I would strongly agree with the mad Russian that the **mind is key** in any training and not something to be overlooked. Training without maximal focus is almost a waste of time versus that done with it. Pavel offers a number of "tricks" to help in this area, and it never hurts to have a few more of these up one's sleeve.

At the core of "Power to the People" are several concepts. Probably the most highly emphasized one is never to train to failure, as many of the HIT philosophy advise, and many bodybuilders swear by.

Comrade Pavel suggests that one always leave a rep or two in reserve, on every set. Train low reps, with heavy but not maximal weight, and keep overall volume to a point that does not leave you fatigued. One rep absolute max efforts should only be done on occasion, but training at 85 - 95 percent frequently is strongly suggested. Doing several sets of triples with a weight you could get 5 reps with in an all-out set is more efficient and more productive, according to Pavel and many of his countrymen.

This idea would be in contrast with those spoken of in Brooks Kubick's "**Dinosaur Training**" manual, the training methods espoused by Tom Platz and also those of Mike Mentzer.

All of the above have made a name for themselves in the fitness arena, so it might be difficult to argue that they have no clue what they are talking about. Of course, 2 of the 3 mentioned above are bodybuilders, so pure strength building was not their primary goal.

Zach Even-Esh

\

Zach is a trainer that I like, as he tells it like it is, trains hard himself, and offers no instant fix BS. His primary training protocol is called the Underground Strength System. He was a High School wrestling coach, personal trainer and competitive bodybuilder before going full time with his fitness info enterprise and this has enabled him to quit a 90K per year job, so it must be doing quite well.

He espouses an eclectic training module and is big on the instinctive training idea. He seldom if ever seems to do the same workout twice, mixing in strongman moves, power and Olympic lifts,

some bodybuilding type stuff, sandbag training, sled dragging/pushing, and doing sprints.

He likes to have running as a component of a program, as most high school and college football and wrestling coaches do. He'll throw in some kettlebell training and one could say he is into high intensity, but he varies from high reps to singles across the matrix of exercises he uses. He is another trainer that will reference old schoolers like **George Hackenschmidt** and others, pointing to their no BS, blood, sweat and tears training work ethics. He blasts classic rock tunes while filming his hard-core training bouts, and he likes to make even the hardest workouts fun. I like that about him. He seems to have the ability to push his trainees to their limits while they still somehow manage to have a good time doing it. That is not easy to do. He instills a can-do attitude and that is great for everyone. He does not harp on genetics or scientific principles, but tells students that they can get strong, lean and mean if they just work hard and keep giving their all. I think if you are looking for a good overall conditioning program, trying to improve in a sport or just muscle up and lose a few pounds of unwanted fat, you could not go too wrong following Zach's ideas for a while.

He is a strong proponent of multi-joint, functional training, and is no stranger to the bench press, squat and deadlift and their many variations.

Another thing I like about Zach is his use of odd objects and in designing cheap methods and equipment you can train anywhere with. He loves to train outside, and I can relate to this. He'd be the first to tell you that you can train hard without lots of fancy or expensive equipment and you will likely never see him at a chrome and mirror spa-like facility. He would probably be in his glory training in **Bob Peoples' dungeon gym**, and so would I!

There are lots of other trainers and fitness experts I could mention, and the list already given is far from exhaustive, but I have mentioned some of my favorites that I thought were deserving of a mention and some coverage in this book. Please do not feel offended if one or more of your favorites has been left out. After all, we have to save some for the sequel, right?

Giants training with Jumpstretch bands

Chapter Twenty-two
Wrapping it up

So, we have discussed great lifters from Steinborn to Simmons & Dr. Squat, as well as their influences. We have looked at bodybuilders, powerlifters, strongmen and Olympic lifters. Have we covered everything from soup to nuts in the strength training world since 100 years ago until the present?

I would have to give a resounding and emphatic "NO, not hardly!" response to that one. We have really only scratched the surface. Even when we are keying on a specific exercise like the squat as our primary point of interest, there are so many variations that it is mind boggling. There are a number of variables with just about any exercise that can be tweaked and experimented with. Range of motion can be limited, foot position and stance can be varied, heels can be elevated or stay flat, footwear can make a difference, the position of the bar on the back can be changed, or the bar can be lifted from the floor, from behind, from the waist, etc. **Time under tension** is an important variable we have not delved deeply into, but one we need to take a look at. We did talk about **the speed of execution on a lift and about being explosive** with lighter weights, as in the Westside "**dynamic**" training mode. One of the reasons that "speed" training is not something to be used exclusively is that it does not provide the best time under tension, which is just what it sounds like; how long the trained muscles are fighting the resistance or are under tension. There are several or more ways of manipulating this variable. One way is to vary the speed of a single repetition, or even to break 1 repetition into components and vary the speed of these. As an example, you could descend very slowly, and then "explode" up out of the whole. Alternatively, you could descend slowly, pause briefly at the bottom, and ascend as slowly as you came down. You can vary the up phase, the down (eccentric) phase, pause anywhere in between for any length of time, or even do "**static holds**" or "**static contractions**" which was touched on earlier.

You could also vary the time of a complete "set" and even **forget about counting repetitions**, but rather continue the set for a given period of time. **HIT and HIIT** training modes incorporate these ideas. Taking a moderate weight and working for a period of 45 seconds to a minute, perhaps a minute and 10 or 15 seconds at the high end, is very challenging method that has been reported to be a tremendous muscle building tool. Varying the rest periods can cause dramatic effects as well, and these are emphasized in HIT and HIIT training modes as much as the speed or duration of the set itself.

HIT training is "**high intensity training**", and HIIT is high intensity **interval t**raining, by the way. Interval training means the speed is not constant for a given cycle of exercise. Jogging or walking at x number of mph for a half an hour becomes interval training when you throw in a sprint or moderately paced short run every now and then.

High intensity training has variations and may be defined a bit differently by those who espouse or use it, but basically it is about maintaining a high heart rate throughout a given session. As you might guess then, high intensity interval training involves training at a high heart rate pace, but with intervals of brief slowdowns or stoppage during the cycle.

Doing weight training bouts for timed sets in which the HR is elevated to 70-80 percent of max, with short (20-30 seconds) rest periods is **a great way to burn fat while building muscle** and strength, though admittedly the fat burning component is emphasized here over the ultimate in strength building.

We did talk earlier about **eccentric training**, which Bob Peoples in particular was a huge fan of. There are variations of eccentric training modes, some more intense than others.

The most brutal forms use **greater than 100 percent of a maximum**, standard 1 rep in a given movement, where the weight is lowered by the exerciser in as controlled a fashion as he is capable of, with spotters (or hydraulics in Peoples case) raising the weight back to the start position. Paul Anderson, as you hopefully recall from earlier sections used a variation on this theme in that his spotters would even push down on the weight to add further resistance on the down phase, and then he would go on to perform multiple reps of both the concentric and eccentric phases of the squat. **He cautioned that this was a method only for the advanced trainee and that even then it should be worked into gradually**.

Well, he was not just whistling Dixie, my friends; that stuff could put a serious hurtin' on you even if you are very strong to begin with! I can tell you that I have done the negatives in which the concentric phase was all spotter and the eccentric phase was all me, and that is about as much a DOMS* producing method as I have come across. These are not something to be done on a regular or frequent basis.

- *DOMS =Delayed onset muscle soreness**

There are **ways to emphasize the eccentric phase** that won't require you to use a walker for several days after, and these methods have even been espoused by the likes of Men's Health and Fitness type magazines, which tend to be geared towards the less extreme trainee.

This involves **taking more time in the descent phase**, and or pausing at the bottom and/or somewhere else in the ROM. Taking 5 seconds to descend as opposed to 1 or 2 both **increases the time under tension** overall and puts the emphasis on the eccentric phase, both of which can have some interesting results.

You can also throw in **partial range movements** during a set such as something I saw in Men's Health that they called a **1 ¼ squat**. This involves a 3 second descent, followed by a 1 second pause. From there you would come up just one fourth of the way, and then re-descend to the parallel position, hold for yet another 1 second pause, and then rise.

Start position

Descend slowly to bottom position shown, pause briefly

Ascend just to quarter squat position:

Return to full squat and hold briefly one more time before ascent:

Clearly, you could improvise the timing and the range of motion components of this type of movement for different effect. We mentioned also something about the "**slow continuous tension**" technique, which is employed primarily by bodybuilders. Typically, one uses a relatively light weight but does it painfully slowly in both phases, and never locks out the weight, so that the tension is never removed during the set. This is a valid method, but keep in mind that time is not the only factor here, otherwise, one might choose to just use bodyweight and do one repetition that lasts a very long time. Time under tension is important, but the amount of tension is also very crucial. In a sense, tension over a certain threshold will by itself create more time under tension because **max and near max loads will slow you down**, at least in the typical powerlifting movements.

Using a very light weight (let's say 50 percent max and under) and concentrating on "**slow continuous tension**" is not that beneficial in terms of building real muscle and power. In fact, very little of the workload, if any, in a strength seeker's workout should consist of weights in that range, other than warm ups. Even guys who train with just bodyweight realize that doing countless reps with a standard pull-up or pushup movement has diminishing returns for those who are at an advanced level in that format. What can be done about that situation? The answer is very simple; **make the exercise more difficult;** present the body with something new it must adapt to. This can mean elevating the feet, using only one arm at a time, putting a towel around a chin-up bar to create a grip deficit that must be overcome, or adding weight to the exercise (or other forms of resistance, such as bands or even a partner pushing against you). We mentioned the old bodyweight style squats called Hindu Squats above, and there has been an interesting tool developed to make these more challenging also. There is actually a "machine" for this at some gyms, but the concept lends itself to easy DIY replication, as seen with my own version here:

DIY Sissy squat harness made by the author

The handles you see in the photo do not come into play for the "**Sissy Squat**", but one puts a pad on the bar, puts it behind the knee area and does squats, supported by the harness from falling backward. The shins remain strictly vertical, and this is considerably more challenging than a standard bodyweight free style squat. You could also **increase the difficulty by adding weight or band resistance.**

I did not invent this concept, so I am not trying to credit myself with inventing it, please understand.

While I have come up with an original concept or two on my own, I like making my own cheapo versions of things I find on the net and elsewhere.

Sometimes, however, there is nothing like the real thing, and if you can afford to drop the coin, having the good stuff is nice. You can often find great bargains on used equipment in places like thrift stores, yard sales and on craigslist or eBay, and I am always looking in one or another of these areas for that next gem of a find. People buy nice equipment and find their physical commitment does not match the financial one they have already made, and vultures like me are quick to pounce on their misfortune. You should, too

My website, Christianiron.com, has a page devoted to Cheap & DIY fitness ideas, and I suggest you check it out for some cool ideas, here:

http://christianiron.com/FrugalFitness.aspx

One of the ideas you will find there is my lever system for attachment to a power rack. (I got the rack from a Craigslist seller for 100 $, and it came with some extras). While I used discarded pieces of an old bench as my main lever arm, you can use any number of other easy & cheap methods with a bit of DIY ingenuity.

Here are a couple of pictures of my lever system in action.

Chapter Twenty-Three
One last subject

While most of the coverage in this manual has concentrated on old school stuff, there are some relatively newer ideas that have come forth in the realm of nutritional supplementation. We touched on various forms of protein intake with Paul Anderson, and Jim Brewster's revamped 20 rep squat program ended with a nice little modern nutrition primer as follows:

(Repeated from pg 167) Here's a great stack for use with the 20 rep squat routine:

Protein
Multi vitamin
a pre workout drink, e.g. No-Explode by BSN, or SuperPump250 by Gaspari Nutrition

Creatine Monohydrate
Nitric oxide
Glutamine
A good testosterone booster or prohormone, e.g. Anabolic-Matrix Rx or 1-Andro Rx by Iron-MagLabs

In my humble opinion, this set of supplements is not bad, but it could be added to and updated slightly. I first would caution you that some of the prohormone type supplements contain things which could cause you to fail a drug screen for a competition, even though it may not be actual steroids.

Mr. Brewster also mentions pre-workout drinks and names a couple of brand names for these, and then also later on mentions Nitric Oxide, which is also known as AAKG, a form of the amino acid Arginine. Both of the pre-workout products Jim suggests contain Nitric Oxide as one of their main ingredients. Both of these, and the majority of such products also contain considerable doses of caffeine and or other stimulants, and again, one must be careful in this area with drug screenings flagging some of these substances. Even high doses of caffeine are banned in some lifting and sports federations, as is the herb ephedra and a few others. Be aware of what you are ingesting!

One good, safe pre-workout supplement this author has tried is a sublingual spray or dropper formulation of good old B12. No side effects or drug screen issues, and provides a nice energy burst. Also, you might enjoy a nice big juicy Navel orange or a piece of Grapefruit as an energy booster before training.

A few additional items are worthy of noting, I think;

Beta Alanine is another supplement along the lines of creatine that has been reported to provide strength enhancing qualities and it has found its way into a number of pre and post workout products of late, though it does not yet have the proven track record of creatine.

Speaking of creatine, there are a lot more options now besides the plain vanilla creatine monohydrate that is still the cheapest and most widely used and available form. There are some formulations that are supposed to be better absorbed, like effervescent creatine, for example, which fizzes when mixed with water or juice much like alka-seltzer. Other forms contain additional components or different molecular structures of creatine. You may wish to experiment with other formulations, but good old creatine monohydrate may still provide the best bang for your buck, though I'm sure various supplement manufacturers would beg to differ with me on that point.

This supplement does have a couple of minor downsides; bloating and digestive issues, especially at higher dose levels is one problem. Another is cramping of muscles if hydration is not adequate. Since creatine causes water retention within muscle tissues, one must consume a lot of water while on a creatine cycle, especially during training bouts. Also, if using a plain creatine monohydrate supplement, it is advised to consume the doses along with a high glycemic index juice (apple or grape juice, etc) for better absorption and utilization.

Fish oil capsules have become a standard supplement, especially among older fitness enthusiasts, as it is beneficial for fighting bad lipid profiles as well as being good for joint lubrication. In the joint supplement area, Glucosamine, msm, Chondroitin, Hyaluronic acid and a number of herbs are good for fighting the problems associated with aging, arthritis, etc. There are a number of proprietary formulations containing most of the above items and perhaps some additional ones, like Osteo-Biflex, Flexamin, etc.

In the Testosterone boosting or hormonal balancing arena, there are a number of herbs worth investigating, such as Maca, Terrestris Tribulus, Avena Sativa, Saw Palmetto, Horny Goat weed, Ginseng and a few others. Most of these are advised for older men whose natural testosterone levels are starting to fall off, and they don't seem to be as beneficial for younger men. It is often assumed that any of the herbs that are found in an herbal "male enhancement" or "libido enhancing" formulas work by boosting testosterone, but this is not always true. Some such herbs simply provide stimulus to the uro-genital tract without changing hormonal balance at all.

Yohimbe would be one of these, and this herb contains some alkaloids which may make you feel a little strange or uncomfortable as a side effect. Every time I have taken a supplement containing this herb, it gives me what I term, very scientifically, as "the heebie geebies"

Any herbal formulas should be approached with caution. Read warning labels and take low doses when starting any new regimen to see how it may affect you.

On **protein supplements**, many doctors and nutrition experts will tell you that you can get plenty enough from a good normal diet. The general consensus among hard training iron sport aficionados is that some supplementation in this department can't hurt, unless one throws all moderation to the wind. While you can certainly survive on less protein, as strength athletes we are trying to super compensate our torn down muscle tissues with protein, the building block of muscle. ¾ of a gram to one gram of protein per pound of bodyweight per day can reasonably be considered a minimal requirement for those who train hard with weights. Many lifters suggest considerably more, even as much as 2 grams per pound of BW per day, but keep in mind that extra calories even in the form of pure protein will be converted to fat ultimately. Also, the lever and kidneys have to process the nutrients we take in and huge excesses of anything are not a good idea. With all that being said, unless you are eating 5 or 6 relatively high protein meals or snacks daily, a scoop of extra whey or casein based protein thrown in here and there is probably not a bad idea, especially after a particularly grueling session with the iron. Complex carbohydrates also must be consumed in good amounts to keep muscle glycogen stores at optimal levels, and fats should not be avoided completely either, especially the friendlier fats like extra virgin olive oil, avocados, fish oils, borage oil, etc.

While many lifters in the heavier weight classes consume massive amounts of calories in an effort to gain or maintain bulk and strength, many are coming to the realization that eating "clean" is much more advisable in the long term. Your cardio-respiratory system will thank you for it and your overall health and longevity will be far better off. While the old school guys often consumed copious amounts of raw milk, big juicy, fat laden steaks and burgers, lots of whole eggs, etc, leaner sources of protein should be the target for most of your meals. Going off the tracks occasionally with a big fat steak is OK, but having one every night for dinner is a bad idea.

Avoid junk, white bread, pastries and cakes, candy, overly salty foods, soda and other sugary soft drinks (check those energy drink labels); even a lot of the protein bars we commonly consume can be loaded with crap. Seek out less processed and more organic foods and you can't go too wrong. Sound nutrition is a key component of a strength training program and this is one area that often is not given enough attention relative to one's training regimen. If you don't eat well, sleep well and allow your body to get everything it needs to fully recover from tough workouts, you are really short changing yourself and you will not make the true progress you are capable of.

Keep alcohol ingestion within moderation, as well as stimulants and other potential toxins. Don't put an extra burden on your system on top of the stress of hard training and expect the best results. This is just common sense.

I just wanted to finish the book with a few words to the wise in the nutrition realm, though this is a subject we could discuss at great length. That is not within the intended scope of this book.

I hope you have enjoyed the book and found it informative and at least somewhat entertaining. I know I learned quite a bit in the process of doing the research for it and putting it together, and I trust you have also learned something that will help you to become a better, stronger athlete going forward.

Thanks for reading!!

You may also enjoy a few of my other books, several of which are shown here:

Forgotten Secrets of the old time Strongmen

*Autometrics
A complete manual on how to workout in your car*

The Secrets of Age Defying Strength and how to obtain it

You can find links with purchasing info here:

http://christianiron.com/suggestedreading.aspx

I also have a **Facebook** group page which keys on Old School methods, DIY stuff, and has a number of pictures and videos as well as a discussion board, should you wish to interact.

You can find that here:

http://www.facebook.com/apps/application.php?id=2361831622&b#!/pages/Forgotten-Strength-Secrets/120175808017032?ref=ts

If you are local to the greater Philadelphia, Allentown, and Bethlehem area (or even if not), please consider dropping in and subscribing to my online column:

http://www.examiner.com/x-20420-Allentown-Weight-Lifting-Examiner

Thanks so much for your purchase. If you enjoy the book, please tell a friend. If you don't, please tell me!

Email me at:

dy@christianiron.com

Train Hard!!!!! ☺☺☺